D0142843

EXPULSIONS

EXPULSIONS

Brutality and Complexity
in the Global Economy

Saskia Sassen

THE BELKNAP PRESS OF
HARVARD UNIVERSITY PRESS

Cambridge, Massachusetts
London, England
2014

To Richard

Copyright © 2014 by the President and
Fellows of Harvard College
All rights reserved
Printed in the United States of America

Library of Congress Cataloging-in-Publication Data

Sassen, Saskia.
Expulsions : brutality and complexity
in the global economy / Saskia Sassen.
pages cm
Includes bibliographical references and index.
ISBN 978-0-674-59922-2 (alk. paper)
1. Economics—Sociological aspects. 2. Economic
development—Social aspects. 3. Economic development—
Moral and ethical aspects. 4. Capitalism—Social aspects.
5. Equality—Economic aspects. I. Title.

HM548.S275 2014
330—dc23   2013040726

Contents

Introduction

The Savage Sorting

We are confronting a formidable problem in our global political economy: the emergence of new logics of *expulsion*. The past two decades have seen a sharp growth in the number of people, enterprises, and places expelled from the core social and economic orders of our time. This tipping into radical expulsion was enabled by elementary decisions in some cases, but in others by some of our most advanced economic and technical achievements. The notion of expulsions takes us beyond the more familiar idea of growing inequality as a way of capturing the pathologies of today's global capitalism. Further, it brings to the fore the fact that forms of knowledge and intelligence we respect and admire are often at the origin of long transaction chains that can end in simple expulsions.

I focus on complex modes of expulsion because they can function as a window into major dynamics of our epoch. Further, I select extreme cases because they make sharply visible what might otherwise remain confusingly vague. One familiar example in the West that is both complex and extreme is the expelling of low-income workers and the unemployed from government social welfare and health programs as well as from corporate insurance and unemployment support. Beyond the negotiations and the making of new law required to execute this expulsion, there is the extreme fact that the divide between those with access to such benefits and those denied

it has sharpened and may well be irreversible under current conditions. Another example is the rise of advanced mining techniques,
notably hydraulic fracturing, that have the power to transform
natural environments into dead land and dead water, an expulsion
of bits of life itself from the biosphere. Together the diverse expulsions I examine in this book may well have a greater impact on the
shaping of our world than the rapid economic growth in India, China,
and a few other countries. Indeed, and key to my argument, such
expulsions can coexist with economic growth as counted by standard
measures.

These expulsions are made. The instruments for this making range
from elementary policies to complex institutions, systems, and techniques that require specialized knowledge and intricate organizational formats. One example is the sharp rise in the complexity of
financial instruments, the product of brilliant creative classes and
advanced mathematics. Yet, when deployed to develop a particular
type of subprime mortgage, that complexity led to the expulsion a
few years later of millions of people from their homes in the United
States, Hungary, Latvia, and so on. Another is the complexity of the
legal and accounting features of the contracts enabling a sovereign
government to acquire vast stretches of land in a foreign sovereign
nation-state as a sort of extension of its own territory—for example,
to grow food for its middle classes—even as it expels local villages
and rural economies from that land. Another is the brilliant engineering that allows us to extract safely what we want from deep inside
our planet while disfiguring its surface en passant. Our advanced political economies have created a world where complexity too often
tends to produce elementary brutalities.

The channels for expulsion vary greatly. They include austerity
policies that have helped shrink the economies of Greece and Spain,
environmental policies that overlook the toxic emissions from enormous mining operations in Norilsk, Russia, and in the American
state of Montana, and so on, in an endless array of cases. The specif-

ics of each case matter in this book. For instance, if our concern is environmental destruction rather than interstate politics, the fact that both these mining operations are heavy polluters matters more than the fact that one site is in Russia and the other in the United States.

The diverse processes and conditions I include under the notion of expulsion all share one aspect: they are acute. While the abjectly poor worldwide are the most extreme instance, I do include such diverse conditions as the impoverishment of the middle classes in rich countries, the eviction of millions of small farmers in poor countries owing to the 220 million hectares of land, or over 540 million acres, acquired by foreign investors and governments since 2006, and the destructive mining practices in countries as different as the United States and Russia. Then there are the countless displaced people warehoused in formal and informal refugee camps, the minoritized groups in rich countries who are warehoused in prisons, and the able-bodied unemployed men and women warehoused in ghettos and slums. Some of these expulsions have been taking place for a long time, but not at the current scale. Some are new types of expulsions, such as the 9 million households in the United States whose homes were foreclosed in a short and brutal housing crisis that lasted a mere decade. In short, the character, contents, and sites of these expulsions vary enormously across social strata and physical conditions, and across the world.

The globalization of capital and the sharp rise in technical capabilities have produced major scaling effects. What may have been minor displacements and losses in the 1980s, such as deindustrialization in the West and in several African countries, had become devastations by the 1990s (think Detroit and Somalia). To understand this scaling as more of the same inequality, poverty, and technical capacity is to miss the larger trend. Similarly with the environment. We have been using the biosphere and producing localized damage for millennia, but only in the last thirty years has the damage grown to become a planetary event that boomerangs back, often hitting sites that had nothing to do with the original destruction, such as the Arctic permafrost. And so on with other domains, each with its own specifics.

The many diverse expulsions examined in this book together amount to a savage sorting. We tend to write about the complex organizational capacities of our modern world as producing societies capable of ever more complexity, and conceive of this as a positive development. But often it is so in a partial way or holds for a short temporal frame. Expanding the range of situations and the temporal frame makes visible the fact of sharp edges that obscure what might lie beyond. This raises a question: is much of today's society tending toward the condition of brutal simplicity against which the great historian Jacob Burckhardt warned in the nineteenth century? From what I have observed, complexity does not inevitably lead to brutality, but it can, and today it often does. Indeed, it often leads to simple brutality, not even grand brutality of a sort that might be an equal, even if negative, to that complexity, as is today's scale of our environmental destruction.

How does complexity produce brutality? Part of the answer, I will argue, concerns the logics organizing some of today's major order-making systems in domains as diverse as global environmental protection and finance. Let me illustrate very briefly my argument with two cases, developed at length in this book. The main policy "innovation" in interstate agreements to protect the environment is carbon trading, which means, practically and brutally speaking, that countries will tend to fight for expanding their right to pollute so as to either buy or sell a bigger quota of carbon emissions. In the case of finance, its organizing logic has evolved into a relentless push for hyperprofits and a need to develop instruments that enable it to expand the range of what can be financialized. That led to a willingness to financialize even the livelihoods of those who lose everything if the instrument backfires. It was the case with the type of subprime mortgage launched in 2001 in the United States. What is perhaps still misunderstood is that this was a financial project aimed at profits for high finance. It was not aimed at helping modest-income people buy a house, and hence the opposite of the state projects launched decades earlier, such as the GI Bill and loans under the FHA. The capacities furthering the developments of these systems and innovations are not necessarily intrinsically brutalizing. But when they function within particular types of organizing logics they become so. The capacity of finance to make capital is not inherently destructive, yet it is a type of capital that needs to be put to the test: can it be materialized into a transport infrastructure, a bridge, a water-cleaning system, a factory?

There is a social conundrum here. These capacities should have served to develop the social realm, to broaden and strengthen the well-being of a society, which includes working with the biosphere. Instead they have too often served to dismember the social through extreme inequality, to destroy much of the middle-class life promised by liberal democracy, to expel the vulnerable and the poor from land, jobs, and homes, and to the expulsion of bits of the biosphere from their life space.

A question running through this book is whether the mix of cases I discuss here, which cut across the familiar divisions of urban versus rural, Global North versus Global South, East and West, and more, are the surface manifestation, the localized shape, of deeper systemic dynamics that articulate much of what now appears as unconnected. These systemic dynamics might be operating at a more subterranean level, with more to connect them than we can grasp when we divide the world into familiar, discrete categories—capitalist economy, communist China, sub-Saharan Africa, the environment, finance, and so on. We use these labels to give familiar shapes and meanings to conditions that might actually be originating in deeper, unfamiliar trends. This possibility is a key driver in each of the chapters of this book.

I use the notion of subterranean trends as a shorthand for what are, strictly speaking, *conceptually* subterranean trends. They are hard to see when we think with our familiar geopolitical, economic, and social markers. The one domain where they are perhaps most visible is that of the environment. We know that we are using and destroying the biosphere, but our "environmental policies" do not connect with or reflect a clear understanding of the actual condition of the biosphere. Thus carbon trading as a way of protecting the environment makes sense only from an interstate perspective, and makes little sense from a planetary perspective where local destructions scale up and hit us all. New dynamics may well get filtered through familiar thick realities—poverty, inequality, economy, politics—and thereby take on familiar forms when in fact they are signaling accelerations or ruptures that generate new meanings.

Using the notion of subterranean trends is one way of calling into question familiar categories for organizing knowledge about our economies, our societies, and our interaction with the biosphere. It helps us assess whether today's problems are extreme versions of old troubles or manifestations of something, or some things, disturbing and new. I explore whether the sheer variety of expulsions taking place obscures larger subterranean dynamics that may underlie that variety at ground level. The prevalence of this one feature—the possibility of expulsions—across our familiar differentiations is what led me to the notion of such subterranean trends. The specialization of research, knowledge, and interpretation, each with its own canons and methods for protecting boundaries and meanings, does not always help in this effort of detecting subterranean trends that cut across our familiar distinctions. But specialization does give us detailed knowledge about specifics, bringing us back to basics that can be compared with one another.

Rather than giving meaning to facts by processing them upward through theorization, I do the opposite, bringing them down to their most basic elements in an effort to de-theorize them. Through such de-theorizing I can then revisit inequality, finance, mining, land grabs, and much more in order to see what we would miss with more abstract categorizations; one instance is seeing the more radical fact of expulsions rather than merely more inequality, financial speculation, mining advances, etc. In short, one aim of the book is to stay close to the ground, in order to discover by suspending the overwhelming weight of the familiar categories through which we interpret current trends.

At its sharpest, my hypothesis is that beneath the country specifics of diverse global crises lie emergent systemic trends shaped by a few very basic dynamics. For that reason, empirical research and conceptual recoding must happen together. Empirically a phenomenon may look "Chinese" or "Italian" or "Australian," but this may not help us detect the DNA of our epoch, even if such labels capture certain features. China may still retain many features of a communist society, but growing inequality and the recent impoverishment of its modest middle classes might be rooted in deeper trends that are also at work in, for instance, the United States. Despite enduring differences the two countries may both be hosting major contemporary logics that organize the economy, notably speculation-driven finance and a push for hyperprofits. These parallels and their consequences for people, places, and economies may well turn out to be more significant for understanding our times than differences between communism and capitalism. Indeed, at a deeper level, these "parallels" may be the multisited materializations of trends that are deeper than speculation and hyperprofits but are as yet invisible in that they have not been detected, named, or conceptualized. My focus on the materializing of global trends inside countries contrasts with the far more common focus on the deregulation of national borders where the border is seen as the site for our current transformation.

The problem as I see it is one of interpretation. When we confront today's range of transformations—rising inequality, rising poverty, rising government debt—the usual tools to interpret them are out of date. So we fall into our familiar explanations: governments that are not fiscally responsible, households that take on more debt than they can handle, capital allocations that are inefficient because there is too much regulation, and so on. I do not deny that these explanations have some use, but I am more interested in exploring whether other dynamics are at work as well, dynamics that cut across these familiar and well-established conceptual/historical boundaries.

The far-ranging sets of facts and cases I use throughout this book point to limits in our current master categorizations. Notwithstanding all the differences, whether under communism or liberal democracy, in Africa or North America, particular practices dominate how we mine, manufacture, use people, and get away with murder, figuratively speaking. The politico-economic orderings within which these practices take place imbue them with distinct meanings, and one question for me is whether these meanings camouflage more than they reveal. I use the cases in the book as facts on the ground, as material instances that can help detect *conceptually* subterranean trends that cut across our geopolitical divisions. Is today's sharp increase of displaced people in sub-Saharan Africa *systemically* akin to the sharp growth of the permanently unemployed and frequently incarcerated in the United States? Are the impoverished middle classes in Greece systemically akin to the impoverished middle classes in Egypt, even though these two countries have very different political economies? Is the large mining complex in Norilsk, Russia, a long-term source of acute toxicity in the area, systemically akin to the Zortman-Landusky mining operations in Montana, United States, with their own long-term toxicities? These facts on the ground help do away with old conceptual superstructures, such as capitalism versus communism.

The epochal transformations that interest me here are rooted in diverse and often old histories and genealogies. But my starting point is the 1980s, a vital period of change both in the South and in the North, in capitalist and communist economies alike. To mark the period I highlight two profound shifts from the vast and rich histories that take off in the 1980s. These two shifts happen across the world. But they evolve with highly specific characteristics in each locality, and it is this feature that makes those shifts a useful backdrop for the research in this book.

One is the material development of growing areas of the world into extreme zones for key economic operations. At one end this takes the shape of global outsourcing of manufacturing, services, clerical work, the harvesting of human organs, and the raising of industrial crops to low-cost areas with weak regulation. At the other end, it is the active worldwide making of global cities as strategic spaces for advanced economic functions; this includes cities built from scratch and the often brutal renovation of old cities. The network of global cities functions as a new geography of centrality that cuts across the old North-South and East-West divides, and so does the network of outsourcing sites.

The second is the ascendance of finance in the network of global cities. Finance in itself is not new—it has been part of our history for millennia. What is new and characteristic of our current era is the capacity of finance to develop enormously complex instruments that allow it to securitize the broadest-ever, historically speaking, range of entities and processes; further, continuous advances in electronic networks and tools make for seemingly unlimited multiplier effects. This rise of finance is consequential for the larger economy. While traditional banking is about selling money that the bank has, finance is about selling something it does not have. To do this, finance needs to invade—that is, securitize—nonfinancial sectors to get the grist for its mill. And no instrument is as good for this as the derivative. One result that illustrates this capacity of finance is that by 2005, well before the crisis started brewing, the (notional) value of outstanding derivatives was $630 trillion; this was fourteen times global gross domestic product (GDP). In some ways, the nonalignment between the value of GDP and that of finance is not unprecedented in Western history. But that misalignment has never been so extreme. Moreover, it is a major departure from the Keynesian period, when economic growth was driven not by the financializing of everything but by the vast expansion of material economies such as mass manufacturing and mass building of infrastructures and suburbs.

We can characterize the relationship of advanced to traditional capitalism in our current period as one marked by extraction and destruction, not unlike the relationship of traditional capitalism to precapitalist economies. At its most extreme this can mean the immiseration and exclusion of growing numbers of people who cease being of value as workers and consumers. But today it can also mean that economic actors once crucial to the development of capitalism, such as petty bourgeoisies and traditional national bourgeoisies, cease being of value to the larger system. These trends are not anomalous, nor are they the result of a crisis; they are part of the current systemic deepening of capitalist relations. And, I will argue, so is the shrinking economic, as distinct from financial, space in Greece, Spain, the United States, and many other developed countries.

People as consumers and workers play a diminished role in the profits of a range of economic sectors. For instance, from the perspective of today's capitalism, the natural resources of much of Africa, Latin America, and central Asia are more important than the people on those lands as workers or consumers. This tells us that our period is not quite like earlier forms of capitalism that thrived on the accelerated expansion of prosperous working and middle classes. Maximizing consumption by households was a critical dynamic in that earlier period, as it is today in the so-called emergent economies of the world. But overall it is no longer the strategic systemic driver that it was in most of the twentieth century.

What is next? Historically, the oppressed have often risen against their masters. But today the oppressed have mostly been expelled and survive at a great distance from their oppressors. Further, the "oppressor" is increasingly a complex system that combines persons, networks, and machines with no obvious center. And yet there are sites where it all comes together, where power becomes concrete and can be engaged, and where the oppressed are part of the social infrastructure *for* power. Global cities are one such site.

These are the contradictory dynamics I examine in this book. Bits and pieces of this account have been recorded in the general literature on contemporary affairs, but it has not been narrated as an overarching dynamic that is taking us into a new phase of a certain type of global capitalism. What I seek to contribute is a theorization that begins with the facts at ground level, freed from the intermediation of familiar institutions, and takes us to the other side of traditional geopolitical, economic, and cultural differentiations.

CHAPTER 1

Shrinking Economies, Growing Expulsions

The aim of this chapter is to put some flesh on the idea that we may have entered a new phase of advanced capitalism in the 1980s, one with reinvented mechanisms for primitive accumulation. Today's is a form of primitive accumulation executed through complex operations and much specialized innovation, ranging from the logistics of outsourcing to the algorithms of finance. After thirty years of these types of development, we face shrinking economies in much of the world, escalating destructions of the biosphere all over the globe, and the reemergence of extreme forms of poverty and brutalization where we thought they had been eliminated or were on their way out.

What is usually referred to as economic development has long depended on extracting goods from one part of the world and shipping them to another. Over the past few decades this geography of extraction has expanded rapidly, in good part through complex new technologies, and is now marked by even sharper imbalances in its relation to, and use of, natural resources. The mix of innovations that expands our capacities for extraction now threatens core components of the biosphere, leaving us also with expanded stretches of dead land and dead water.

Some of this is old history. Economic growth has never been benign. But the escalations of the past three decades mark a new epoch in that they threaten a growing number of people and places throughout the world. Such growth still takes on distinctive formats and contents in the mix of diversely developed countries we refer to as the Global North versus the mix of less or differently developed countries we refer to as the Global South. For instance, predatory elites have long been associated with poor countries that have rich natural resources, not with developed countries. Yet increasingly we see some of this capture at the top also in the latter, albeit typically in far more intermediated forms.

My thesis is that we are seeing the making not so much of predatory elites but of predatory "formations," a mix of elites and systemic capacities with finance a key enabler, that push toward acute concentration.[1] Concentration at the top is nothing new. What concerns me is the extreme forms it takes today in more and more domains across a good part of the world. I see the capacity for generating extreme concentration in some of the following trends, to mention just a few. There has been a 60 percent increase in the wealth of the top 1 percent globally in the past twenty years; at the top of that 1 percent, the richest "100 billionaires added $240 billion to their wealth in 2012—enough to end world poverty four times over."[2] Bank assets grew by 160 percent between 2002, well before the full crisis, and 2011, when financial recovery had started—from $40 trillion to $105 trillion, which is over one and a half times the value of global GDP.[3] In 2010, still a period of crisis, the profits of the 5.8 million corporations in the United States rose 53 percent over 2009, but despite skyrocketing profits, their United States corporate income tax bills actually shrank by $1.9 billion, or 2.6 percent.

Rich individuals and global firms by themselves could not have achieved such extreme concentration of the world's wealth. They need what we might think of as systemic help: a complex interaction of these actors with systems regeared toward enabling extreme concentration. Such systemic capacities are a variable mix of technical, market, and financial innovations plus government enablement. They constitute a partly global condition, though one that often functions through the specifics of countries, their political economies, their laws, and their governments.[4] They include enormous capacities for intermediation that function as a kind of haze, impairing our ability to see what is happening—but unlike a century ago, we would not find cigar-smoking moguls in this haze. Today, the structures through which concentration happens are complex assemblages of multiple elements, rather than the fiefdoms of a few robber barons.

Part of my argument is that a system with the capacity to concentrate wealth at this scale is distinctive. It is different, for instance, from a system with the capacity to generate the expansion of prosperous working and middle classes, as happened during most of the twentieth century in the Global North, in much of Latin America, and in several African countries, notably Somalia. This earlier system was far from perfect: there were inequality, concentration of wealth, poverty, racism, and more. But it was a system with a capacity to generate a growing middle sector that kept expanding for several generations, with children mostly doing better than their parents. Also, these distributive outcomes were not simply a function of the people involved. It took specific systemic capacities. By the 1980s, these earlier capacities had weakened, and we saw the emergence of capacities that push toward concentration at the top rather than toward the development of a broad middle. Thus the fact, for example, that the top 10 percent of the income ladder in the United States got 90 percent of the income growth of the decade beginning in 2000 signals more than individual capacity—it was enabled by that complex mix I conceive of as a predatory formation.

In the first section of this chapter I elaborate on how economic growth can get constituted in diverse ways with diverse distributive effects. I find that in our global modernity, we are seeing a surge of what are often referred to as primitive forms of accumulation, usually associated with earlier economies. The format is no longer something like the enclosure of farmers' fields so that wool-bearing sheep can be raised there, as was done in England to satisfy textile manufacturers' demands during the industrial revolution. Today, enormous technical and legal complexities are needed to execute what are ultimately elementary extractions. It is, to cite a few cases, the enclosure by financial firms of a country's resources and citizens' taxes, the repositioning of expanding stretches of the world as sites for extraction of resources, and the regearing of government budgets in liberal democracies away from social and workers' needs. I return to these subjects in the third section.

The second section examines global inequality through this critical lens. Inequality, if it keeps growing, can at some point be more accurately described as a type of expulsion. For those at the bottom or in the poor middle, this means expulsion from a life space; among those at the top, this appears to have meant exiting from the responsibilities of membership in society via self-removal, extreme concentration of the wealth available in a society, and no inclination to redistribute that wealth. Building on the discussion of extreme instantiations of inequality, the third section focuses on familiar situations that, when taken to extremes, become unfamiliar—the other side of the curve. To render visible today's accelerated systemic capacity to make the familiar extreme, I focus on the developed world. Greece and Spain particularly have entered a phase of active shrinkage of their economies to a point we would not have thought possible in the developed world only a few years ago.

These first three sections of the chapter bring out the speed with which what was experienced as more or less normal can evolve into its opposite. The final two sections focus on acute types of expulsions that are likely to become more widespread in particular areas of the world. One is the growth over the past two decades of the displaced population, mostly in the Global South, and the other is the rapid increase of the incarcerated population in a growing number of countries in the Global North. These and so many other old but mutating conditions point to a multisited systemic transformation. In the Global South, both the diverse causes of displacement and the futures of those who have been displaced are calling into question the United Nations' formal classifications of displaced persons, because mostly such people will never go back home—home is now a war zone, a plantation, a mining operation, or dead land. An equivalent shift is evident in the Global North, where what until recently was incarceration as response to a crime (whether the crime was actually committed or not) is now becoming the warehousing of people, which, furthermore, is increasingly done for profit—with the United States in a vanguard all its own.

Unsustainable Contradictions? From Incorporation to Expulsion

The ways in which economic growth takes place matter. A given growth rate can describe a variety of economies, from one with little inequality and a thriving middle class to one with extreme inequality and concentration of most of the growth in a small upper tier. These differences exist across and within countries. Germany and Angola had the same rate of GDP growth in 2000 but clearly had very different economies and saw very different distributive effects. Although Germany is reducing the level, it still puts a good share of government resources into countrywide infrastructure and offers a wide array of services to its people, from health care to trains and buses. Angola's government does neither, choosing to support a small elite seeking to satisfy its own desires, including luxury developments in its capital city, Luanda, now ranked as the most expensive city in the world. These differences can also be seen in a single country across time, such as the United States just within the past fifty years. In the decades after World War II, growth was widely distributed and generated a strong middle class, while the decade beginning in 2000 saw the beginnings of an impoverished middle class, with 80 percent of the growth in income going to the top 1 percent of earners.

In the post–World War II era, the critical components of Western market economies were fixed-capital intensity, standardized production, and the building of new housing in cities, suburbs, and new towns. Such patterns were evident in a variety of countries in North and South America, Europe, Africa, and Asia, most prominently Japan and Asia's so-called Tiger economies. These forms of economic growth contributed to the vast expansion of a middle class. They did not eliminate inequality, discrimination, or racism. But they reduced systemic tendencies toward extreme inequality by constituting an economic regime centered on mass production and mass consumption, with strong labor unions at least in some sectors, and diverse government supports. Further deterrents to inequality were the cultural forms accompanying these processes, particularly through their shaping of the structures of everyday life. For instance, the culture of the large suburban middle class evident in the United States and Japan contributed to mass consumption and thus to standardization in production, which in turn facilitated unionization in manufacturing and distribution.[5]

Manufacturing, in tandem with state policies, played a particularly strong role in this conjunction of trends. As the leading sector in market-based economies for much of the twentieth century, mass manufacturing created the economic conditions for the expansion of the middle class because (1) it facilitated worker organizing, with unionization the most familiar format; (2) it was based in good part on household consumption, and hence wage levels mattered in that they created an effective demand in economies that were for the most part fairly closed; and (3) the relatively high wage levels and social benefits typical of the leading manufacturing sectors became a model for broader sectors of the economy, even those not unionized nor in manufacturing. Manufacturing played this role in non-Western-style industrial economies as well, notably in Taiwan and South Korea, and, in its own way, in parts of the Soviet Union. It has also played a significant part in the growth of a middle class in China since the 1990s, though not as consequential a role as it did in the West in the twentieth century.

By the 1990s, these economic histories and geographies had been partly destroyed. The end of the Cold War launched one of the most brutal economic phases of the modern era. It led to a radical reshuffling of capitalism. The effect was to open global ground for new or sharply expanded modes of profit extraction even in unlikely domains, such as subprime mortgages on modest residences, or through unlikely instruments, such as credit default swaps, which were a key component of the shadow banking system. Thus I see China's rapid manufacturing growth as part of this new phase of global capitalism that takes off in the 1980s;[6] this also helps explain why that growth did not lead to the vast expansion of a prosperous working and middle class in China. Such a difference also marks manufacturing growth in other countries that have become part of the outsourcing map of the West.

Two logics run through this reshuffling. One is systemic and gets wired into most countries' economic and (de)regulatory policies—of which the most important are privatization and the lifting of tariffs on imports. In capitalist economies we can see this in the unsettling and de-bordering of existing fiscal and monetary arrangements, albeit with variable degrees of intensity in different countries.

The second logic is the transformation of growing areas of the world into extreme zones for these new or sharply expanded modes of profit extraction. The most familiar are global cities and the spaces for outsourced work. Each is a type of thick *local* setting that contains the diverse conditions *global* firms need, though each does so at very different stages of the global economic process, for instance, computers for high-finance versus manufacturing components for those computers. Other such local settings in today's global economy are plantations and places for resource extraction, both producing mostly for export. The global city is a space for producing some of the most advanced inputs global firms need. In contrast, outsourcing is about spaces for routinized production of components, mass call centers, standardized clerical work, and more, all of it massive and standardized. Both these types of spaces are among the most strategic factors in the making of today's global economy, besides intermediate sectors such as transport. They concentrate the diverse labor markets, particular infrastructures, and built environments critical to the global economy. And they are the sites that make visible, and have benefited from, the multiple deregulations and guarantees of contract developed and implemented by governments across the world and by major international bodies—in both cases, work mostly paid for by the taxpayers in much of the world.

Inequality in the profit-making capacities of different sectors of the economy and in the earning capacities of different types of workers has long been a feature of advanced market economies. But the orders of magnitude today across much of the developed world distinguish current developments from those of the postwar decades. The United States is probably among the most extreme cases, so it makes the pattern brutally clear. Figures 1.1 and 1.2 show the extraordinary

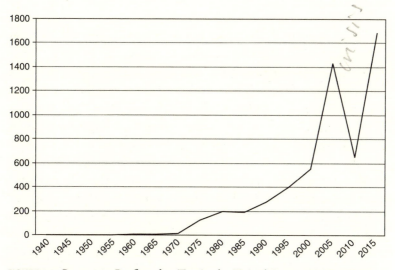

FIGURE 1.1 Corporate Profits after Tax in the United States, 1940s–2010s (in $ billions)

Data source: Federal Reserve Bank of St. Louis 2013a.

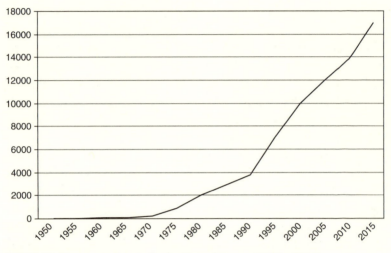

FIGURE 1.2 Corporate Assets in the United States, 1950s–2010s (in $ billions)

Data source: Federal Reserve Bank of St. Louis 2013b.

rise in corporate profits and assets over the past ten years, and this in a country that has long had extraordinary corporate results.

The decade of the 2000s helps illuminate this relentless rise in corporate profits and reduction of corporate taxes as a share of federal tax revenues. The crisis late in the decade brought a sharp but momentary dip in corporate profits, but overall these kept growing. The extent of inequality and the systems in which inequality is embedded and through which these outcomes are produced have generated massive distortions in the operations of diverse markets, from investment to housing and labor. For instance, using Internal Revenue Service data on corporate tax returns, David Cay Johnston finds that in 2010 the 2,772 companies that own 81 percent of all business assets in the United States, with an average of $23 billion in assets per firm, paid an average of 16.7 percent of their profits in taxes (down from 21.1 percent in 2009), even though their combined profits rose 45.2 percent, a new record.[7] Profits growing three times faster than taxes means their effective tax rates fell.[8] The effects are visible in the composition of federal tax revenues: a growing share of individual taxes and a declining share of corporate taxes. The share of individual taxes is estimated to rise from 41.5 percent of federal revenues in fiscal 2010 to 49.8 percent in fiscal 2018. In contrast, corporate income taxes—assuming current rates—are expected to grow by only 2.4 percentage points over the same period, from 8.9 percent of federal revenues in 2010 to 11.3 percent in 2018.[9]

The trajectory of governments in this same period is one of growing indebtedness. Today, most of the developed-country governments could not engage in the large-scale infrastructure projects common in the postwar decades. Using International Monetary Fund (IMF) data, the Organisation for Economic Co-operation and Development (OECD) finds widespread growth of central government debt as a percentage of GDP. Table 1.1 presents numbers for several, mostly developed countries. The trend holds for very different types of governments: Germany saw its central government debt increase from 13 percent of GDP in 1980 to 44 percent in 2010; U.S. government debt increased from 25.7 percent of GDP in 1980 to 61 percent in 2010; and China's rose from 1 percent of GDP in 1984 to 33.5 percent in 2010.

The rise of government deficits has also been fed by the increase in tax evasion, partly facilitated by the development of complex accounting, financial, and legal instruments. In a 2012 research project for the Tax Justice Network, accountant Richard Murphy estimates tax evasion globally at $3 trillion in 2010, which represents 5 percent of the global economy and 18 percent of global tax collections in 2010.[10] The study covered 145 countries with $61.7 trillion of gross product, or 98.2 percent of the world total. The estimated tax evasion is based on a juxtaposition of World Bank data on the estimated size of shadow economies with a Heritage Foundation analysis of average tax burdens by country.[11] Figure 1.3 presents

TABLE 1.1: Central Government Debt (% of GDP) in Eleven Countries, 1980–2010

Country	Year			
	1980	1990	2000	2010
Australia	8.0	6.1	11.4	11.0
Canada	26.1	46.6	40.9	36.1
China	1.0[a]	6.9	16.4	33.5
Germany	13.0	19.7	38.4	44.4
Greece	n/a	97.6[b]	108.9	147.8
Italy	52.7	92.8	103.6	109.0
Japan	37.1	47.0	106.1	183.5[c]
Portugal	29.2	51.7	52.1	88.0
Spain	14.3	36.5	49.9	51.7
Sweden	38.2	39.6	56.9	33.8
United States	25.7	41.5	33.9	61.3

Data source: OECD 2014.
Notes: a. Data for 1984
b. Data for 1993
c. Data for 2009

tax evasion estimates for several developed countries, including those generally seen as well governed and well functioning, such as Germany, France, and the United Kingdom. It ranges from 8.6 percent of GDP in the United States to 43.8 percent in Russia. Murphy finds that a key reason for this tax evasion is the combination of weak rules on accounting and disclosure combined with inadequate budgets to enforce tax laws. The United States has the largest amount of absolute tax evasion, clearly a function partly of the size of its economy. Murphy estimates U.S. tax evasion at $337.3 billion, which is 10.7 percent of global evasion; this is not too different from

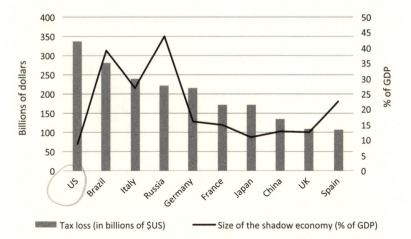

FIGURE 1.3 Countries with the Largest Absolute Levels of Tax Evasion, 2011
Data source: Johnston 2011.

the official U.S. Internal Revenue Service tax gap estimates. Given the measures used in the report, it excludes "lawful" tax evasion, which we know has increased sharply over the last decade thanks to extremely creative accounting, including the use of private contractual arrangements that can bypass state regulations *lawfully,* so to speak.[12]

The losers in much of this are the majority of citizens and their governments. Governments become poorer, partly as a result of tax evasion and partly because more of their citizens are impoverished and therefore less capable of meeting their social obligations. The Genuine Progress Indicator (GPI) is a comprehensive measure that includes social conditions and environmental costs; it adjusts expenditure using twenty-six variables so as to account both for costs such as pollution, crime, and inequality and for beneficial activities where no money changes hands, such as housework and volunteering. An international team led by Ida Kubiszewski from Australian National University collected GPI estimates for seventeen countries, which together account for over half the world's population and

GDP, to generate a global overview of GPI changes over the last five decades. They found that GPI per person peaked in 1978 and has been declining slowly but steadily ever since.[13] In contrast, GDP per capita has been rising steadily since 1978. The research team argues that this signals that social and environmental negatives have outpaced the growth of monetary wealth. Clearly, an additional factor is the distribution of that monetary wealth, which, as we know from other data examined in this chapter, has become increasingly concentrated at the top.

Using IMF data on public expenditures and adjustment measures in 181 countries, Isabel Ortiz and Matthew Cummins examine the impact of the crisis, from 2007 through the forecasts for 2013–2015. The authors find that the IMF data used in 314 studies show that a quarter of the countries are undergoing excessive contraction. "Excessive contraction" is defined as a cut in government expenditures as a percentage of GDP in the 2013–2015 postcrisis period compared to the equivalent measure in the precrisis levels of 2005–2007. Fiscal contraction is found to be most severe in the developing world. Overall, sixty-eight developing countries are projected to cut public spending by 3.7 percent of GDP on average in 2013–2015, compared to 2.2 percent in twenty-six high-income countries. In terms of population, austerity will affect 5.8 billion people, or 80 percent of the global population, in 2013; this is expected to increase to 6.3 billion, or 90 percent of people worldwide, by 2015. This leads the authors to question the desirability of fiscal contraction as the way out of the crisis. They argue that the worldwide propensity toward fiscal consolidation is likely to aggravate unemployment, produce higher food and fuel costs, and reduce access to essential services for many households in all these countries. These households are bearing the costs of a "recovery" that has passed them by.[14]

Some of the major processes feeding the increased inequality in profit-making and earnings capacities are an integral part of the advanced information economy; thus this growing inequality is not an anomaly nor, in the case of earnings, the result of low-wage immigrant labor, as is often asserted. One such process is the ascendance and transformation of finance, particularly through securitization, globalization, and the development of new telecommunications and computer-networking technologies. Another source of inequalities in profit making and earnings is the growing service intensity in the organization of the economy generally, that is to say, the increased demand for services by firms and households.[15] Insofar as there is a strong tendency in the service sector toward polarization in the levels of technical expertise that workers need, and in their wages and salaries, the growth in the demand for services reproduces these inequalities in the broader society.

The exceptionally high profit-making capacity of many of the leading service industries is embedded in a complex combination of new trends. Among the most significant over the past twenty years are technologies that make possible the hypermobility of capital at a global scale; market deregulation, which maximizes the implementation of that hypermobility; and financial inventions such as securitization, which liquefy hitherto illiquid capital and allow it to circulate faster, hence generating additional profits (or losses). Globalization adds to the complexity of these service industries, their strategic character, and their glamour. This in turn has contributed to their valorization and often overvalorization, as illustrated in the unusually high salary increases for top-level professionals that began in the 1980s, a trend that has now become normalized in many advanced economies.[16]

Of all the highly developed countries, it is the United States where these deep structural trends are most legible. National-level data for the United States show a sharp growth in inequality. For instance, earnings growth during the precrisis level for 2001 to 2005 was high but very unequally distributed. Most of it went to the

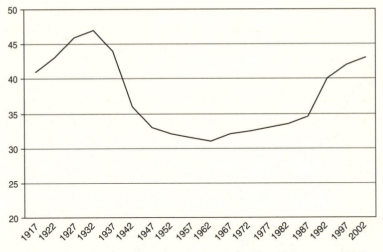

FIGURE 1.4 Share (in %) of Income[a] Going to the Top 10 Percent of U.S. Households, 1917–2002

Data source: Mishel 2004, table 1.

Note: a. Income is defined as market income but excludes capital gains.

upper 10 percent and, especially, the upper 1 percent of households. The remaining 90 percent of households saw a 4.2 percent decline in their market-based incomes.[17] Figure 1.4 traces a longer-term pattern from the boom and bust of the 1920s, the growth of the middle sectors in the decades of the Keynesian period, and the return to rapidly rising inequality by 1987. It was in that immediate postwar period extending into the late 1960s and early 1970s that the incorporation of workers into formal labor market relations reached its highest level in the most advanced economies. In the United States, it helped bring down the share of total job earnings going to the top 10 percent from 47 percent at its height in the 1920s and early 1930s to 33 percent from 1942 until 1987. The formalization of the employment relation in this period helped implement a set of regulations that, overall, protected workers and secured the gains made by often violent labor struggles. Not that

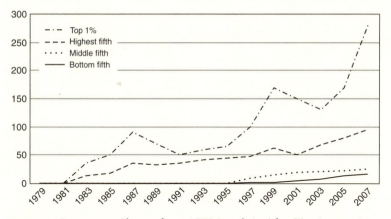

FIGURE 1.5 Percentage Change from 1979 Levels in After-Tax Income in the United States, 1979–2007

Data source: Sherman and Stone 2010.

all was well, of course. This formalization also entailed the exclusion of distinct segments of the workforce, such as women and minorities, particularly in some heavily unionized industries. Whatever its virtues and defects, this golden period for organized labor came to an end in the 1980s. By 1987, inequality was on its way up again, and sharply. Figure 1.5 shows that the top 1 percent of earners had a 280 percent rise in their household income between 1979 and 2007, a trend that was confirmed in the 2010 census and continues today.

The Global South has had its own version of shrinkage, a subject I develop at greater length in Chapter 2. Very briefly, after twenty or more years of IMF and World Bank restructuring programs, many of these countries now carry a far larger burden of debt to diverse private lenders represented by the IMF than they did before international financial intervention. Their governments now pay more to their lenders than they invest in basic components of development such as health and education. Table 1.2 presents data for some of the governments that owe the most.

TABLE 1.2: Low- and Lower-Middle Income Governments with the Highest Foreign Debt Payments, 2012

Country	Debt payment (% government revenue)
Belize	28.1
Philippines	27.1
Bhutan	26.6
El Salvador	25.8
Sri Lanka	24.1
St Vincent	18.6
St Lucia	18.1
Angola	17.1
Maldives	14.4
Gambia	13.9
Paraguay	13.3
Guatemala	12.7
Indonesia	11.9
Laos	11.5
Pakistan	10.5

Source: Jubilee Debt Campaign 2012, table 3.

These are some of the key destructive trends that began in the 1980s, took off globally in the 1990s, and reached some of their highest levels in the 2000s. Although many of them began before the 2008 crisis, they were not quite visible. What was visible was the redevelopment and gentrification of vast urban areas, which produced an *impression* of overall prosperity, from Paris to Buenos Aires, from Hong Kong to Dublin. Now these formerly invisible trends have been exacerbated and have become visible. In their extreme forms they can function as windows into a more complex and elusive reality of impoverishment in the making, one partly engendered by what was mostly visible as explosive growth in wealth and profits, a twenty-year process I have examined in great detail elsewhere.[18]

In what follows I examine the sharp shifts in a number of very diverse domains. They range from the rapid growth in corporate profits alongside the rapid increase in government budget deficits to the rise of displaced populations in the Global South and the rising rates of incarceration in the Global North. Each of the domains examined is highly specific and functions within a particular assemblage of institutions, laws, aims, and obstacles. As conditions become acute, they contribute to a third phase that is just beginning, one marked by *expulsions*—from life projects and livelihoods, from membership, from the social contract at the center of liberal democracy. It goes well beyond simply more inequality and more poverty. It is, in my reading, a development not yet fully visible and recognizable. It is not a condition faced by the majority, though it might become one in some cases. It entails a gradual generalizing of extreme conditions that begin at the edges of systems, in microsettings. This is important, because much of this sharp shift I am seeking to capture is still invisible to the statistician. But it is also to the passerby—the impoverished middle classes may still be living in their same nice houses, with their losses hidden behind neat facades. Increasingly these households have sold most of their valuables to afford payments, have started to sell their basics, including furniture, and are doubling up with grown-up children. My assumption is that in their extreme character these conditions become heuristic and help us understand a larger, less extreme, and more encompassing dynamic in our political economies.

Next I begin by describing general trends in the growth of inequality in both rich and poor countries, to be followed by a more detailed examination of the active shrinking of the Greek, Spanish, and Portuguese economies.

Income Inequality in the World

The growth of inequality in the past thirty years has been relentless.[19] Rather than providing an overview of a by now familiar subject, I want to recover particular aspects of inequality. Beyond disagreements of measures, time frames, and interpretation, much evidence shows substantial income and wealth inequalities both among and within countries across the globe. Most of this inequality can be accounted for by differences among countries as measured by country means.

While there is general agreement that the overall level of economic inequality in the world has risen sharply over the past century and a half (see Figure 1.6), there is ongoing debate over the past twenty years. Various authors have demonstrated that much depends on

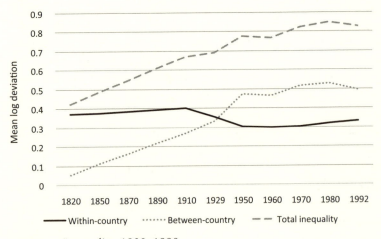

FIGURE 1.6 Inequality, 1830–1990

Data source: Bourguignon and Morrison 2002, table 2.

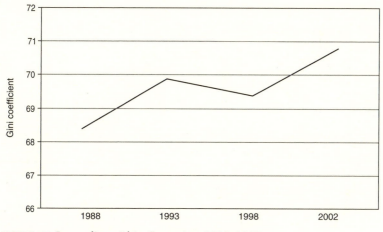

FIGURE 1.7 Inequality within Countries, 1988–2002
Data source: Milanovic 2009.

how global inequality is measured. If rather than using country means, we would use the sum of the actual numbers of poor in each country according to basic standards, we would arrive at yet another measure of global inequality. Yet it is clear that the gap between incomes in rich and poor nations is large and growing. In one measure of the inequality among national incomes, Milanovic shows that the poorest quintile of certain high-income nations (which includes countries such as Denmark) will be richer on average than the richest quintile in low-income nations (which includes countries such as Mali).[20]

Though inequality among countries still accounts for most of global inequality, its share has been declining since the late 1980s, which confirms some of the trends I discuss: according to Atinc et al., it fell from 78 percent in 1988 to 74 percent in 1993 and 67 percent by 2000.[21] What supports my thesis is that since the 1980s, intracountry inequality—inequality *within* countries—has been increasing (see Figure 1.7), even if not necessarily in all countries. Further, there were significant rises in several OECD member countries

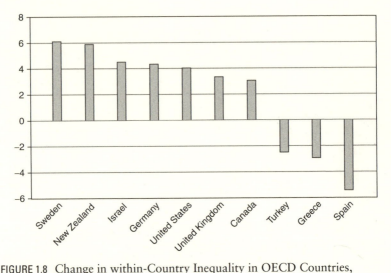

FIGURE 1.8 Change in within-Country Inequality in OECD Countries, 1980s–2000s

Data source: OECD 2013b.

for which long-term data are available (see Figure 1.8 for a sampling). For some OECD countries—notably the United States, United Kingdom, and Israel—within-country income inequality has been on the rise since the late 1970s. In the 2000s, within-country income inequality began to rise quickly in traditionally low-inequality countries such as Germany, Finland, and Sweden. The evidence for OECD countries points to growing within-country inequality.

Income Inequality in the United States

The United States can serve as a kind of natural experiment, showing us how bad income inequality can get in what is commonly categorized as a "highly developed country" (see Figure 1.9). According to Milanovic, even though the poorest people in the United States may, on average, fare much better than the poorest in many devel-

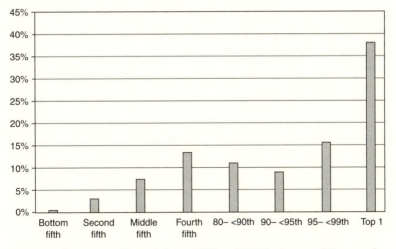

FIGURE 1.9 Percentage Growth from 1979 to 2006 in Average Wages and Salaries in the United States, by Household Rank

Data source: Economic Policy Institute 2011d.

oping nations, inequality *within* the United States is among the highest in the world. In 2010, the top fifth of income-earning families in the United States accounted for 47 percent of total national income, with 20 percent going to the top 5 percent of income-earning families alone; these numbers exclude inherited wealth, capital gains, and other non-job income. Meanwhile, the bottom fifth accounted for only 3.8 percent of this income.[22] Critically, the disparity between the top and the bottom has grown: the share of income going to the top 10 percent of the U.S. population has increased sharply since the 1980s, while the bottom 90 percent has seen only modest increases over the same time period. In the United States the top 1 percent of wage earners saw their wages and salaries increase by 144 percent between 1979 and 2006 (right before the crisis), while the bottom 90 percent of wage earners saw an increase of only 15 percent over the same period.[23] Between 2000 and 2007 the average income in the United States grew by $1,460, but *all* gains went to the richest 10 percent, while income for the bottom 90 percent declined.[24]

Wealth disparities in the United States tend to mirror disparities in income. The distribution of wealth in the United States is heavily skewed not only to the top quintile of wealth holders but in particular to the top 1 percent (see Figure 1.10). Moreover, the top 1 percent of wealth holders in the United States saw their wealth increase over the 1980s and 1990s, peaking in 2007 at 103 percent greater than in 1983 before falling after the financial crisis to 48 percent greater than in 1983.[25] During this same period, median household wealth in the United States peaked in 2007 at 48 percent higher than 1983 levels, before falling sharply after the financial crisis to 13.5 percent *less* than 1983 levels.[26]

Even more so than income, gains in real wealth were heavily skewed toward the wealthiest Americans in the period from 1983

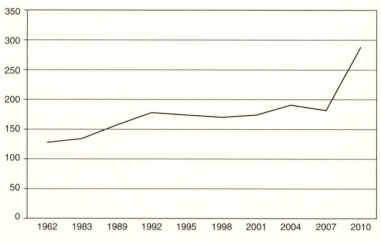

FIGURE 1.10 Ratio of Wealth of Top 1 Percent to Median Wealth in the United States, 1962–2010

Data source: Economic Policy Institute 2011e.

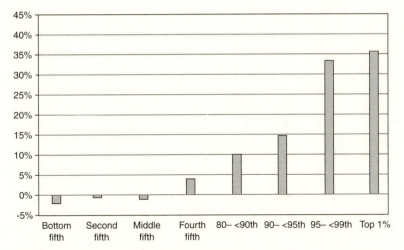

FIGURE 1.11 Change in Share of Total Wealth from 1983 to 2010 in the United States, by Household Rank

Source: Economic Policy Institute 2011g.

to 2009. During this period, *all* gains in wealth went to the top two quintiles, with the wealthiest 5 percent of Americans accounting for 81.7 percent of the total wealth gained. The middle, lower middle, and lowest quintiles, meanwhile, all saw decreases in their wealth over this time (see Figure 1.11).

Extreme Conditions in Rich Countries

If the United States shows us how bad intracountry inequality can get, Greece, Spain, and Portugal can show us how sharply a whole economy can shrink. I use these three countries as but the most extreme sites of what is a broad trend within the developed world, including the rest of the eurozone: the shrinking space of the economy in developed countries. Such shrinking is an unusual trend in developed countries when not at war with each other. The more common language to describe these trends is that of low growth and high unemployment. I will argue that this language is too vague given the extreme condition of large parts of the population and economy in these three countries, and in fact many other countries, including the United States. Modest increases in employment growth are not enough to eliminate this shrinking. The aim here is not to provide a detailed description of the well-documented rise in unemployment and bankruptcies. My aim is to use these trends to explore the shrinking of economic space and its consequences.

There is a de facto redefinition of "the economy" when sharp contractions are gradually lost to standard measures. The unemployed who lose everything—jobs, homes, medical insurance—easily fall off the edge of what is defined as "the economy" and counted as such. So do small shop and factory owners who lose everything and commit suicide. And so do the growing numbers of well-educated students and professionals who emigrate and leave Europe all together. These trends redefine the space of the economy. They make it smaller and expel a good share of the unemployed and the poor from standard measures. Such a redefinition makes "the economy" presentable, so to speak, allowing it to show a slight growth in its measure of GDP per capita. The reality at ground level is more akin to a kind of economic version of ethnic cleansing in which elements considered troublesome are dealt with by simply eliminating them. This shrinking and redefinition of economic space so that economies can be represented as "back on track" holds for a growing number of countries in the European Union and elsewhere. One difference is the central role of the IMF and the European Central Bank in narrating what it takes to return to growth. To some extent they are succeeding, insofar as theirs are almost the only voices being heard on the matter, and the language they use is not of contracting economies but of a return to GDP growth. Indeed, in early January 2013, the European Central Bank said that Greece's economy was on the path back to growth, and Moody's upgraded Greek debt by a point; the country's rating is still low, but such shifts matter because investors take them into account. What is left out of these measures showing a return to some growth is that a significant portion of households, enterprises, and places have been expelled from that economic space that is being measured. The expelled become invisible to formal measurements, and thereby their negative drag on growth rates is neutralized.

A second major feature of the position of European Union institutions and governments heading the so-called rescue effort for Greece is to consider it a unique case—a poor country with extreme tax fraud and a dysfunctional government bureaucracy. To some extent Portugal and Spain are also seen as extreme, though for different reasons than Greece. That is to say, they are not seen as indicative of a trend that might also affect the rest of the eurozone. But if we look at the other European Union (EU) countries that are confronting low growth, relatively high unemployment, and pressures to cut social programs, the picture changes.

I argue that we cannot assume that Greece, Spain, and Portugal are unique cases. We need to examine whether they are. What takes an extreme form in Greece, and to some extent in Portugal and Spain, may well also be present elsewhere in the eurozone and beyond. This would alert us to a deeper structural condition in this phase of advanced capitalism, which took off in the 1980s and became entrenched in the 1990s. The explanation would thus not be confined to exceptional conditions, such as Greece's poverty and corruption, but would have to address structural features of the political economy present throughout the European Union.

The data in Figures 1.12 and 1.13 offer evidence for this thesis that Greece and Spain are extreme examples of a larger trend affecting the eurozone more generally.[27] Greece's government debt almost tripled from 2000 to 2013. While Spain's debt actually declined in the roaring 2000s, by 2011 its private debt was surpassing the eurozone average. Notwithstanding sharp differences among countries, the eurozone overall saw declining economic growth and, as

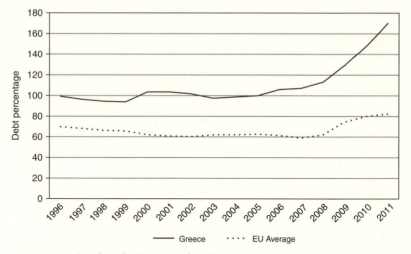

FIGURE 1.12 Greek Debt Compared to Eurozone Average, 1996–2011

Data source: Eurostat, "Government Deficit and Debt," 2013a.

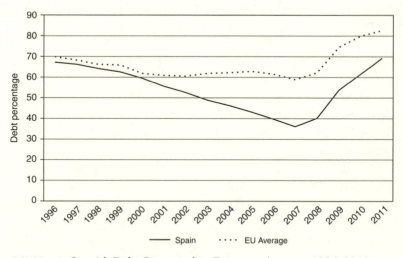

FIGURE 1.13 Spanish Debt Compared to Eurozone Average, 1996–2011

Data source: Eurostat, "Government Deficit and Debt," 2013a.

FIGURE 1.14 General Government Financial Balance, 1999–2012

Data source: OECD 2012.

Figure 1.14 shows, a considerable rise in government indebtedness. And workers across Europe have staged protests against rising unemployment and austerity measures.

In a detailed examination of the G20, a group that includes many non-European countries, the International Labour Organization and the OECD found that in "postcrisis" 2012, seventeen of these countries had unemployment levels above the precrisis levels of 2007.[28] Only Germany, Russia, and Brazil had a decline in unemployment. More specifically, in over half of the countries examined, long-term unemployment as a share of total unemployment remains above precrisis levels. Finally, in Europe the unemployment rate rose further overall, and particularly so in France, Italy, and Spain. Europe's 2012 youth unemployment rate exceeded 20 percent in most countries (see Figure 1.15), in some cases by a lot. It was below 5 percent in only four G20 countries (China, India, Japan, and the Republic of Korea).

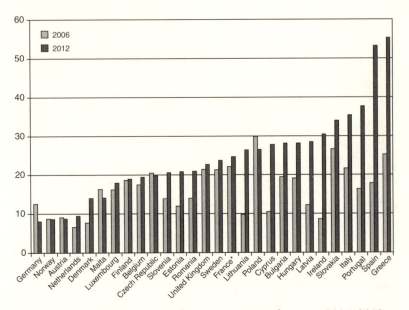

FIGURE 1.15 European Youth (under Age 25) Unemployment, 2006, 2012
Data source: Eurostat 2013b.

A second variable, the ratio of the employment rate for women to the rate for men, changed little since 2007, signaling a relatively gender-neutral impact of the crisis on job loss that is probably an indication of the depth of job losses.[29] The exceptions are Spain and Turkey, where this ratio did rise. A third variable considers 2012 youth unemployment, which was over twice as high as adult unemployment in the G20. High as it is, this rate is known to be a severe undercount, since a substantial proportion of youth in G20 countries are neither in the labor force nor in school or a training program. More generally, youth labor force participation rates have dropped in nine of the G20 countries. The median youth labor force participation rate stands at 60 percent, ranging from a low of 49.4 percent in Italy to a high of 69.8 percent in China, which suggests that where jobs are available, as in China, youth participation is high.

This type of evidence helps us see that a good part of the world's richer economies is experiencing negatives two years after the crisis was supposedly over. The extreme cuts in social benefits, declines in workforce numbers, and increases in income taxes imposed on Greece and Spain years after the 2008 crisis, make visible a deep restructuring project. But milder versions of such restructuring are taking place throughout the eurozone, as well as in other wealthy countries such as the United States.

One project that seems to be part of this restructuring involves keeping the increasingly privatized and corporatized economy going by getting rid of excessive social contract–related expenditures. Debt repayment and austerity programs are disciplining mechanisms that serve this larger project of protecting a particular type of economy. They do not help or aim at maximizing employment and production. Greece's recession, entering its fifth year in 2012, is deepening as a result of privileging debt repayment, job cuts, reductions in social programs, and higher taxes. These policies keep intensifying, with the Greek government regularly announcing further cuts: for instance, at the end of 2012, a 22 percent cut in the private sector minimum wage, abolishing permanent jobs in state enterprises, and eliminating a further 150,000 jobs in the public sector by 2015. Recognition of the limits and counterproductive effects of such policies is widespread. Regarding Greece, Charles Dallara, managing director of the Institute of International Finance (IIF) and the spokesman for Greece's creditors, said that responses to the Greek debt crisis placed too much emphasis on short-term austerity and not enough on improving the country's longer-term competitiveness. Further, concerning what it would take to pay Greece's foreign creditors, he argued that it would take "only some €15bn–€20bn. . . . This can easily be realised in part by reducing interest rates on the loans which Europe and the IMF made to Greece on more concessional terms."[30]

Whatever the logic behind Europe's sorting of winners and losers, it is important to note it tends to cut deep into the social and economic fabric of a country. Economic output in Greece, Spain, and Portugal has fallen over the past several years. This challenges the prevailing European view that fiscal belt-tightening will foster growth. Official data make this clear, even if they undercount the shrinkage because they exclude a direct measure of what has been expelled from the formal economy. In the first three months of 2013, Greece's economy contracted for a nineteenth straight quarter as consumption and investment declined—a 16 percent drop in its GDP since the end of 2007. Moreover, this decline is accelerating: Greece's GDP fell by 5.6 percent in the first quarter of 2013 alone, a steeper decline than had been estimated given a return to growth, as formally measured, in several of Europe's economies. Portugal's GDP decline is speeding up as well, according to the country's National Statistics Institute. In the last quarter of 2012, Portugal's GDP fell by an estimated 5.3 percent, for a total decline of 3.2 percent for the year. Further, Portugal's contraction in the first quarter of 2013 exceeded initial projections.[31] Spain, the eurozone's fourth-largest economy, has contracted each year for the last several years; both the government and the International Monetary Fund predicted further contraction in 2013.[32] First-quarter 2013 figures show that Spain did indeed fall deeper into recession, for a seventh straight quarter of economic shrinkage. The expectation is that expansion will not happen until 2014. While the rate of contraction in Spain might be lower than that in Greece, official unemployment, at 27.2 percent, was just as high.

These economies are testing grounds for Europe's major policy setters, who posit that reducing government spending and raising taxes will bring about economic recovery and a revival of investor confidence. It is important to note that the severe economic contractions in Greece and Portugal have not significantly affected eurozone GDP.[33] Those two economies combined account for only 4 percent of the bloc's €9.5 trillion ($12.6 trillion) economy. But Spain is another matter; this may be reflected in the 100 million IMF loan exclusively for Spain's banks. Significantly, this loan was clearly not intended to enable government delivery of needed health and education services or to stimulate employment via government services generally. Such uses were explicitly excluded in the loan's conditions. More generally, all three economies may be making visible deep trends at work across Europe, as indicated by data presented in the next section.

So far, there is no evidence that the strategy for economic growth is working in the stated way. The Greek, Portuguese, and Spanish economies have kept contracting. And while Greece's GDP has seen mild growth since early 2013, this measure of growth excludes all that has been expelled from the space of the economy, as we have seen. Thus it is a growth measure that exists alongside rising poverty, joblessness, homelessness, hunger, use of soup kitchens, suicide rates among owners of small businesses that are going under, and more. It leads one to wonder if this brutal restructuring was undertaken precisely in order to achieve a smaller but workable economic space that would show growth in GDP according to traditional metrics—even if it necessitates the expulsion from the economy, and its measures, of significant shares of the workforce and the small business sector. After all, a mere hint of GDP growth can be a positive signal to investors and financial markets, and this is a key achievement from the perspective of current IMF and European Central Bank policy—and not only in the EU. The alternative survival economies that are emerging exist in a different economic space, one that falls outside formal measures and indicators. For now they are not enough to meet the needs of the expelled and of the merely impoverished.

Adverse Conditions for Economic Prosperity

The sharp contraction of the space of what is considered to be the formal economy, especially though not exclusively in Greece, Portugal, and Spain, has multiple negative impacts on people. More unemployment, poverty, suicides, and austerity measures have become part of everyday life for most Greeks, Portuguese, and

Spaniards. Following two decades of unprecedented economic growth as new European Union member states, today Greece, Portugal, and Spain face some exceptionally adverse conditions for economic recovery. In the following sections, I focus briefly on employment, out-migration, foreclosures, and poverty, placing Greece, Portugal, and Spain in conversation with other EU member countries as well as other developed countries in the Global North, such as the United States.

Employment

The extreme employment condition in Greece and Spain becomes evident when these two countries are compared to countries as diverse as China and the United States (see Figure 1.16).[34] The Greek and Spanish labor force has unemployment rates two to three times as large as that in the United States; one qualifier here is that Europe's unemployment measures include a far larger share of

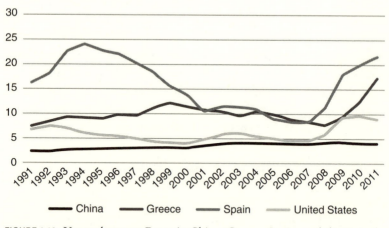

FIGURE 1.16 Unemployment Rates in China, Greece, Spain, and the United States, 1991–2011

Data source: "Unemployment and Inflation (11–19)" and "Key Supply Side Data (20–22)" in OECD 2012; IMF 2012b.

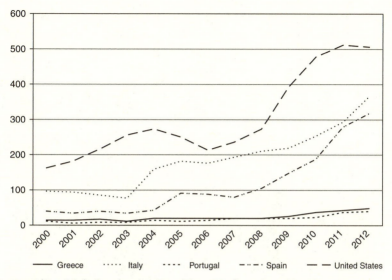

FIGURE 1.17 Male Involuntary Part-Time Workers Ages 25–54 in Greece, Italy, Portugal, Spain, and the United States, 2001–2011 (in thousands)
Data source: OECD 2013c.

the unemployed than do United States measures. In 2013, youth unemployment rates surged past 56 percent in Spain, and Greece now leads the Global North with an astonishing 62.5 percent of its youth workforce jobless.[35]

The number of involuntary part-time workers has grown in the past ten years. Figures 1.17 and 1.18 indicate the extent to which the adult labor market has become increasingly precarious in Greece, Italy, Portugal, Spain, and the United States. Important to note is that there is a sharp overrepresentation of women among involuntary part-time workers. For instance, in Spain their number grew from under 300,000 to almost 1 million, an overrepresentation that cannot be explained by the economic crisis alone. In Italy, Spain, and the United States, the number of men in involuntary part-time work has doubled, while it has tripled for women.

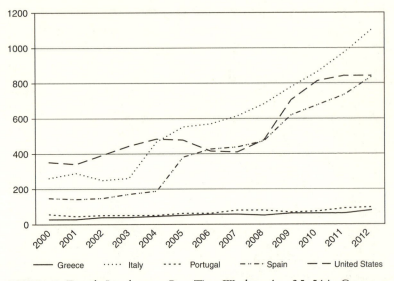

FIGURE 1.18 Female Involuntary Part-Time Workers Age 25–54 in Greece, Italy, Portugal, Spain, and the United States, 2001–2011 (in thousands)
Data source: OECD 2013c.

Out-migration

The shrinking economies of southern Europe have generated novel patterns of geographic mobility, especially among their resident immigrant populations.[36] Figure 1.19 shows an upward trend in out-migration from Spain by citizenship, especially after 2007. The increasing unemployment in the past two years has most probably only added to this emigration.[37] These novel patterns are expected to impact the degree of economic growth and the socioeconomic standards of southern Europe in the near future.

Among immigrants, those of European and Latin American origin exhibit the highest rates of out-migration, especially when compared to Africans and Asians (Figure 1.20). Given the long history of European emigration to Latin America and the ease with which

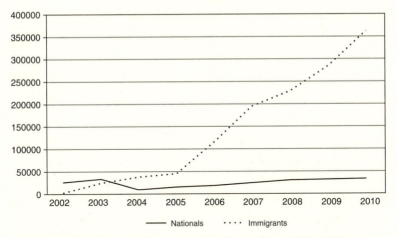

FIGURE 1.19 Out-migration from Spain by Citizenship, 2002–2010
Data source: Eurostat 2012c.

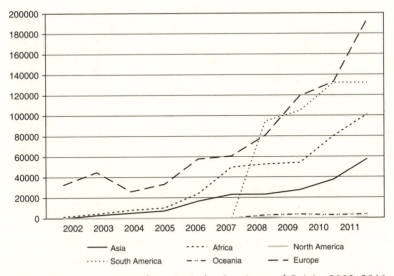

FIGURE 1.20 Out-migration from Spain by Continent of Origin, 2002–2011
Data source: Eurostat 2012c.

Latin Americans in Europe can repatriate, it is no surprise that so many Europeans and Latin Americans have left for South America. In contrast, the restrictions that Africans and Asians face in crossing borders make them more likely to remain in the country of residence, in this case Spain.

Foreclosures

One of the most brutal forms of expulsion is the eviction of people from their homes for failure to pay outstanding debt on their home. This is an especially devastating trend in Europe because there the evicted remain responsible for the full amount of their loan even after foreclosure.

In Spain, where the percentage of homeownership (80 percent) is one of the highest in Europe, foreclosures have reached the highest numbers.[38] This is partly a function of the home construction boom in the 2000s and banks' willingness to innovate on the mortgage front. There have been thousands of evictions every month since 2008; in 2009 alone, there were more than 93,000. By the end of 2012, foreclosures in Spain had surpassed 400,000 since 2007.

But foreclosure rates have increased generally in Europe (see Table 1.3). The most comprehensive examination of European trends only goes as far as 2009, and it is after that year that matters generally got worse, as the fragmentary data indicate.[39] The increases range from a maximum of 205 percent between 2008 and 2009 in Latvia to a low of 10.83 percent in Sweden. Some countries have seen a decline in the *rate* of foreclosures, even as their overall numbers of foreclosures have been extremely high. Hungary's foreclosure rate, for example, declined by 70 percent from 2008 to 2009, but that is because it had very sharp increases in foreclosures in 2007 and 2008. By the end of 2012, Hungary had accumulated almost a million foreclosures since 2009.

TABLE 1.3: European Countries with the Highest and Lowest Numbers of Foreclosures, 2007–2009

	Number of foreclosures			% Change		
	2007	2008	2009	2007–2008	2008–2009	Increase?
Highest foreclosures:						
Hungary	225,663	245,597	71,683	8.83	-70.81	No
Germany	91,788	88,379	86,617	-3.71	-1.99	No
Spain	25,943	58,686	93,319	126.21	59.01	Yes
United Kingdom	27,869	46,984	54,014	68.59	14.96	Yes
Lowest foreclosures:						
Bulgaria	449	886	1,570	97.33	77.20	Yes
Finland	506	825	1,036	63.04	25.58	Yes
Denmark	1,015	1,942	2,860	91.33	47.27	Yes
Netherlands	1,811	1,961	2,256	8.28	15.04	Yes

Data source: White 2013.

Of course, these rising numbers need to be interpreted with caution. For instance, the 63 percent increase in Finland sounds high, but the total number of foreclosure procedures is still below 1,000 (and the measure used also includes nonresidential mortgage loans). Foreclosure rates in at least some EU member states started their increase from a very low base. Further, the total volume of foreclosure procedures is relatively small in relation to the total number of outstanding residential mortgage loans. For instance, the 46,825 foreclosures in 2008 in the United Kingdom represent a high number to begin with, but that number was under 1 percent of the total number of outstanding mortgages in 2008.

What is clear from these and from more recent data is that the *total numbers* of foreclosures since 2007 are increasing year after year, even if they may fall in some years. Second, the trend is not yet over, and countries find themselves in different stages of this process. For instance, between year-end 2007 and year-end 2009, default rates in Portugal and the United Kingdom rose only slightly, while default rates in Cyprus, Hungary, and Poland more than doubled and rates in Ireland tripled. Default rates in Denmark, Spain, Estonia, Bulgaria, and Latvia all increased more than threefold. Apart from Bulgaria, Cyprus, Estonia, Greece, Hungary, Ireland, Latvia, and Poland, however, in none of the member states, nor in Norway, do loans that are more than three months in arrears appear to account for more than 3 percent of total outstanding mortgage loans in 2009. Finally, member states have experienced the impact of the crisis very differently. Each of the three member states with the highest increases (Denmark, Estonia, and Latvia), for example, exhibit very different default rates, suggesting that relative increases in default rates must be viewed alongside the absolute default rate, which is low in some of these cases.

Poverty

These rising default rates, even if low, take on added meaning if we consider the growing incidence of poverty in the EU-27. Poverty is rising throughout Europe, regardless of the different levels of socio-economic development. For instance, between 2010 and 2011, the percentage of the population at risk for poverty or social exclusion increased from 41.6 to 49.1 percent in Bulgaria, from 27.7 to 31.0 percent in Greece, from 25.5 to 27.0 percent in Spain, from 29.9 to 31.0 percent in Hungary, and from 15.0 to 16.1 percent in Sweden (see Table 1.4).

At the end of 2012, Eurostat, the statistical office of the European Union, released updated figures on risk of poverty or social exclusion through 2011.[40] It found that 119.6 million people, or 24.2 percent of the population, in the EU-27 were at risk of poverty, severely materially deprived, or living in households with very low work intensity.[41] In that group of twenty-seven countries, 9 percent of the population were severely materially deprived, meaning that they had living conditions constrained by a lack of resources (for example, they were not able to afford to pay their bills, keep their home adequately warm, or take a one-week holiday away from home). The share of those severely materially deprived varied significantly among member states, ranging from 1 percent in Luxembourg and Sweden to 44 percent in Bulgaria and 31 percent in Latvia. In 2011, the highest shares of people at risk of poverty or social exclusion were recorded in Bulgaria (49 percent), Romania and Latvia (both 40 percent), Lithuania (33 percent), and Greece and Hungary (both 31 percent); the lowest were in the Czech Republic (15 percent), the Netherlands and Sweden (both 16 percent), and Luxembourg and Austria (both 17 percent). Furthermore, the report found that 27 percent of children below eighteen years of age were affected by at least one of the three forms of poverty or social exclusion, based on 2010 data. Children were most affected in twenty member states, while the elderly were the most touched in Bulgaria, Slovenia, Finland, and Sweden. In Denmark, it was the working-age population that was the most affected.

Poverty figures are calculated by different measures in Europe and the United States. But some important trends can be noticed for both

TABLE 1.4: Poverty and Social Exclusion in EU Countries and Switzerland, 2008–2011

	% of the total population excluded, by type of social exclusion			% of population excluded			Number excluded, 2011 (in millions)
	Risk of poverty	Severely materially deprived	Households with low work intensity	2008	2010	2011	
EU 27	16.9	8.8	10.0	23.5	23.4	24.2	119.6
Austria	12.6	3.9	8.0	18.6	16.6	16.9	1.4
Belgium	15.3	5.7	13.7	20.8	20.8	21.0	2.3
Bulgaria	22.3	43.6	11.0	38.2	41.6	49.1	3.7
Croatia	21.1	14.8	17.0	n/a	31.3	32.7	1.4
Cyprus	14.5	10.7	4.5	22.4	22.9	23.5	0.2
Czech Rep.	9.8	6.1	6.6	15.3	14.4	15.3	1.6
Denmark	13.0	2.6	11.4	16.3	18.3	18.9	1.0
Estonia	17.5	8.7	9.9	21.8	21.7	23.1	0.3
Finland	13.7	3.2	9.8	17.4	16.9	17.9	0.9
France	14.0	5.2	9.3	18.6	19.2	19.3	11.8
Germany	15.8	5.3	11.1	20.1	19.7	19.9	16.1
Greece	21.4	15.2	11.8	28.1	27.7	31.0	3.4

Hungary	13.8	23.1	12.1	28.2	29.9	31.0	3.1
Iceland	9.2	2.1	6.2	11.8	13.7	13.7	0.0
Ireland	n/a	n/a	n/a	23.7	29.9	n/a	n/a
Italy	n/a	n/a	n/a	25.3	24.5	n/a	n/a
Latvia	19.3	30.9	12.2	33.8	38.1	40.1	0.9
Lithuania	20.0	18.5	12.3	27.6	33.4	33.4	1.1
Luxembourg	13.6	1.2	5.8	15.5	17.1	16.8	0.1
Malta	15.4	6.3	8.3	19.6	20.3	21.4	0.1
Netherlands	11.0	2.5	8.7	14.9	15.1	15.7	2.6
Norway	10.5	2.3	7.1	15.0	14.9	14.6	0.7
Poland	17.7	13.0	6.9	30.5	27.8	27.2	10.2
Portugal	18.0	8.3	8.2	26.0	25.3	24.4	2.6
Romania	22.2	29.4	6.7	44.2	41.4	40.3	8.6
Slovakia	13.0	10.6	7.6	20.6	20.6	20.6	1.1
Slovenia	13.6	6.1	7.6	18.5	18.3	19.3	0.4
Spain	21.8	3.9	12.2	22.9	25.5	27.0	12.4
Sweden	14.0	1.2	6.8	14.9	15.0	16.1	1.5
Switzerland	15.0	1.3	4.7	18.6	17.2	17.3	1.3
United Kingdom	16.2	5.1	11.5	23.2	23.1	22.7	14.0

Source: Eurojobs 2012.

regions in lifetime rates of homelessness (as indexed by household surveys), in income inequality, and in tax and benefit programs that increase or reduce poverty. Such measures show that before the economic collapse, the United States and the United Kingdom had consistently higher lifetime rates of homelessness, more income inequality, and less generous social welfare policies than most European countries.[42] In all countries, racial minorities and people with mental illness experience high rates of homelessness. However, in recent years, in Greece these trends are becoming extreme. NGOs working with the homeless in Greece estimate that their number had reached 20,000 by year-end 2010, if all homeless on the street, houseless, inadequately housed, and insecurely housed are counted. This is up from the 2009 estimate of 17,000 people, pointing to a disturbing trend of rapid increase.

One indication of a people's economic despair is a sharp rise in suicides.[43] This trend is evident in several countries worldwide, from India to the United States, albeit for diverse reasons—from losing land or a business to the experience of absolute abandonment by state and society. What matters for my analysis here is the fact of the increase, not the total number of suicides. In 2011, the Greek minister for health, Andeas Loverdos, reported that suicides in the first five months of the year may have increased 40 percent compared to the same period in 2010. The report also states that most of these suicides were connected to the financial crisis, as bankruptcies increased sharply and unemployment rose from 13.9 to 20.9 percent in the space of twelve months. Klimaka, a major assistance organization, reports that during that same period of time, calls from people thought to be at serious risk more than doubled, to 5,500 in 2011.

The World's Displaced

One way of bringing a global perspective to these extreme conditions of social expulsion in rich countries is to consider key worldwide displacement trends in poor countries over the last few years.

Unemployment, out-migration, foreclosures, poverty, and suicide rates are useful variables in Global North countries. Displacement due to war, disease, and famine are perhaps more useful variables in the Global South. The main agency in charge of tracking the displaced is the United Nations High Commission on Refugees (UNHCR); it counts specific types of displacement linked to armed conflicts, and hence underrepresents the total.[44] Thus UNHCR numbers leave out the displaced due to the large-scale land acquisitions in the Global South discussed in Chapter 2, those displaced in the Global North due to financial manipulation of their debt discussed in Chapter 3, or those displaced by catastrophic climate change worldwide discussed in Chapter 4.

At the end of 2011, the latest year for which comprehensive UNHCR statistics are available at this time, 42.5 million people worldwide had been forcibly displaced from their homes as a result of persistent or new conflicts in different parts of the world. This is the fifth year when the number of forcibly displaced persons worldwide exceeded 42 million. The classification "displaced persons" comprises several different populations. In 2011, the distribution was 15.2 million refugees (10.4 million under UNHCR's care and 4.8 million registered with the UN Relief and Works Agency for Palestine Refugees), 26.4 million displaced within their own country by conflict, and 895,000 asylum seekers (forcibly displaced as refugees across international borders), with nearly one-tenth of this last group in South Africa alone. The 2011 total contains, among others, three alarming growth trends I would like to highlight here. One is that an estimated 4.3 million were newly displaced by conflict or persecution. The second trend is that the above mentioned 895,000 asylum seekers represented the highest number in this category in more than a decade. The third is that another 3.5 million people were newly displaced within the borders of their countries, a 20 percent increase from 2010.

Next I examine some of these trends in greater detail so as to get at how these outcomes are constituted.

56 · EXPULSIONS

Making Mass Displacement

UNHCR had responsibility for 35.4 million of the total internationally recognized 42.5 million displaced people in 2011. Of those 35.4 million, 25.9 million were refugees and internally displaced persons. The increase over 2010 was largely due to renewed conflict-related displacement in Afghanistan, Côte d'Ivoire, Libya, South Sudan, Sudan, and Yemen. Afghanistan remains the world's leading origin of refugees for 2011. On average, one out of four refugees in the world originated from Afghanistan, with 95 percent of them finding asylum in Pakistan or the Islamic Republic of Iran. Iraq ranked second, the source of over 1.4 million refugees, followed by Somalia with almost 1.1 million, Sudan with 500,000, and the Democratic Republic of the Congo with 491,500.   *Syria .*

Protracted displacement of five years or more affects 7.1 million refugees—almost three-quarters of the refugee population under the UNHCR mandate. A protracted refugee situation is defined by UNHCR as one where 25,000 or more refugees from the same country have been in exile for five or more years. This is of particular concern to human rights activists: they have coined the term *refugee warehousing* to describe the multiyear impact of such restricted mobility, enforced idleness, and dependency in camps or other segregated settlements.[45] These are the expelled who are probably never going back to a normal life.

Table 1.5 shows the global breakdown of forcibly displaced people in 2011 by category. Table 1.6 provides a list of those countries reporting the largest numbers of new internally displaced people, and Table 1.7 summarizes some of the key facts and figures for global internal displacement trends in 2011. Finally, Table 1.8 shows where all forcibly displaced people are seeking refuge, by category of displacement and continent of asylum. These numbers are visually integrated in the world map included as Figure 1.21, which shows internally displaced people by country of asylum *and* cate-

TABLE 1.5: Global Forced Displaced under UNHCR Care, 2011

Categories of displaced population	Number of people (millions)
Refugees	10.4
Asylum seekers (pending cases)	0.9
Returned refugees	0.5
IDPs assisted by UNHCR	15.5
Returned IDPs	3.2
Stateless persons	3.5
Various	1.4
Total	35.4

Data source: UNHCR 2012b.

TABLE 1.6: Countries with the Largest Reported Numbers of Internally Displaced People, 2011 (in thousands)

Country	Beginning 2011	End 2011	% Change
Afghanistan	351	448	27
Azerbaijan	592	599	1
Colombia	3672	3888	6
Côte d'Ivoire	517	127	−75
Democratic Republic of the Congo	1721	1709	−1
Iraq	1343	1332	−1
Kenya	300	300	0
Pakistan	952	452	−52
Somalia	1463	1356	−7
Sudan	1526	2340	53

Data source: UNHCR 2012b.

Syria?

TABLE 1.7: Key Facts and Figures on Displaced People, 2011

Number of people internally displaced by the end of 2011	15.5 million
Most affected region	Africa (7 million IDPs)
Region with the largest relative increase in number of IDPs in 2009	South and Southeast Asia (with a 23 percent year-on-year increase from 2.5 million to 4.3 million)
Countries with more than a million people identified as IDPs	5 (Colombia, Democratic Republic of the Congo, Iraq, Somalia, Sudan)
Countries with at least 200,000 people identified as IDP at the end of 2011	14 (Afghanistan, Azerbaijan, Colombia, Democratic Republic of the Congo, Georgia, Iraq, Kenya, Myanmar, Pakistan, Serbia, Somalia, South Sudan, Sudan, Yemen)
Countries with at least 200,000 people returning during 2009 (in order of scale)	6 (Pakistan, Democratic Republic of the Congo, Uganda, Sudan, Kenya, Philippines)
Countries with new displacement in 2009	23
Countries with a significant proportion of IDPs living in protracted displacement	At least 34
Countries in which almost all IDPs lived in identified sites	3 (Burundi, Chad, Uganda)
Countries with IDPs in urban environments	At least 48
Countries with legislation or policies specifically addressing internal displacement	16

Data source: UNHCR 2012b.

TABLE 1.8: Estimated Number of Forcibly Displaced People by Category of Displacement and Continent of Asylum, 2011 (in thousands)

Continent of asylum	Total refugees[a]	Refugees assisted by UNHCR	Asylum seekers	IDPs protected/ assisted by UNHCR[b]	Returned IDPs[c]	Stateless persons[d]	Various[e]	Total population of concern
Africa	2,924	2,562	391	6,961	2,196	21	174	13,054
Asia	5,104	3,302	83	4,254	1,048	2,759	1,132	14,526
Europe	1,534	91	313	370	1	697	104	3,021
Latin America and the Caribbean	378	101	50	3,888	n/a	n/a	n/a	4,316
Northern America	430	n/a	54	n/a	n/a	n/a	n/a	483
Oceania	35	2	5	n/a	n/a	n/a	n/a	40
Total	10,405	6,058	896	15,473	3,245	3,477	1,412	35,440

Data source: UNHCR 2012b.

Notes: a. Includes people in refugee-like situations.

b. Includes people in IDP-like situations.

c. IDPs protected by UNHCR who have returned to their place of origin during the calendar year.

d. Persons who are not considered nationals by any state under the operation of its laws. It covers de jure and de facto stateless persons, and persons who are unable to establish their nationality.

e. Individuals who do not fall directly into any of the other categories, but to whom UNHCR may protect and offer assistance services, on humanitarian or other special grounds.

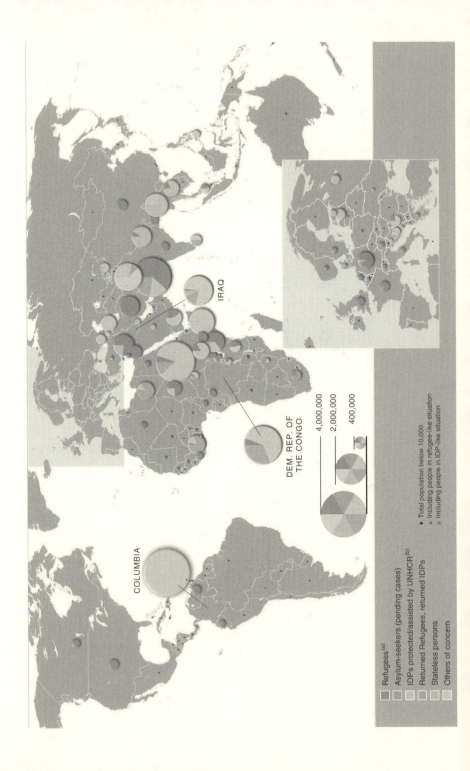

COLUMBIA

IRAQ

DEM. REP. OF
THE CONGO

4,000,000

2,000,000

400,000

- Refugees (a)
- Asylum-seekers (pending cases)
- IDP's protected/assisted by UNHCR (b)
- Returned Refugees, returned IDPs
- Stateless persons
- Others of concern

♦ Total population below 10,000
a Including people in refugee-like situation
b Including people in IDP-like situation

gory. None of these numbers take into account the surge in refugees after 2011, notably due to the conflict in Syria.

Bearing the Burden of Displacement

As the above numbers indicate, Global South countries hosted 80 percent of the world's refugees. Almost 5 million refugees resided in countries where the per capita GDP was below $3,000. The forty-eight least-developed countries provided asylum to about half of these refugees. In 2011, Pakistan, Iran, and Syria hosted the largest refugee populations, at 1.7 million, 886,500, and 755,400 respectively. The Global North country with the largest refugee population was Germany, hosting well over half a million people.

The refugee population has a much greater economic impact on the Global South than on the Global North. Pakistan experienced the biggest economic impact, with 605 refugees for each U.S. dollar of its per capita GDP, followed by Democratic Republic of the Congo and Kenya with 399 and 321 refugees for each dollar of per capita GDP, respectively. In contrast, Germany experienced a minimal impact on its economy from its refugee population, with 15 refugees for each dollar of per capita GDP. Clearly, economic impact might be minimal even as social impact can be high.

António Guterres, the United Nations high commissioner for refugees, attributed this imbalance in refugee hosting to xenophobia. "Fears about supposed floods of refugees in industrialized countries are being vastly overblown or mistakenly conflated with issues of migration," Guterres said in a statement. "It is poorer countries that are left having to pick up the burden."[46]

FIGURE 1.21 Total Population of Concern to UNHCR by Country of Asylum and Category, 2011
Source: UNHCR 2012a, map 1.

Reconceptualizing the Key Forces of Displacement

While the vast majority of displaced persons across the globe continue to be forcibly expelled from their homes due to persistent or new political conflicts, there is also an increase in those expelled due to environmental disasters.[47] Factors such as poverty and political conflict, which themselves can drive global dynamics of expulsion, also intensify the impact of environmental disasters on the world's poor. Bangladesh and Mozambique provide two illustrative case studies.

Bangladesh is widely recognized as one of the countries most vulnerable to cyclones and flooding, both of which have increased in severity and frequency in recent years. Currently almost 40 million people in Bangladesh live in coastal zones threatened by sea-level rises. It is estimated that around 3 percent of coastal land will be lost to the sea by the 2030s and 6 percent by the 2050s. As climate change advances, however, this loss of land to rising sea levels is expected to generate a far more disastrous impact on those living in coastal regions. Rising sea levels exacerbate flooding, bringing larger storm surges during cyclones and increased salinity levels in coastal areas; this will damage crops and drinking water supplies. Increasing salinity along Bangladesh's coastline is a major emergent problem among communities there, as it destroys livelihoods by making vast stretches of arable land unfarmable and contaminating drinking water for both people and livestock. Beyond such impending coastal disasters, in the interior, severe droughts and heavy flooding are causing both temporary and long-term displacements. An estimated 6.5 million people in Bangladesh have already been displaced by climate change, a number that is only expected to rise.

Mozambique is among a handful of countries suffering from both desertification and sea-level rise. Major flooding occurred in 2001, 2007, 2008, 2010, and 2012. Mozambique has been relatively successful at resettling its climate-displaced populations, but as United

Nations migration researchers report, resettlement removes people from the physical danger of extreme floods but can lead to other environmental, social, and economic difficulties. Subsistence farmers and fishers lose access to fertile lands on riverbanks and are confined to higher, drought-prone areas. And even if some regularly return to the fertile land and waters, they are unlikely to maintain land ownership and their livelihoods as farmers. They increasingly become dependent *"on governmental and international aid."*[48] As in Bangladesh, the loss of livelihoods from climate change has also been the major driver of displacement in Mozambique.

Together, these global dynamics of extreme poverty, mass displacement, environmental disasters, and armed conflicts have created heretofore unseen levels of social expulsion, especially in the Global South but now also beginning in the Global North, albeit through different events.

Imprisonment as Expulsion

A final mechanism of expulsion must be considered if we are to fully appreciate the nuances of advanced capitalism that we are living through: the rapid increase in incarceration. At the limit, it is becoming a brutal form of expulsion of surplus labor populations in the Global North, especially in the United States and increasingly in the United Kingdom. From a global perspective, one can see systemic resonances between the mass-incarcerated, warehoused refugees, and forcibly displaced people. All three signal the presence of larger foundational dynamics of expulsion that surface through the thick realities of diverse localities and systemic sites. These thick realities on the ground, along with the very different specialized research fields for each of these subjects, take us away from conceptualizations that might point to systemic parallels. From my interpretive stance, they are indeed diverse localized forms of deeper conceptually subterranean trends that cut across established differentiations.

Mass incarceration has long been present in extreme dictatorships. But today it is also emerging as inextricably linked to advanced capitalism, albeit via the formal link of crime. Most of the people who are being incarcerated are also the people who do not have work and for whom work will not be found in our current epoch; this was less the case twenty years ago, when a prisoner had a better chance to be considered rehabilitated and deserving of a job. In this sense, then, today's prisoners in the United States and in the United Kingdom are increasingly today's version of the surplus laboring population common in the brutal beginnings of modern capitalism.

Three trends can be seen when we look at incarceration, an old process, but one that today is reaching new orders of magnitude and diversifying its institutional spaces to include private for-profit prisons.[49] Most notable is the increase in the numbers of the incarcerated, a trend evident in a growing number of countries. The United States is the most dramatic case and in that regard (again) tells us how bad it can get. The imprisoned population in the United States has increased 600 percent in the past four decades. The 2.3 million prisoners in the United States account for 25 percent of those incarcerated globally, giving the United States the largest single imprisoned population in the world. Second is the sharp growth globally in those under some form of protracted correctional supervision. In the United States alone, an additional 5 million people are currently on probation or parole, which means they are effectively second-class citizens, not easily hired for a job or able to get housing. Third is the growth in the privatization of prisons and prison services, most developed in the United States but taking hold in more and more countries. The privatizing of prison services is taking place in fields as diverse as policing, courts, community supervision (electronic monitoring), parole, probation, and halfway houses for those who obtain early release from prison.

On each of these trends, global statistics are uneven in their criteria and coverage. Measures of the world's prison population often leave out those who are on parole or other such forms of carceral surveillance. In its many guises, carceral surveillance outside the prison setting is becoming a significant mechanism for social exclusion, which at the limit can become yet another mechanism for expulsion. It is difficult to measure in most countries, let alone on a global scale. Similarly, the global rise of privatization across the many facets of the global carceral assemblage, from prisons to prison services, is also difficult to track. Current data on private prison facilities center on the United States as the pioneering country in this development, followed by a mix of countries with diverse initiatives at different stages of development, including Mexico, New Zealand, Peru, South Africa, and the United Kingdom.[50]

To gain a handle on this emergent condition of expulsion through imprisonment, I begin by analyzing U.S. incarceration in the global context, then move to a detailed analysis of the rise of prison privatization in the past four decades.

U.S. Incarceration in Global Context

At present, 1 in 100 Americans is incarcerated in a U.S. state or federal prison or detained in a local jail awaiting trial.[51] When those on probation or on parole are added, the total figure tops 7 million people—1 in 31 Americans. And if all people with an arrest or conviction record are counted, the number reaches 65 million people—1 in 4 Americans. That the United States criminal justice system now touches overall 25 percent of the population is quite extreme compared with most Global North countries. If there was ever an argument to be made for American exceptionalism, the mushrooming state and private corporate prison complex would likely be the proof. Not only does the United States lead the globe in incarceration rates, but the state of Louisiana has become the world's prison capital, with 1 in 55 Louisianans currently living behind bars.

A state-by-state analysis of incarceration rates in the United States makes it clear that the carceral boom is far from uniform; this also points to the need for finer politico-legal differentiations inside countries in country-by-country analyses across the globe. While the southern states of Louisiana, Mississippi, Oklahoma, Alabama, and Texas lead the nation in residents on lockdown, the New England states of New Hampshire, Massachusetts, Rhode Island, and Maine bring up the rear. States with high incarceration levels are frequently represented as suffering from a regional proclivity toward criminality. Rather, what those states have in common are administrative rules and practices such as protracted pretrial detention, harsh sentencing laws, and minimal opportunities for pre-release. High-incarceration states also share another feature: the proliferation of for-profit prisons and for-profit prison services.

To this list of variables that are part of how a criminal justice system is organized and run, the International Centre for Prison Studies adds several others to establish the specificity of the United States carceral state in global perspective. According to the ninth edition of "World Prison Population List," released in 2011, it is estimated that more than 10.1 million people are held in penal institutions throughout the world, mostly as pretrial detainees/remand prisoners or as sentenced prisoners.[52] This figure excludes seven countries for which data were not available. Note that the 2011 report does not control for differences in carceral practices among countries, which can make a sharp difference in the overall data. Among variables not included is whether all pre-trial detainees and juveniles are held under the authority of the prison administration and whether prisons are used to house people with mental illnesses and/or those detained for drug and alcohol addiction. Moreover, those held in a form of custody not under the authority of the prison administration—for example, the 5 million people in the United States who are on probation or parole—are generally excluded from the official national prison totals.

Despite such discrepancies, the International Centre for Prison Studies draws several key conclusions in its analysis of global prison population trends. One is that "almost half of [those held] are in the

United States (2.29m), Russia (.81m), and China (1.65m sentenced prisoners)," with another 650,000 in detention centers in China. Figure 1.22 shows the steady growth of state and federal prisoners in private facilities from 2000 to 2010.

It is more challenging to estimate a global equivalent to the United States number of 7 million Americans under some form of correctional supervision (jail, prison, probation, parole). Parole is not widely used in much of the world; it remains a judicial practice primarily of wealthy Western countries. On the other hand, poor countries tend to have vastly more people detained while awaiting trial. In 2008, The International Centre for Prison Studies conducted a global analysis of pretrial detainees and other remand prisoners in all five continents, estimating that as many as 2.5 million people worldwide were incarcerated while awaiting trial. In Liberia, Mali, Haiti, Andorra, Niger, and Bolivia, 75 percent or more of the *total* prison population is awaiting trial. In 2008, the Open Society Foundation launched a global pretrial campaign as part of their initiative on

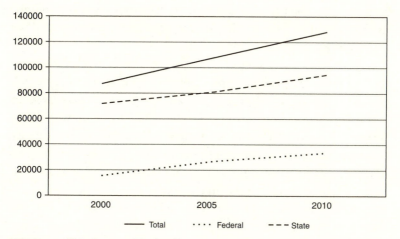

FIGURE 1.22 U.S. State and Federal Prisoners in Private Facilities, 2000–2010
Data source: Guerino, Harrison, and Sabol 2012, appendix table 19.

rights and justice. By their estimates, approximately 3 million people are behind bars awaiting trial on a given day in our world, and the annual estimate is 10 million unduplicated individuals.[53]

Private Prisons

The proliferation of for-profit prisons and for-profit prison services that undergirds big carceral systems in the United States serves as a window on what is actually involved in such a system.[54]

In the case of the United States, historians often trace the *concept* of private prisons to the convict leasing system that emerged in tandem with the Black Codes after the abolition of slavery in the United States. But the rise of discrete, privately operated correctional facilities is decidedly a twentieth-century development. As early as the 1970s, private companies began to take over the operation of halfway houses in the United States at a time of rapidly rising incarceration rates due to drug-related convictions; public facilities could not handle the added numbers. In the 1980s, private corporations further encroached "on the 'soft' end of the correctional continuum" by contracting with the Immigration and Naturalization Service (INS) to detain undocumented immigrants.

In 1984, the Corrections Corporation of American (CCA) became the first for-profit prison company to win a contract to run an entire prison facility, in Hamilton County, Tennessee. Some years later, the Wackenhut Corrections Corporation (now GEO Group) was set up. By the 1990s, both CCA and Wackenhut had set their sights overseas, striving to influence government policy and/or gain prison contracts in the United Kingdom, Australia, and France. A 2001 U.S. Department of Justice report estimated that there were 184 privately operated correctional facilities worldwide, which held a total of 132,346 people in custody. Of these, 158 were in the United States. These were distributed across thirty states, Puerto Rico, and the District of Columbia, but concentrated in the southern and western regions of the country. The remaining twenty-six facilities out of the total 184, included ten in the United Kingdom and twelve in Australia.

Private prisons continued to proliferate throughout the first decade of the twenty-first century in the United States, at rates roughly proportional to the overall growth in the U.S. prison population (see Figure 1.22). By year-end 2010, private facilities in the United States housed 128,195 state and federal prisoners. About 16 percent of United States federal prisoners (33,830) and nearly 7 percent of state prisoners (94,365) were housed in private facilities on December 31, 2010. Table 1.9 provides a regional breakdown of state and federal prisoners held in private prisons in 2000, 2009, and 2010. By 2010, thirty states in the United States had some level of privatization, with seven states housing more than a quarter of their incarcerated in private prisons.

By 2005 prison privatization, often in the form of emergent public-private partnerships, was present on all continents, even if not comparable to the U.S. level.[55] Laura McTighe analyzed a series of briefings on prison privatization released by the Public Services International Research Unit and found the following patterns and conditions in the year 2005:

- In Europe, the countries that made decisions regarding private prisons or private sector involvement in prisons were Belgium, the Czech Republic, France, Germany, Hungary, Ireland, and the United Kingdom. France's famed thirty-facility public-private prison partnership provided the blueprint for the country's expansion into for-profit juvenile detention. The United Kingdom continued to extend the role of the private sector in its carceral system, including a new privatized electronic monitoring program; this expansion proceeded in the face of increased media attention focused on deplorable conditions in private facilities. Hungary started construction of a 700-bed private prison and planned a second to open in 2007, and the Czech Republic

TABLE 1.9: U.S. State and Federal Prisoners in Private Facilities, by Region and States with Largest Populations in Private Prison, 2000–2010

Region	2000	2009	2010	% all prisoners (2010)
U.S. total	87,369	129,333	128,195	8.0
Federal	15,524	34,087	33,830	16.1
State	71,845	95,246	94,365	6.7
Northeast	2,509	5,423	5,301	3.0
New Jersey	2,498	2,950	2,841	11.4
Pennsylvania	0	920	1,015	2.0
Midwest	7,836	4,895	5,885	2.2
Indiana	991	2,479	2,817	10.1
Ohio	1,918	2,195	3,038	5.9
South	45,560	58,737	60,491	9.2
Florida	3,912	9,812	11,796	11.3
Texas	13,985	19,207	19,155	11.0
West	15,940	26,191	22,688	7.3
Arizona	1,430	8,971	5,356	13.3
New Mexico	2,155	2,822	2,905	43.6

Data source: National Prisoner Statistics Program 2013.

planned its first private prison. Ireland drew up plans for its first private prison, opened nine private courts, privatized its electronic monitoring, and converted two empty prisons into for-profit halfway houses. In Germany, the British company Serco was awarded a five-year contract to provide psychological, medical, and educational services; video surveillance, kitchens, workshops, and facility management services; and industrial work for 300 prisoners in conjunction with other companies. Greece rounded out the list with a year-end opening of six new prisons and passage of a new law that provided the framework for future public-private partnerships.

- In Asia and the Pacific, the countries that were developing private prisons in 2005 were Israel, Thailand, Russia, and Hong Kong. Israel awarded its first prison contract. Thailand conducted a substantial feasibility study on prison privatization. Russia's economy ministry was considering private prison construction as a solution to the $9 billion estimated cost to modernize its existing penitentiary system. Members of Hong Kong's Special Administrative Region government made a trip to the United Kingdom to study its public-private partnership prison projects.
- In Africa, South Africa ended the year with its two private prisons running strong and four new facilities under construction. The leadership of the New Partnership for Africa's Development, an economic development program run by the African Union, increasingly looked to South Africa as a model for private-sector financing of prisons and other ailing public services.
- In the Australia and Oceania region, the American company GEO Group lost its only prison contract in New Zealand and was increasingly under investigation surrounding correctional issues in Australia. But by the end of the year Australia had not only privatized the New South Wales government's police stations but also welcomed a new private prison lobbying group on the national scene.
- In South America, Ecuador's interior minister advocated the expedited expansion of prison privatization, while a constitutional court thwarted Costa Rica's attempt to award a private prison contract to a Utah-based company.
- In North America, Canada made a major step toward privatization when it contracted prison monitoring out to a for-profit corporation.

This one-year snapshot of global private prison expansion is instructive for several reasons. While much research has been conducted on prison privatization in the United States, for-profit prisons had become a decidedly global phenomenon by the turn of the twenty-first century. Many of the corporations that led the U.S. privatization boom earned as much as 20 percent of their profits from overseas prison contracts. Furthermore, this global snapshot helps to illuminate the legal and legislative mechanisms through which privatization was often introduced, and the wide variety of prison settings in which private financing was able to flourish. Thus analyses of worldwide private prisons that focus solely on prisons holding sentenced adults and pre-trial detainees can miss key developments. Among such developments are, for instance, the expansion of privatization into juvenile detention facilities in France, halfway houses in Ireland, and electronic monitoring programs in the United Kingdom and Canada. Beyond such dedicated for-profit facilities and correctional supervision strategies, carceral systems also saw the rise of prisons that outsourced to for-profit companies services such as health care, education, food, and transportation, as was the case in Germany. The evolution from public to private prisons was often initiated through parliamentary debates and legislation; this was the case in Greece, Russia, Hong Kong, and Ecuador. Finally, lobbying efforts by private prison companies often served to expand privatization even (and especially) in the face of media and independent monitoring evidence of the failures of private prisons, as was the case in Australia.

Private prisons and prison services corporations in the United States pursue their goals as a regular private firm might (see Figure 1.23). Campaign contributions in the 2000s by two major corporations had reached several million dollars by the 2010 election cycle in Washington, DC (see Figure 1.23) and even more at the state level. In economies where privatization has been seen as efficient the argument for private prisons is easy to make. Yet prisons are not just any way of making profits.[56] Profits come from filling beds and selling state prison services. Indeed, there is evidence of bribes to keep prison beds full and profits up. In what is probably an extreme case, the Penn-

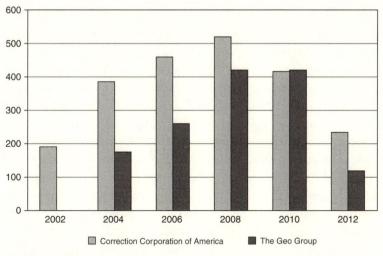

FIGURE 1.23 Washington Campaign Contributions (in thousands of dollars), 2002–2012

Source: Kirkham 2012.

sylvania Supreme Court in 2011 overturned about 4,000 convictions issued by Judge Mark Ciavarella, dubbed the "kids-for-cash" judge after he accepted $1 million in bribes from developers of privatized juvenile detention centers and then presided over trials that sent youth to those same centers.[57] There are multiple instances across the United States, albeit in milder versions, of this push to keep prison beds occupied: the rise in longer sentences even for minor offenses, three-strikes-and-you're-out legislation (whereby a third felony conviction mandates life imprisonment), the greater likelihood that even the very elderly and impaired are being kept in prison. Together these and other measures result in an expanding prison population that generates a greater demand for prison beds; directly or indirectly, this generates a greater demand for private prisons and prison services. Despite such gross miscarriages of justice, the myth that privatization decreases costs and increases safety has remained largely untouched.

Beyond the privatization of prisons, jails, juvenile facilities, half-way houses, electronic monitoring programs, and in-prison services, many transnational corporations have set up satellite factories inside prisons. This is often facilitated by for-profit prison contracts, as was the case in Germany when the British company Serco took over the majority of operations. Throughout the Federal Bureau of Prisons in the United States, all sentenced prisoners are required to work so long as they are medically able. Institution assignments vary, and wages are a meager 12¢ to 40¢ per hour. Those employed in Federal Prison Industries make slightly more for the metals, furniture, electronics, textiles, and graphic arts they are required to produce; pay ranges from 23¢ to $1.15 per hour, of which up to 50 percent can be garnished to cover court-ordered fines, victim restitution, child support, and other monetary judgments.[58] Federal Prison Industries is a U.S. government-owned corporation created in 1934 to provide job skills training to federal prisoners, who work for the federal government; it is a very different arrangement from that used by corporations who use prison labor. Private corporations can benefit from such low-wage labor in several ways: (1) from directly using prisoner labor for manufacturing and service jobs, (2) by contracting with other companies to purchase products or services made by prisoners, and (3) by investing in the private prison corporations responsible for the ever-expanding global correctional system. Available evidence suggests that the majority of corporations profiting from prison labor, including Chevron, Bank of America, AT&T, Starbucks, and Walmart, fall into the second mode.

In prisons and jails across the United States, increasingly the commodity being bought and sold is prisoners themselves. This has been facilitated by a shift in the way that prisons are funded by the government: from cost reimbursement to fixed-rate per diem systems, whereby a prison receives a flat fee per incarcerated person per day. Recently, several state prison systems have transitioned from cost reimbursement to per diem systems for their entire facilities. The practice is also starting to extend to local jails: New Orleans became the first major U.S. city to finance its local jail through a per diem system.

Until the 1880s, the Department of the Interior and its U.S. Marshals Service were responsible for federal prisoners at facilities across the United States, including local jails. Historically, the U.S. Marshals Service housed federal prisoners at facilities across the United States, including local jails. Per diem funding dates back to that time, when the federal government began to "rent" beds in state prisons and local jails for housing those serving federal time. However these federal prisoners were by far the exception. This is an important point to underscore if we are to understand why mass incarceration has become such a powerful vehicle of expulsion under our current phase of advanced capitalism.

This may seem like little more than a logistical change in the way that prison operators are reimbursed by the state or local municipality. In practice, however, reimbursement for incarcerated bodies rather than actual prison operating costs has created a perverse incentive to lock up more people for longer periods of time at taxpayers' expense. If a person is held in custody for even twenty-five hours, a prison or local sheriff's office is reimbursed for two days. After basic operating costs are covered, anything left over is profit for the sheriff. (In contrast, one might posit that if the bottom line is operating costs, it would seem that fewer prisoners for less time is the ideal, and it would mean using less of the taxpayers' money.) The capacity for profit generation through the warehousing of incarcerated people has been leveraged in critical ways outside of the dynamics of prison privatization discussed thus far. For example, it has now been well documented that sheriffs in rural Louisiana parishes trade prisoners among facilities to keep all beds full and, thus, reimbursement rates at the highest possible amount.

CONCLUSION: PREDATORY FORMATIONS

A long chapter with many diverse strands deserves a short and sharp conclusion. There is one organizing proposition across all these diverse strands: since the 1980s, there has been a strengthening of dynamics that expel people from the economy and from society, and these dynamics are now hardwired into the normal functioning of these spheres. One outcome is the shrinking of the recognized economy—recognized in standard measures. I see this as a rupture with the preceding period—the Keynesian period in some parts of the world, and, with its own modes, the working communist state period in others. In both these types of political economy the systemic tendency was toward incorporating people, especially as workers, notwithstanding social exclusions of all sorts. In this sense they contrast with the expulsion dynamics I see as prevailing in the current post-1980s period across diverse types of political economies (though this chapter has largely focused on political economies in the Global North; Chapter 2 will concentrate on the Global South).

Getting at those expulsions meant getting at a mix of very diverse conditions and local specifics—in short, getting to ground level. To do this I used established data sets, albeit to explore an idea that is far from established. In the established data, each condition is specific to a country and a sector, and each has been researched and conceptualized on its own terms. And yet at ground level, a level not intermediated by the specifics of nation and sector, each of the examined conditions contains within it an expulsion dynamic—marked by extremes in unemployment, poverty, suicide, displacement from home and land, incarceration, or suicide.

Beyond the empirics of each condition, the second strand organizing the chapter is the need to conceptualize these diverse conditions inside countries and across countries in ways that make visible deeper shared dynamics across sectors and countries. A prison in the Global North is not the same entity as a displaced-persons camp in the Global South. The "long-term unemployed" and small business bankruptcies in each Greece, Italy, and India are not the same as the "excess suicides" in each country. The emigration of Spain's middle-class citizens because they have been expelled from the prosperity zone of their country's economy is not the same event as smallholder farmers migrating to urban slums because they have been expelled from their land. Each one of these cases is specific, and each one has been researched and conceptualized on its own terms via the existing data. In this chapter I have sought to capture the fact itself of this mix of local events and situated meanings. And yet, at ground level, not intermediated by the specifics of country and sector, they all go in one direction—toward pushing people out.

I conceive of the mix of elements that generates each of the particular expulsions examined in this chapter as a kind of predatory formation. That is to say, these expulsions are not simply the result of an individual's, a firm's, or a government's decision or action. Yes, such decisions and actions matter, but they are part of larger assemblages of elements, conditions, and mutually reinforcing dynamics. Suicide is a very personal decision, but the demographic concept of "excess suicides" in specific places and situations is partly a function of a larger assemblage of conditions. European Central Bank and IMF officials have made the decision to insist on government debt reduction via cuts in basic services and the jobs of mostly modest-salaried government employees. Yet we cannot simply say that the IMF and the bank are guilty of the extreme outcomes discussed in this chapter; the decisions of these powerful actors are part of a larger assemblage of institutional changes implemented in the name of the "proper way of running an economy," an idea that goes back to the 1980s and has now spread worldwide. Similarly, each of the cases discussed in this chapter arises partly out of the application of complex knowledges and the deployment of complex technologies.

x powerlines

Yet we cannot simply say that such knowledges and technologies are the cause of the extreme outcomes analyzed here.

There is a kind of systemic logic at work in each of these predatory formations. It is this logic that led me to the notion of a formation rather than simply a collection of powerful individuals and firms that make decisions with major consequences for people and places worldwide. At the heart of this logic is a distortion when compared to the prior period—that of rising welfare states in many market economies as well in many communist countries.

Perhaps this systemic logic is clearest in the case of private prisons and, as I examine in Chapter 2, land grabs. Profit-driven private prisons are not the same as government prisons. Strictly speaking, the latter are part of a government's larger obligation to protect its citizens from genuinely dangerous individuals. Since it is meant to be a public good financed through citizens' taxes, the goal of a government prison is to imprison those who are a danger and only for as long as is necessary: citizens' taxes should not be used on frivolous imprisonment and unnecessarily long terms (though in practice, the right balance among these imperatives—protecting citizens and using citizens' taxes wisely—is rarely fully achieved). When prisons become a corporate business whose logic is not unlike the logic of a motel owner—fill those beds—the goals are opposite from those of government prisons: to imprison more people and to keep them there for longer periods. As I examined in this chapter, the proliferation of private for-profit prisons has coincided with far longer sentences for trivial acts and a further increase in the rate of incarceration. There are decision makers at each step of the process, but they are caught in a sticky web of systemic logics. Finally, the profits of private prisons are represented as a positive addition to a country's GDP even as they are a government cost; in contrast, government-run prisons are only represented as government debt.

It is this type of predatory logic embedded in an assemblage of diverse elements, each only a bit of a larger formal institutional domain, that marks much of our current period. In Chapter 2 I focus on yet another such systemic logic: when a corporation or a foreign government acquires a large tract of land to grow palm to make biofuels, it expels whole floras and faunas, small farmers, rural manufacturing setups, and more. But it all translates into a rise in corporate profits and an increase in a country's GDP. Each of the predatory formations discussed in this book also tells us something about the larger challenge we confront—one that goes beyond powerful individuals and institutions.

CHAPTER 2

The New Global Market for Land

The acquisition of local land by foreign governments and foreign firms is a centuries-old process in much of the world. But we can detect specific phases in the diverse histories and geographies of such acquisitions. A major such shift began in 2006, marked by a rapid increase in the volume and geographical spread of foreign acquisitions, as well as the diversity of the buyers. More than 200 million hectares of land are estimated to have been acquired from 2006 to 2011 by foreign governments and firms. Much of the purchased land is in Africa, but a growing share is now in Latin America and, a first since the post–World War II era, in several countries in Europe and Asia, notably Russia, Ukraine, Laos, and Vietnam. Finally the buyers are increasingly diverse, including purchasers from countries of origin that range from China to Sweden, and firms from sectors as different as biotechnology and finance.

What matters for my analysis is this extremely sharp change in the total level and geographical range of foreign land acquisitions. It represents a break in a long-term trend and thereby becomes an indicator of a larger systemic shift, one that goes beyond the old, established patterns of acquisition. Two significant factors contribute to this sharp increase in acquisitions. One is the growing demand for industrial crops, notably palm for biofuels, and for food crops, the latter still coming largely from the states of the Persian

Gulf and from China. The second is that growing demand for land and the sharp rise in global food prices in the 2000s made land a desirable investment, even for speculative reasons. It is now public knowledge that the major banks were already concerned in 2006 about signs of the extraordinary financial crisis that was about to break. It is no coincidence that land then surged as a destination for investment capital, both because of its materiality (the thing itself, rather than a derivative representing land) and as a means of access to an expanding range of commodities (food, industrial crops, rare earth minerals, and water).

The acquisition of foreign land is not a lone-wolf event. It requires, and in turn stimulates, the making of a vast global market for land. It entails the development of an also vast specialized servicing infrastructure to enable sales and acquisitions, secure property or leasing rights, develop appropriate legal instruments, and even push for the making of new law to accommodate such purchases in a sovereign country. This is an infrastructure that goes well beyond supporting the mere act of purchasing. It not only facilitates but also stimulates further foreign acquisitions of land. This increasingly sophisticated specialized service sector invents new types of contracts and forms of ownership, and creates innovative accounting, legal, and insurance instruments.[1] As it develops, this specialized sector, in turn, depends on further acquisitions of foreign land as a source of profits. We see the beginnings of a large-scale commodification of land, which may in turn lead to the financializing of the commodity we still call, simply, land.

The scale of land acquisitions leaves a large global footprint. It is marked by a vast number of microexpulsions of small farmers and villages, and by rising levels of toxicity in the land and water surrounding the plantations constructed on the acquired land. There are growing numbers of displaced people, rural migrants moving to slums in cities, destroyed villages and smallholder economies, and, in the long run, much dead land. What actually happens when a new owner/leaser, whether national or foreign, has acquired 2.8 million hectares of land to grow palm for biofuels? Mostly, dozens of villages, whole smallholder agriculture districts, and whole manufacturing operations in these rural regions are expelled from the land. Some may receive compensation and some may be resettled in equivalent terrain. But generally speaking, the losses are far larger than the compensations. Finally, flora and fauna are expelled to make room for monocultures. All this brings degradation of the land and the earth itself, through loss of diversity of nutrients and of insect life. After a few decades, the land will be exhausted, clinically dead, as we have seen in older plantation zones in Central America, the Caribbean, and parts of Africa. In the very long term the land may recover, but the descendants of the expelled farmers and rural manufacturers will most likely not benefit, and instead find themselves living in crammed slums at the edges of large cities.

Let me emphasize that this trajectory has become the norm, regardless of who is purchasing land and where. Millions of Brazilian smallholders have been expelled from their farmland, which has been taken over by vast soya plantations that produce for export. The developers may be national or foreign corporations and individuals. One outcome has been hunger in areas where there used to be little if any hunger even if they were poor: soya has replaced black beans, which were a source of income and food for poor farmers. And many of them have had no option other than to migrate to the slums of large cities. The new hunger is further accentuated by the toxicity that large plantations bring to the surrounding area, making it difficult for the households of plantation workers to use their small plots to grow food.

The actual material practices that underlie these large-scale foreign acquisitions vary enormously. I am interested in these material practices, which transform sovereign national territory into a far more elementary condition—land for usufruct. This process, at least indirectly, degrades the governments that sold and leased the land. The eviction of farmers and craftspeople, villages, rural man-ufacturing districts, and districts of agricultural smallholders simi-larly degrades the meaning of citizenship for local people. And when the mines and plantations occupy land where there are no people, they degrade water and earth. Such material practices re-constitute territory in vast stretches of the nation-state: territory becomes merely land in the case of plantations and dead land in the case of mines.

These are accelerated histories and geographies in the making. Right now we know that many millions of people are dramatically affected by the scale of these processes. The fact that the vast ma-jority of acquisitions since 2006 have been by foreign governments and firms may or may not prove decisive for the people of those areas. Sometimes host governments have agreed to these deals for the benefit of local elites; other times they have simply succumbed to pressures and commissions. Researchers can find it easier to track foreign rather than national acquisitions of land, as informa-tion about the former is more likely to be in the public domain. But large-scale national acquisitions are also happening, with implica-tions similar to those I discuss for foreign acquisitions. The critical dimension explored in this chapter is the empirical one: the scale, geography, purpose, and diversity of foreign acquisitions.

This empirical examination aims at laying down the facts in or-der to signal the devastating consequences that rural populations and rural land may face. Given the recency of this new wave of ac-quisitions, we do not yet fully know the consequences for all the people and the land caught up in this vortex of large-scale acquisi-tions. But we do know enough to be worried.

Debt as a Disciplining Regime: Preparing the Ground for Land Acquisitions

Today's large-scale acquisitions of foreign land are enabled by the explicit aims and unplanned consequences of the IMF and World

Bank restructuring programs implemented in much of the Global South in the 1980s. To this we can add the demands of the World Trade Organization (WTO) in the 1990s and into the 2000s to lift import-export barriers in the name of "free trade." The resulting mix of constraints and demands had the effect of disciplining governments not yet fully integrated into the regime of free trade and open borders pursued mostly by large firms and the governments of dominant countries.

The aim was compliance with what was then an emerging body of rules and conditionalities that eventually were represented as self-evident norms for the proper governing of an economy if a country was to have growth and prosperity. Among the better-known of these quasi-norms were the control of inflation even if it meant sacrificing economic growth and employment, reduction of apparent government waste at just about any cost; payment of debt even if it meant cutting social benefits, health care, and infrastructure development; and privatization of all the basic service functions, from telecommunications to banking.[2] These norms, imposed on Global South countries through IMF and World Bank restructuring programs beginning in the 1980s, resonate with what today goes under the name of "austerity" in Europe.

In my reading, then, it is not merely the fact that governments of poor countries are burdened with debt repayment that creates suffering, as much well-meaning discussion of the Global South and the eurozone describes. What also matters is the larger assemblage of elements within which debt functions and which the dynamics of debt helped constitute. Let me bring in the qualifiers later and for now put it brutally for the sake of clarity. Even if privatization and the lifting of trade barriers are not by themselves destructive forces, they tend to become so in the context of weak governments weighed down by costly debt restructuring programs. Indeed, they have become mechanisms for the direct and indirect destabilizing of a large number of governments in the Global South. For instance, many national manufacturing and consumer services firms have gone under because they could not compete with cheap mass imports by global firms. In short, these diverse programs had the effect of reconditioning national sovereign frameworks in ways that enabled the insertion of national territory into the new or emerging global corporate circuits. Once there, territory became land for sale on the global market.

My core conceptual move here is to see these programs of the 1980s and onward as regimes of discipline. These regimes aimed at a major restructuring of the role of government and at making the executive branch of government beholden to powerful international organizations such as the IMF, the World Bank, and the WTO. These regimes do not exist simply to push for repayment of debt and a few policy changes, though perhaps the work of the IMF and the WTO did, decades ago, begin with such limited goals. Nor have the IMF, World Bank, and WTO programs in the Global South succeeded in what they presented as necessary policies to achieve economic growth. Where followed, their advice has not delivered either economic development or strong democratic government. The effect in most of the program countries was, rather, a massive increase in indebtedness to foreign lenders and a sharp shrinkage in government funds for education, health, and infrastructure. Nor did the private economic sector fare well: there were widespread bankruptcies among local enterprises after the entry of well-capitalized foreign mass-market firms. Indeed, the IMF has had to face up to this by implementing special debt relief programs for the forty-one so-called HIPCs (highly indebted poor countries).

The language of failed states, the most common way to describe these weakened, often devastated nation-states, leaves out many of the negative effects that key actors of the international governance system, notably the IMF and the WTO, have had on program countries. Such language represents these states' decay as endogenous, a function of their own weaknesses and corruptions. These states are indeed mostly weak, corrupt, and uncaring about the well-being of their citizens. But it is important to remember that it often is and was the vested interests of foreign governments and firms that enabled the corruption and weakening of these states. And good leaders who resisted Western interests did not always survive; consider, notably, the now-recognized murder of the Congolese leader Patrice Lumumba by the United States government. Further, the extensive land acquisitions now under way, with the expulsions of small farmers and poisoning of land they are causing, cannot be understood simply as a consequence of the corruption of host states.

IMF and World Bank restructuring programs prepared the ground for the systemic deepening of advanced capitalism. This is not a novel point, and while I agree with the well-known critiques of these programs, my focus here is on something that has received less attention: detecting how those restructuring programs partly enabled the ease with which foreign buyers can purchase land in many of the countries subjected to such programs, and the ease with which governments are willing to allow those acquisitions. Greed and money are not enough to explain the outcome. Further, notwithstanding the similarities to older imperial epochs, there is now clear treaty law that asserts the authority of all national states over their territory. As a result, it is actually not so simple for a government to acquire vast stretches of land in a foreign country, nor for a government to sell or lease its land to a foreign government. Enablements, which include corruption and a government's overwhelming foreign debt, can play a role in the negotiation. But so can innovative lawyering, accounting, and business deal-making.

There are (at least) two vectors through which we can identify the bridge between restructuring programs and today's massive land acquisitions. One is the debt regime as a factor that helps weaken and impoverish national governments in much of the Global South. This in turn has often been a factor in governments' extreme corruption and disregard for the nation's well-being, especially in underdeveloped but resource-rich countries. It can also be a factor in a government's willingness to sell vast amounts of land and expel whole villages from their land to do so. The other vector is the debt regime: it can function as a strong and "legitimate" point of entry into a sovereign nation-state; what was once open access to the economies of Global South countries for the IMF and World Bank seems to have eventually been extended to foreign governments and firms. The debt regime, in turn enabled extensive fiscal disciplining and prioritized the payment of foreign debt over national priorities such as education and economic development. To put it bluntly, it is easier for rich foreign governments and investors to acquire vast stretches of land in sub-Saharan Africa and parts of Latin America and Asia if their dealings are with weakened and/or corrupt governments and local elites, with little if any voice and political representation left for the population.

This is not to argue that rich countries, global firms, and international organizations have long conspired to weaken poor countries specifically to enable purchases of land. I am extracting the older history alluded to earlier in this chapter, which begins in the 1980s with restructuring programs, and arguing that it weakened and impoverished those national governments. As I will discuss later, many of these countries had developed both mass manufacturing and a middle class employed in government bureaucracies; for instance, Mogadishu, Somalia, was a middle-class city, with a large educated workforce and a prosperous working class. When national debt exploded in the 1980s in much of sub-Saharan Africa, partly due to the recycling of so-called post-1973 OPEC dollars, much of this progress was thwarted. Key reasons were the imposition of debt repayment priorities and the opening of markets to powerful foreign firms. This weakened the state, thereby impoverishing the middle classes, and it destroyed the indigenous manufacturing sector, which could not compete with large mass-market foreign firms. A downward cycle was put in motion that in turn enabled the much later large-scale acquisition of land by foreign governments and firms.

One way of reading this earlier history in the Global South is to see it as an antecedent of what has begun to crawl into the Global North through the venue of state deficits as those deficits began to rise sharply over the last few years.[3] A key component of these rising deficits among Global North governments is the falling share of corporate taxes in total state tax revenue; to this we can add in some countries, massive transfers of state tax revenue to fund bail-outs or cheap money for banks. The growing dependence of states on individual tax payments makes the state even more vulnerable given a financial crisis with massive repercussions on the economy, notably a sharp rise in unemployment. Add to this the bankruptcies of growing numbers of small enterprises, often family-owned, which are unlikely to use tax havens, and states experience an additional loss of revenue. These losses proceed alongside the sharp rise in corporate profits—public resources decline and private resources grow, as examined in Chapter 1. Under its own specific modalities, the Global North experiences an asymmetry between the fortunes of governments and major firms similar to what I examine here for the Global South. In the Global South this facilitated, among other things, the concentration of benefits at the top (including the upper levels of the middle class), thinned out the modest middle classes, and sharpened the meaning of poverty. This looks remarkably similar to the major trends in Greece today, even though Greece's wealthy elites mostly do not live in that country, unlike what is the case in Angola and Nigeria, for instance. The structural adjustment programs imposed on Global South countries echo the austerity politics of the Global North, not just in Greece but also in countries as diverse as the United States and the Netherlands.

Debt and debt-servicing problems have long been a systemic feature of the developing world. But the particular features of debt negotiated by the IMF, rather than the fact of debt per se, are what concern me here: this was not just about debt, but rather about using the issue of debt to reorganize a political economy. The second feature that concerns me is how the gradual destruction of traditional economies in rural areas prepared the ground, literally, for some of the new needs of advanced capitalism, notably land for plantation agriculture and for access to water, metals, and minerals. While the pursuit of these needs is familiar and has happened before, my argument is that they are now part of a new organizing logic that changes their valence and their macro-level effects. This notion or proposition is based on a methodological and interpretation practice I develop at length elsewhere.[4]

With few exceptions, poor countries subjected to the restructuring regime that began in the 1980s now have larger shares of their populations that are in desperate poverty and are less likely to enter the "modern" economy via consumption than they did even twenty years ago, a dynamic that parallels certain developments in the Global North (see Chapter 1). When this new era began in the 1980s, many sub-Saharan countries had functioning health and education systems and economies, and less absolute destitution than today. Also, resource-rich countries have seen more of their people become destitute and expelled from basic survival systems because of those resources, even as another part of their population becomes a rich middle class, also because of those resources; Nigeria and Angola are probably the most familiar cases of this common pattern in the current decade. The dominant dynamic at work for these populations is, to a good extent, the opposite of the old Keynesian dynamic of valuing people as workers and as consumers. Expulsions from home, land, and job have also had the effect of giving expanded operational space to criminal networks and to the trafficking of people, as well as greater access to land and underground water resources to foreign buyers, whether firms or governments. Systemically, the role of rich donor countries has also shifted: overall they give less in foreign aid for development than they did thirty years ago. As a result, in many cases the remittances sent by low-income immigrants to countries of origin are now larger than foreign aid to those countries. Further, since the late 1990s an increasing share of foreign aid comes through NGOs and philanthropic organizations, further marginalizing many a government's role in development. One extreme outcome is the de facto downgrading of governments to the status of predatory elites.

These systemic shifts contribute to explain a complex difference that can be captured in a set of simple numbers. Generally, the IMF asked poor program countries in the 1980s and 1990s to pay 20 to 25 percent of their export earnings toward debt service. In contrast, in 1953, the Allies cancelled 80 percent of Germany's war debt and only insisted on 3 to 5 percent of export earnings for debt service. They asked 8 percent from central European countries in the 1990s. Against these past levels, the debt service burdens on poor countries beginning in the 1980s are extreme. It does suggest that the earlier aim of policy for Europe—first Germany after World War II and more recently central Europe—was reincorporation into the capitalist world economy. In contrast, the aim for the Global South in the 1980s and 1990s was more akin to transformative discipline, starting with forced acceptance of both restructuring programs and loans from the international system. It is in this sense that the restructuring programs were about more than debt service: they aimed at shaping a political economy and a repositioning of these countries as sites for extraction, ranging from natural resources to the consumption power of their populations.

After twenty years of this regime, it became clear that it did not deliver on the basic components for healthy development. The discipline of debt service payments was given strong priority over infrastructure, hospitals, schools, jobs, and other people-oriented goals. The primacy of this extractive logic became a mechanism, perhaps mostly unintended, for systemic transformation that went well beyond debt service payment. It contributed to the devastation of large sectors of traditional economies, often the destruction of a good part of the national bourgeoisie and petty bourgeoisie, the sharp impoverishment of the population and, in many cases, of the state. Again, beyond the many differences there are worrisome resonances with today's austerity politics in Europe and other developed countries.

Even before the economic crises of the mid-1990s that hit a vast number of countries as they implemented privatization and open-border policies, the debt of poor countries in the Global South had grown from $507 billion in 1980 to $1.4 trillion in 1992.[5] Debt service payments alone had increased to $1.6 trillion, more than the actual debt in 1980. From 1982 to 1998, indebted countries paid in interest four times the amount of their original debts, and at the same time their indebtedness went up fourfold. These countries had to use a significant share of their total revenues to service these debts. For instance, Africa's debt service payments reached $5 billion in 1998; that year, for every $1 in foreign aid African countries paid $1.40 in debt service. By the late 1990s, debt-to-GDP ratios (see Table 2.1) were especially high in Africa, where they stood at 123 percent, compared with 42 percent in Latin America and 28 percent in Asia.[6] As of 2006, the poorest forty-nine countries (countries with annual per capita income of less than $935) had debts of $375 billion. If to these poor countries we add the "developing countries," in 2006 a total of 144 countries had debt amounting to $2.9 trillion and paid $573 billion to service that debt.[7]

Generally, IMF debt management policies from the 1980s onward have not halted the worsening situation for the unemployed and poor.[8] Much research on poor countries documents the link between hyperindebted governments and cuts in social programs. These cuts tend to affect women and children in particular through reductions in education and health care, both investments necessary to ensure a better future.[9]

TABLE 2.1: Debt Service Amount and as a Percentage of GDP in Selected Countries, 2009

Country	Total external debt ($billions)	Total external debt payment ($billions)	Total health spending (% GDP)	Total spending on debt service payments (% GDP)
Angola	15.1	1.6[a]	1.5	6.8
Ecuador	17.1	4.1[a]	2.2	11.4
Egypt	34.4	2.5[a]	2.4	2.8
Georgia	1.9	0.2[a]	2.4	2.9
Jamaica	6.5	1.0[a]	2.4	10.1
Lebanon	23.3	3.5[a]	2.4	16.1
Lesotho	0.7	54.2[a]	2.4	3.7
Moldova	2.0	0.3	4.2	8.6
Morocco	16.4	2.7	1.7	5.3
Pakistan	33.7	2.4	0.4	2.2
Panama	9.8	2.0	5.2	13.4
Papua New Guinea	1.9	0.4	3.0	6.7
Paraguay	3.1	0.5	2.6	6.7
Philippines	61.5	9.9[a]	1.4	10.0
Ukraine	333.3	5.9	3.7	6.6

Source: Jubilee Debt Campaign 2013.
Note: a. Yearly payment

There is now a larger history in the making. In my reading it includes as one key element a repositioning of much of Africa and substantial parts of Latin America and Central Asia in a new massively restructured global economy with a growing demand for land and the many things it allows access to, from food to minerals and water. Weakened governments and the destruction of traditional economies have facilitated access to that land by foreign governments and firms. After decades of debt service and competition from mass-market foreign firms, there is little left of what were once modern economic sectors in many of these countries. Thus modest middle-class sectors that may once have had the possibility of active participation in the new consumer economy, and even in the current land and resource boom, are simply no longer there, for reasons ranging from brain drain and military conflicts to IMF restructuring programs. To this we can add corruption on both sides of many international deals, which enabled the emergence of what can only be described as predatory elites in resource-rich countries. By the early 2000s, this mix of processes and conditions had launched a new phase of wealth accumulation for some and a struggle merely to survive for growing components of society, economy, and government.

The Who, Where, and What of Foreign Land Acquisitions

What is actually being measured in general descriptions of land grabs can vary considerably depending on the study. I have chosen the data of the Land Matrix project, which were generated collectively in collaboration with the International Land Coalition. It provides the most comprehensive overall measure.[10]

But before discussing the Land Matrix findings, I briefly mention several focused investigations into specific sectors and countries; each contributes to the larger, rapidly moving overall process of data gathering.[11] GRAIN, a French NGO, developed its own database on land acquisitions in 2012. It can account for about 14 million hectares acquired by foreign investors in 416 separate land deals. GRAIN's methodology is stricter than Land Matrix's. It collected information specifically on post-2006 land deals led by foreign investors involving "large areas of land . . . for the production of food crops."[12] A second focused study comes from HighQuest Partners, an OECD contracted consulting firm specializing in farmland investing. They interviewed twenty-five financial groups that invested in farmland in 2010, and were managing a total of $7.44 billion in agricultural assets. HighQuest Partners also generated estimates for total investment of private capital in farmland and agricultural infrastructure of between $10 billion and $25 billion. Finally, HighQuest also found that twenty of the twenty-five funds surveyed were at the time raising money for further investments.[13] In short, this is a live story. A third study, by Ellen Aabø and Thomas Kring for the United Nations Development Programme, found that the total global area of farmed land in 2007 was 1,554 million hectares. Land for pasture expanded by 2.5 million hectares per year between 1990–2007, for a total global pasture area of 3,400 million hectares in 2007. They also report that plantation forestry expanded by 2.5 million hectares per year between 1990 and 2005, to a total of 140 million hectares globally. And while Aabø and Kring do alert the reader that "data on the exact scale of large land acquisitions are scarce and incomplete, due to the lack of transparency that often accompanies these investments," their figures show that a large share of these acquisitions was in developing and transition economies: 54 percent in the case of plantation forestry, accounting for 75 million hectares.[14]

Several other estimates suggest similarly dramatic numbers.[15] A recent report from the Oakland Institute suggests that during 2009 alone, foreign investors acquired nearly 60 million hectares of land in Africa. The Commercial Pressures on Land Research Project, a project of the International Land Coalition and the French group Centre de Coopération Internationale en Recherche pour le Développement, has documented more than 2,000 projects covering as much as 227 million hectares of land since 2001, with most purchases since 2011. Oxfam uses the Land Matrix data to report that an area eight times the size of the United Kingdom was sold or leased in land grabs between 2000 and 2010. Further, Oxfam estimates that between 2008 and 2009, deals by foreign investors for agricultural land increased by approximately 200 percent. And Sofia Murphy, a researcher at the Institute for Agriculture and Land Policy, reports that "the World Bank estimates some ten million hectares of land were contracted in just five African countries (Ethiopia, Liberia, Mozambique, Nigeria and Sudan) between 2004 and 2009."[16]

Each of the above findings and measures contributes insights into what is a vast global operation with multiple sites in very diverse countries and with very diverse buyers and sellers. The Land Matrix project provides a good overview of that large-scale phenomenon. To begin with, consider how Land Matrix defines the types of land acquisitions to be included in measurements. This is worth looking at, as it indicates some of the limitations of existing data. According to this definition, pertinent land transactions

1. Entail a transfer of rights to use, control, or own land through sale, lease, or concession
2. Imply a conversion from land used by smallholders, or for important environmental functions, to large-scale commercial use
3. Are 200 hectares or larger and were not concluded before the year 2000, when the FAO food price index was lowest

The Land Matrix database contains information about two types of data: "reported" and "cross-referenced." "Reported" data cover deals presented in published research reports, media reports, and government registers where these are made public. "Cross-referenced" data refer to deals about which information is obtained from multiple sources; the cross-referencing process involves an assessment of the reliability of the source of the information, triangulation with other information sources, and, if necessary, confirming with in-country partners in the Land Matrix networks. Media reports are not considered sufficient for cross-referencing. Research reports based on fieldwork, confirmation by known in-country partners, and official land records are considered sufficient evidence.

While the explosion in food demand and food prices in the mid-2000s was certainly a key factor in this post-2006 phase of land acquisitions, it is crops for biofuels that now account for most of the acquisitions. Cross-referenced data from the Land Matrix show that biofuel production accounts for over 37 percent of land acquired after 2006. In comparison, food crops account for 25 percent of cross-referenced deals, followed by 3 percent for livestock production and 5 percent for other nonfood crops. Farming broadly understood, including food and industrial agriculture, accounts for 73 percent of cross-referenced acquisitions. The remaining 27 percent of land acquired is for forestry and carbon sequestration, mineral extraction, industry, and tourism (see Figure 2.1).

A second major pattern is the massive concentration of foreign acquisitions in Africa. Of the publicly reported deals, 948 land ac-

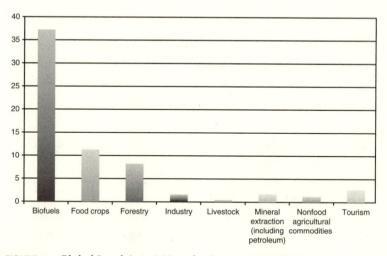

FIGURE 2.1 Global Land Acquisitions by Sector, 2006–2010 (in millions of hectares)

Data Source: Anseeuw, Wily, et al. 2012, figure 5.

quisitions totaling 134 million hectares are located in Africa; 34 million of these hectares have been cross-referenced. This compares with 43 million hectares reported for Asia (of which 29 million hectares have been cross-referenced) and 19 million hectares in Latin America (of which 6 million hectares have been cross-referenced). The remainder (5.4 million hectares reported and 1.6 million hectares cross-referenced) is in other regions, particularly eastern Europe and Oceania (see Figures 2.2 and 2.3).

It is important to note that acquisitions in OECD countries are generally not reflected in the data. One reason is that the Land Matrix only counts private transactions that involve a conversion of tenure system (e.g., land that formerly was held in common by a social group is transferred to private ownership) or a move away from smallholder production. Several major OECD countries, notably the United States and Australia, have had precisely such histories of land appropriation, from indigenous societies and from

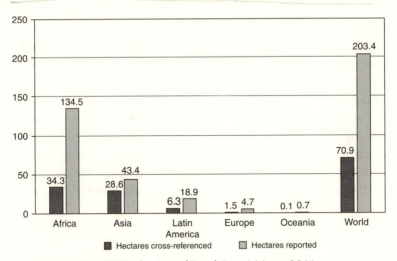

FIGURE 2.2 Regional Distribution of Land Acquisitions, 2011 (in millions of hectares)

Source: Anseeuw, Wily, et al. 2012, figure 4.

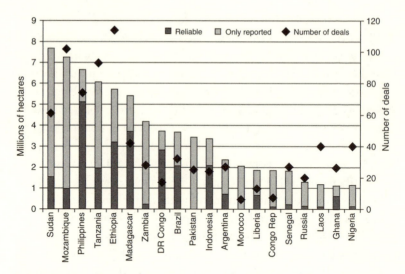

FIGURE 2.3 Most-Targeted Countries According to Size of Total Reported Acquisitions, 2012

Source: Anseeuw, Boche, et al. 2012, figure 4.

small farmers, but they took place decades and centuries ago. Further, this definition of "land grabs" also holds for several OECD countries today, among which are the United States, Mexico, Australia, Brazil, to mention just a few, where small farmers have lost their land to corporate buyers. It is worth noting that land grabs are also happening in Europe, but through a different venue—basically, preventing small farms from expanding and new small farms from being developed. This mode of land grabs falls outside the current definition and tends to fall below the 200 hectares minimum to be included in the Land Matrix measure.

The data on acquisitions also point to a sort of regionalism that is not just geographic but also geopolitical—that is, a tendency for buyers from certain regions to acquire land in a specific set of regions. The Land Matrix project finds that this might be linked to regional trade agreements. Thus, 75 percent of land acquisitions in Southeast Asia are by regional players within the context of growing regional integration.[17] I would venture that the role of geopolitics is exemplified by the interest of some Gulf States in land deals in Muslim countries such as Pakistan and Sudan, or by Libya's earlier acquisitions under Qhadaffi in the Sahel. A third example capturing elements of both is the fact that intraregional trade in Africa has become dominated by South African actors, who account for a reported 40.7 million hectares in land acquisitions since 2009.[18] Figure 2.4 shows the top investor countries, while Table 2.2 shows the regional origin of investors by region of land acquisition.

A brief elaboration of the case of biofuels and timber illustrates some additional features of land acquisitions. What stands out is how much land is needed to meet demand for biofuels, often implemented in the name of greening energy supplies, even though there is little greening involved. For example, the EU's renewable fuels target requires that 10 percent of transport fuels be supplied by renewables

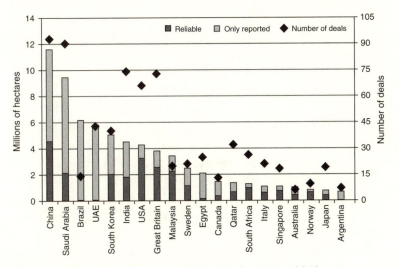

FIGURE 2.4 The Origin of Investment: Top 20 Countries, 2012

Source: Anseeuw, Boche, et al. 2012, figure 11.

TABLE 2.2: Who Buys Where, 2011 (millions of hectares)

Origin of investors	Regions where land acquired				
	Africa	Asia	Latin America	Europe	Oceania
Africa	6.4	0	0.1	0	0
Central Asia	12.3	25.3	0.6	0	0.1
Latin America	0.1	0	1.7	0	0
Europe	6.0	0.6	0.5	1.5	0
North America	3.3	0.4	1.6	0	0
Oceania	0	0.3	0.1	0	0
Western Asia	3.7	1.6	0	0	0

Data source: Anseeuw, Wily, et al. 2012, figure 3.

Note: Western Asia used by authors to indicate mostly Muslim Asia.

by 2020, with the expectation that 80–90 percent of this target is likely to be met by biofuels. The result has been widespread corporate investments in biofuel production both inside and outside Europe.[19] The Netherlands Environment Assessment Agency estimates that these targets require 20–30 million hectares of production, of which 60 percent will be imported. A very different biofuel case, but with the same land-intensive features, is palm oil production for biodiesel in the Peruvian forest; it already uses 52,829 hectares and the plan is to expand to 307,329 hectares in the short- to medium-term.[20]

The demand for timber might become another major stimulus for land acquisitions. Augusta Molnar and colleagues report that in nine tropical countries studied, concessions in forest areas have already been granted for 258 million hectares; the demand for forest lands is rising fast due to the growing commodification of forest products.[21] Most forest land deals are not reported in the Land Matrix because they do not necessarily imply a conversion of the total concession area. The researchers suggest that demands on forests are rising sharply as more forest products are being turned into commodities.[22] Louis Putzel and coworkers report that since 2000, China has obtained 121 concessions over 2.67 million hectares of forest in Gabon and is negotiating rights in the Democratic Republic of Congo and Cameroon.[23] Further pressure on forests comes from clearance for oil palm plantations. An estimated 7.5 million hectares of land are already under oil palm cultivation in the Indonesian forest, with a rate of land clearance in the late 2000s exceeding 600,000 hectares per year.[24]

While it belongs to a different economic domain and requires far less land than crops or timber, manufacturing is increasingly competing for land in particular areas. For example, case studies from the International Land Coalition show this is occurring with the establishment of special economic zones (SEZs) in densely populated areas

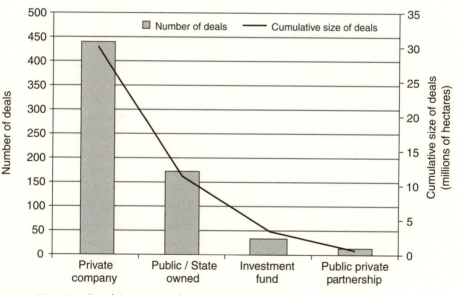

FIGURE 2.5 Land Acquisition by Type of Investor
Data source: Anseeuw, Boche, et al. 2012, figure 12.

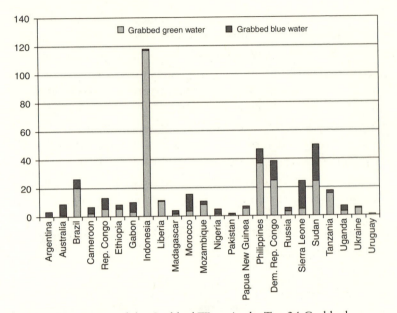

FIGURE 2.6 Assessment of the Grabbed Water in the Top 24 Grabbed
Countries, 2012 (in billions of cubic meters)

Data source: Rulli, Saviori, and D'Odorico 2013, figure 3. Note that the word "grabbed" is in the original source.

in Benin and India.[25] In India, 571 SEZs have been approved covering
140,000 hectares in total, leading to conflicts with displaced land users in a number of cases. Such zones are also being developed in Africa: China is setting up eight major SEZs around the continent.[26]
Besides land, manufacturing generates a demand for raw materials
from rural areas, which may impinge on traditional rural economies.

Figure 2.5 provides an overview of land acquisition by type of
investor, and Table 2.3 provides an overview by country.

A final set of findings concerns water use or needs as part of land
acquisition. The researchers were particularly interested in how
transnational land deals entailed water access and use (see Figure
2.6). They gathered data on land acquisitions from multiple sources,
accounting for 90 percent of all known acquired land, and used a

TABLE 2.3: Countries with the Largest Foreign Acquisitions of Land, 2012

Grabbed country[a]	Grabbed land (hundreds of thousands of hectares)	% of total global grabbed land	% of country's cultivated land	% of country's area
Argentina	6.31	1.34	1.97	2.26
Australia	46.45	9.90	9.78	0.60
Brazil	22.55	4.80	3.29	0.26
Cameroon	2.95	0.63	4.01	0.62
Congo, Democratic Republic of	80.50	17.15	1.08	3.43
Congo, Republic of	6.64	1.41	8.91	0.28
Ethiopia	10.01	2.13	6.68	0.91
Gabon	4.07	0.87	85.75	1.52
Indonesia	71.39	15.21	16.76	3.75
Liberia	6.50	1.38	106.52	5.83
Madagascar	3.69	0.79	10.40	0.63
Morocco	7.00	1.49	7.73	1.57
Mozambique	14.97	3.19	28.24	1.87
Nigeria	3.62	0.77	0.98	0.39
Pakistan	3.34	0.71	1.57	0.42
Papua New Guinea	3.14	0.67	32.75	0.68
Philippines	51.71	11.02	49.48	17.24
Russia	28.31	6.03	2.29	0.17
Sierra Leone	4.94	1.05	40.62	6.88
Sudan	46.90	9.99	23.00	1.87
Tanzania	20.27	4.32	17.63	2.14
Uganda	8.59	1.83	9.70	3.56
Ukraine	12.08	2.57	35.53	2.00
Uruguay	3.46	0.74	18.08	19.61

Data source: Rulli, Saviori, and D'Odorico 2013, table 1. Note that the use in this table of the word "grabbed" is in the original source. In some countries the grabbed land is a substantial fraction of their cultivated land (FAO 2009).

TABLE 2.4: Land and Water Resources Available in the Grabbed Countries, 2012

Grabbed Country	Cultivated area (thousands of hectares)	Land suitable for crops (thousands of hectares)	Yield gap	% Renewable freshwater resources withdrawn	Grabbed water per capita (m³ per year)	Malnourishment (%)
Argentina	32,000	96,644	-0.57	3.99	12.71	0
Australia	47,511	134,146	-0.31	4.58	120.53	0
Brazil	68,500	512,983	-0.59	0.41	86.29	10
Cameroon	7,363	33,119	-0.78	0.34	676.51	29
Congo, Democratic Republic of	7,450	161,026	-0.80	0.05	307.35	37
Congo, Republic of	560	23,227	-0.78	0.01	2,382.25	32
Ethiopia	14,985	39,946	-0.80	4.56	185.27	49
Gabon	475	16,838	-0.80	0.08	4,428.47	8
Indonesia	42,600	49,351	-0.55	5.61	60.25	6

Liberia	610	5,323	-0.78	0.08	385.74	46
Madagascar	3,550	28,764	-0.75	4.36	73.27	40
Morocco	9,055	8,353	-0.90	43.45	172.51	5
Mozambique	5,300	60,437	-0.90	0.35	1,041.06	58
Nigeria	37,000	60,478	-0.78	3.60	34.91	8
Pakistan	21,280	4,438	-0.55	74.35	40.61	20
Papua New Guinea	960	11,603	-0.41	0.05	393.44	29
Philippines	10,450	8,734	-0.58	17.03	29.67	21
Russia	123,541	287,045	-0.70	1.47	139.40	6
Sierra Leone	1,215	3,753	-0.80	0.31	853.36	43
Sudan	20,391	89,285	-0.85	57.58	1,844.26	18
Tanzania	11,500	62,505	-0.81	5.39	1,131.01	41
Uganda	8,850	12,795	-0.75	0.48	139.14	30
Ukraine	33,376	49,338	-0.72	27.56	128.26	5
Uruguay	1,912	14,152	-0.65	2.63	51.46	4

Data source: Rulli, Saviori, and D'Odorico 2013, suppl. table 2. Note that the use in this table of the word "grabbed" is in the original source.

hydrologic model to determine the associated rates of freshwater use. They found that transnational deals for land and water are occurring in all continents except Antarctica. More important, they established that the amount of grabbed water lowered water supplies to a point below what is required to ensure the per capita volume necessary for a balanced diet and what would be sufficient to improve food security and abate malnourishment in the pertinent countries.[27] Table 2.4 gives an overview of land and water resources available in countries where water is being mined.

MATERIAL PRACTICES OF LARGE-SCALE LAND ACQUISITIONS

Investments in large-scale land acquisitions have crowded out other material economies, especially in sub-Saharan Africa. One outcome that has received little attention is the sharp decline in the share of foreign direct investment (FDI) going to mass manufacturing, a sector that can generate good jobs and feed the growth of a middle class. This decline took place just as several countries of the Global South were beginning to experience significant growth in mass manufacturing. If we consider Africa, for instance, the data show a sharp decline in foreign direct investment in manufacturing. Both South Africa and Nigeria, Africa's two top FDI recipients in 2006 (accounting for 37 percent of FDI stock in Africa), have seen a sharp transformation in the composition of investment: a fall in FDI in manufacturing and a sharp rise in FDI in the primary sector—mining, crops, oil, and such.[28] In Nigeria, where foreign investment in oil has long been heavy, the share of the primary sector in FDI stock stood at 75 percent in 2005, up from 43 percent in 1990. Other African countries have seen similar shifts. Even in Madagascar, one of the (mostly small) countries where manufacturing FDI inflows began to increase as recently as the 1990s, this increase was well below that of FDI in the primary sector.[29] There is much evidence showing that this shift from investment in manufacturing to investment in mining, oil, and land is not good for the development of national economies.

The current phase of land acquisitions dwarfs investments in manufacturing. A few examples assembled by von Braun and Meinzen-Dick signal the range of buyers and of locations, with Africa a major destination. South Korea has signed deals for 690,000 hectares and the United Arab Emirates for 400,000 hectares, both in Sudan. Saudi investors are spending $100 million to raise wheat, barley, and rice on land leased to them by Ethiopia's government; they receive tax exemptions and export the crop back to Saudi Arabia.[30] China secured the right to grow palm oil for biofuels on 2.8 million hectares of Congo, making it the world's largest palm oil plantation. It is negotiating to grow biofuels on 2 million hectares in Zambia. Perhaps less well known than these African cases is the fact that privatized land in the territories of the former Soviet Union, especially in Russia and Ukraine, is also becoming the object of much foreign acquisition. In 2008 alone, these acquisitions included the following: a Swedish company, Alpcot Agro, bought 128,000 hectares in Russia; South Korea's Hyundai Heavy Industries paid $6.5 million for a majority stake in Khorol Zerno, a company that owns 10,000 hectares in eastern Siberia; Morgan Stanley bought 40,000 hectares in Ukraine; Gulf investors are planning to acquire Pava, the first Russian grain processor floated on the financial markets (the intention was to enable the sale of 40 percent of its landowning division to international investors), which will give them access to 500,000 hectares. Also less noticed is Pakistan's intended lease of 500,000 hectares of land to Gulf investors, with the bonus of a security force of 100,000 to protect the land.

In what follows I focus on one set of countries in more detail. It helps understand the variety of buyers and deals underlying the overall counts.

Six Destinations for Acquiring Land

In an analysis of 180 large land acquisitions in Africa, Cecilie Friis and Anette Reenberg identify major types of investors in this current period: (1) oil-rich Gulf states of Saudi Arabia, United Arab Emirates, Qatar, Bahrain, Oman, Kuwait, and Jordan; (2) populous and capital-rich Asian countries such as China, South Korea, Japan, and India; (3) Europe and the United States; (4) private companies from around the world. Investors are mostly energy companies, agricultural investment companies, utility companies, finance and investment firms, and technology companies.[31]

Using the Friis and Reenberg data, I constructed the representations of this geography (shown in Figures 2.7 and 2.8) by focusing on the top six sellers in Africa and their investors.[32] They are Ethiopia, Madagascar, Sudan, Tanzania, Mali, and Mozambique—all sub-Saharan, and all, except Mali, in East Africa. In all these countries both private investors and government agencies have acquired land.

No specific investor dominates in five of these top-selling countries. The exception is Mozambique, where Agri SA, the South African farmers' association, is the largest buyer, and overwhelmingly so. However, when we measure by national origin, each "seller country" does have a dominant "buyer country" in terms of size of acquisitions: India in Ethiopia, South Korea in Madagascar, Saudi Arabia in Sudan, and China in Mali. In Tanzania, it is a multinational group. There are few cases of cross acquisition; among them are Sun Biofuels' purchase of land in Tanzania and Mozambique, China's acquisitions in Mozambique and Mali, Qatar's in Madagascar and Sudan, and those by the United Arab Emirates and Jannat, a Saudi Arabia conglomerate, in Sudan and Ethiopia.[33]

Overall there are forty-seven different countries of origin among investors in these six countries. Among the countries with the most

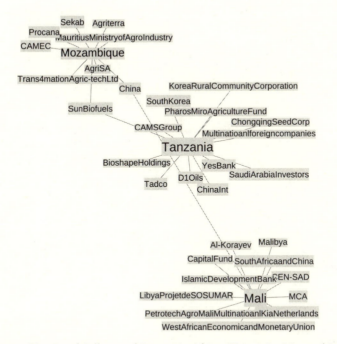

FIGURE 2.7 Top Land Sellers and Buyers in Africa (Tanzania, Mozambique, Mali), 2010

Data source: Friis and Reenberg 2010.

diverse group of investors by country of origin are Madagascar, with twenty-four foreign investors from fifteen countries, and Ethiopia, with twenty-six investors from twelve countries. Asian countries (China, South Korea, India, and Japan) make up almost 20 percent of investors in these six countries. Middle Eastern countries (Saudi Arabia, United Arab Emirates, Egypt, Jordan, Qatar, Lebanon, and Israel) account for almost 22 percent of investors. European countries (United Kingdom, Sweden, Netherlands, Germany, Italy, Denmark, and France) account for 30 percent of investors.

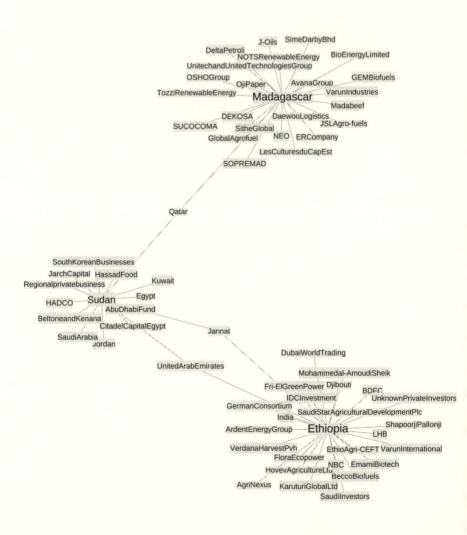

FIGURE 2.8 Top Land Sellers and Buyers in Africa (Madagascar, Sudan, Ethiopia), 2010

Data source: Friis and Reenberg 2010.

African countries (South Africa, Mauritius, Libya, and Djibouti) account for about 10 percent of investors. The remaining investors are from Australia, Brazil, and the United States.

Three countries have a significant share of all investments. The United States, United Kingdom, and Saudi Arabia account for 25 percent of all investors in these six countries. Each has investments in four countries. It is worth noting that private companies dominate among buyers for some countries, and states for others.

ONE CASE: PALM PRODUCTION AT GROUND LEVEL

Palm oil, traded on international commodities and futures market as crude palm oil, is a component of huge numbers of products, including livestock feed, prepared foods, cooking oils, cosmetics, lubricants, and fuels. Between 2000 and 2010, consumption of palm oil doubled to reach 46.8 million tons, surpassing soybean oil in 2005 to become the world's most popular vegetable oil.[34] By 2020, consumption of all vegetable oils is expected to increase 25 percent, with palm oil continuing to be a leader in the category.[35]

In its raw state, crude palm oil is fragile: oil in freshly picked palm fruits begins to decay in as little as forty-eight hours after harvest, meaning that producers need ready access to processing sites. Mills that extract and stabilize palm oil require between 4,000 and 5,000 hectares of cropland to produce output at maximum efficiency. The transportation systems, infrastructure, and economies of scale required for profitable production of palm oil mean that the growing demand is being met by monoculture farming, usually on massive plantations or government-supported smallholder groups.[36]

Eighty percent of commercial palm oil is produced in Malaysia (4 million hectares of land in palm oil production) and Indonesia (7.5 million hectares of land in palm oil production).[37] A scarcity of arable land in Malaysia is pushing new production into Indonesia, where Malaysian conglomerates are the majority investors in approximately two-thirds of all palm oil production ventures.[38] The Indonesian government has promoted palm oil as pro-poor, pro-job, and pro-growth: 85 percent of palm oil consumed in Indonesia is used as food, especially as affordable cooking oil, and 3.5 million small farmers produced 40 percent of the Indonesian palm oil crop.[39]

The outlook for locals, however, is not sunny. In the Indonesian province of Riau, protests by small farmers against the palm industry started in the early 1980s. That is when government officials required the forfeit and redistribution of collectively held land to develop palm oil plantations.[40]

Indonesian land rights are nebulous, unclear, and often insecure. Customary law, known as *adat* in Indonesia and Malaysia, was codified and integrated into Dutch colonial law; it remains an important, if contested, part of the Indonesian legal framework. While *adat* varies greatly among Indonesia's ethnic groups, many indigenous peoples hold land through *hak ulayat* (communal tenure) or *hutan adat* (customary forest license).[41] The Basic Agrarian Law of 1960 limits government recognition of *adat* land rights to claims where "the land is under the ownership of a recognized adat community[,] the boundaries are defined and understood and the community is recognized and functioning as such under adat law principles."[42] These types of issues are also overlooked in the framework for resolving claims between overlapping rights and concessions on land such as conflicts between mining and agricultural claims.[43] Further, Indonesia's land registration system is insufficient; two-thirds of all land in forest administration within the country is without title.[44] These ambiguities and inadequacies leave significant room for vested interests to challenge community land rights. Various Indonesian governments (especially the Suharto regime) actively sought to bring more territory directly under the control of the state, while various businesses have successfully challenged inadequately documented claims of ownership.[45]

Land conflict has come to a head in Indonesia's Riau Province, on the island of Sumatra. Local people have opposed the spread of palm oil plantations since the 1980s; opposition to the industry was suppressed under the Suharto dictatorship but has spread like wildfire since regime change in 1998.[46] Seventy percent of all palm oil plantations in Riau are owned by Malaysian interests; many of these companies have engaged in questionable land acquisitions and failed to respect the rights of local communities that hold land collectively.[47] Under the Basic Agrarian Law of 1960, communities can be forced to forfeit land; this is especially the case in areas where local groups maintain traditional collective land ownership but are engaged in commodity production rather than following indigenous lifeways.

Here is a case that illustrates some of these tensions going back years and the lengthy process of the state recognizing the rights of smallholders. In 1998, PT Mazuma Agro Indonesia (MAI) seized 5,508 hectares of land in the village of Rokan Hulu, Riau, without the consent of village leaders, and began to illegally expel local farmers and their families.[48] Legal action was able to prevent further development until 2012. In February of that year, MAI began development on the land despite the unresolved court case. At 8:30 a.m. on February 2, 2012, a hundred local villagers tried to prevent bulldozers and excavators from clearing their land; at 11:00 a.m., officers of the Northern Sumatran Regional Police opened fire on the protesters, wounding five.[49] This was not the first time land conflicts in Rokan Hulu had become violent. Since 1998, MAI and the leadership of a nearby village had conspired to burn at least eighty-nine houses and destroy twenty-six palm oil processing plants owned by members of the community.[50] In 2004, two men from Rokan Hulu protesting a land claim by palm oil company PT Suraya were killed by the company's security guards; local police deployed to the area prevented the conflict from escalating but failed to apprehend the killers.[51]

Responding to these abuses by firms, in May 2013, the pertinent court in Indonesia transferred millions of hectares of forest from government control to the control of local communities, at least nominally.[52] However, the strength of these new land rights remains dependent on government records and agencies that have proved fallible in the past. It remains to be seen if indigenous people in Indonesia can use their land to produce commodity crops for the global economy without sacrificing their right to communal ownership.

CONCLUSION

These are the elements of a larger history in the making. It includes a repositioning of growing areas of Africa, Latin America, and Asia in a massively restructured global economy. Weakened governments that function as comprador bourgeoisies and the destruction of smallholder economies have launched a new survival phase in expanding parts of the world for rising numbers of people

The key empirical trends that matter for the larger argument in this chapter are the sharp growth in foreign land acquisitions after 2006, a year when the banking crisis was already brewing, and the rapid international diversification of the buyers. It is not the fact of foreign acquisition per se that is the issue here, as foreign ownership has long been part of the world's economic history, and further, there are positive reasons for some acquisitions, such as creating a nature reserve. What matters for my argument is that this sharp growth in foreign ownership is significantly altering the character of local economies, notably land ownership, and diminishing the sovereign authority of the state over its territory. The process of acquisition may be less violent and disruptive than the imperial conquests of the past. But that does not mean they should be confused with more benign examples of foreign ownership—the placement of a job-generating Ford Motors plant in Europe or a Volks-wagen plant in Brazil.

Emphasizing the juxtaposition of formal sovereign authority and growing foreign land acquisitions leads to two conceptual issues that are easily bypassed if we simply emphasize the power asymmetry between those acquiring land and host governments. One of these is the role of IMF and World Bank restructuring, eventually amplified by WTO rules, in weakening the economies, social development, and governments of various countries. The complex of trends and conditions associated with this restructuring actually facilitated the massive foreign land acquisition that took off after 2006 and further escalated after the crisis of 2008. These trends prepared the ground for the sudden rise in acquisitions, for the relative ease of the formal execution of many a novel type of contract, and for the rapid diversification of those doing the acquiring.

The other is the repositioning of national sovereign territory resulting from the sharp rise in land acquisitions by foreigners. National territory is not merely vacant land. Lands acquired by foreigners include vast stretches of national territory populated and shaped by villages, smallholder agriculture, rural manufacturing districts, and the actors that make these economies and reproduce them—whether this is recognized by the state or not. Much of this politico-structural complexity is today being erased from its home territory as a result of these acquisitions. At the extreme, we might ask what citizenship is worth when national territory is downgraded to foreign-owned land for plantations, leading to the eviction of everything else—flora, fauna, villages, smallholders, and the traditional rules that organized land ownership or use.

In their aggregate these large-scale land acquisitions have produced a global operational space that is partly embedded in national territories. They produce a partial denationalization deep inside nation-states, a structural hole in the tissue of national sovereign territory. I see acquisition of land by foreigners as one of several such processes that partly disassemble national territory. The contracts developed for these acquisitions become capabilities of an organizing logic that is disarticulated from the national state even as these acquisitions operate deep inside its territory. Further, in so doing, these contracts often go against the interests not only of much of a country's people but also of local capital, one far more likely to generate positive feedback loops for a country's diverse regions. It is important to note that large-scale foreign land acquisitions could be generators of good jobs and local economic effects, especially when committed to workers rights and to environmental sustainability. But the current trends do not promise much along these lines: it is a story of expulsions of people and local economies and of biospheric destruction.

Against this larger context, the materiality and visibility of foreign land acquisitions become heuristic: they tell us something about a larger process that is often not as visible and material as land or the direct participation of the executive branch of government in the execution of contracts. This way of representing economic globalization is very different from the common notion of the whole state as victim. Indeed, to a large extent it is the executive branch of government that is getting aligned with global corporate capital, both in the Global South and in the Global North. This becomes highly visible in the case of foreign land acquisitions. At the same time, in my reading, a key implication of this strategic participation of states in global processes is that, guided by different interests, states could reorient their goals away from the global corporate agenda and toward global agendas concerning the environment, human rights, social justice, and climate change.

CHAPTER 3

Finance and Its Capabilities

Crisis as Systemic Logic

Once it exists, financial profit can be viewed as morally neutral. It can be used for unambiguous good—materialized, for example, into a nonfinancial asset such as a green transport system. It can be materialized for ill—to buy arms for warlords, say. Or it can be left immaterial, used as a platform for ever more speculative financial constructions that can be so complex they challenge empirical analysis, let alone moral examination. The last of these trends, associated most spectacularly with the market for derivatives, has come to dominate finance over the past twenty years. Until the financial crisis, the obscurity of its operations masked how dangerous this market can be. It has generated the extreme levels of financialization now evident in several major developed countries.

The orders of magnitude the financial system has built up over the last two decades are captured in the total value of outstanding derivatives, a form of complex debt that derives its value from another source, ranging from other types of debt to material goods such as buildings and crops; derivatives are presently the most common financial instrument. That total value of outstanding derivatives stood at $600 trillion (more than ten times the value of global GDP) before the crisis exploded in 2008, and then it dipped briefly before rising again. By 2012, a few years after that very costly event that brought down firms, governments, and whole economies, it had risen to over $800 trillion, and by early 2013 it had reached more than $1 quadrillion. Similarly, the value of bank assets, which stood at $160 trillion right before the crisis, had risen to almost $200 trillion by 2010, and it has kept rising since. In contrast, global GDP actually fell sharply from $55 trillion in 2007 to $45 trillion in early 2008, reflecting the crisis in the economy. The power of finance, and what makes it dangerous, is its capacity to build up its own value even as households, economies, and governments lose value.[1]

I conceive of finance as a capability, though one with variable valence; it is not Amartya Sen's or Martha Nussbaum's positively marked concept of capability. Finance needs to be distinguished from traditional banking. Traditional banks sell money in their possession. Financial firms sell something they do not have, and therein lies the push to be far more innovative and invasive than traditional banking. In this regard finance can be thought of as a capability to securitize just about everything in an economy and, in doing so, subject economies and governments to its own criteria for measuring success. Securitization involves the relocation of a building, good, or debt, into a financial circuit where it becomes mobile and can be bought and sold over and over in markets near and far. In the past two decades finance has invented often very complex instruments to securitize extreme instances of familiar items—not just high-grade debt but also used-car loans and modest municipal government debt. Once an input is securitized, financial engineering can keep on building long chains of increasingly speculative instruments that all rest on the alleged stability of that first step. This is, then, a very special, distinctive, and often dangerous capability. (It is worth remembering that particular kinds of derivatives, one of the key enablers of finance, had been declared basically illegal in the United States. It was not until 1973 that derivatives became legal again in the commodity markets of Chicago.)

At the heart of finance is the work of inventing and developing complex instruments. It is the mathematics of physics and its models that are in play here, not the mathematics of microeconomic models. Exemplifying it all, Goldman Sachs's backroom is well stocked with physicists. The mathematics of the backroom is mostly well beyond the understanding of the highly paid executives of the boardroom.

These features make finance a major force in a process that started in the 1980s and took off sharply worldwide beginning in the 1990s. I consider finance a complex assemblage of actors, capabilities, and operational spaces. Elements of this assemblage function as one of the conceptually subterranean dynamics that concern me in this book. Finance can take diverse forms on the surface and adapt to institutional settings as different as China and the United States, with instruments as diverse as securitized student loans and credit-default swaps. But beneath this diversity of encasements lies an epoch-making capability—the financializing of the debt and assets of firms, households, and governments regardless of geopolitics, sovereign authority, legal system, state-economy relation, or economic sector.

We can think of finance as the most accomplished and effective— at least in the short run—of these conceptually subterranean trends that are reshaping our world in so many different ways. In the case of finance, the visible manifestations take the form of multiple microworlds and microtrends, some specialized, some not: credit card loans, this or that government's deficit, a particular firm's debt, and so on. All this disaggregating is partly due to the diverse institutional arrangements through which those debts and assets are generated and become recognizable to third parties. But disaggregation also renders invisible the deeper vortex and in many ways veils what is happening: a large-scale destruction of healthy economies, healthy government debt, and healthy households. In case after case, this destruction takes the form of a flow of capital and resources to financial firms and the impoverishment of other economic sectors. We cannot generalize too much, for there are exceptions to everything, and we can see an enrichment of a range of sectors other than finance, from high-technology to oil. Many of these other sectors depend on finance or make a living providing finance with the highly specialized services it needs.[2]

Yet we can only apprehend finance and its dynamics through the thick worlds within which its diverse invasions happen. For instance, now we see not just the commodification of food, gold, and many other goods, but also the financializing of those commodities. Similarly, there is not only interest on loans but the financializing of interest payments. There are particularly brutal cases that reveal the economic violence that can ensue when something goes wrong. One example is the expulsion of huge numbers of people from their foreclosed homes in countries as different as the United States, Spain, and Latvia over a short and sharp history. Another is the massive losses arising from financial speculation and borne by the funds of municipal governments in countries as unlike as the United States and Italy.

I begin with a microcosm where all these aspects come together in thick, often elementary ways: how modest households seeking to own modest houses were brought into the financializing machinery in a growing number of countries. I focus on the United States because it was ground zero for this development and the innovation that enabled it. The case serves to illustrate some of the features of financialization, specifically the use of complex instruments in the making of a short, highly profitable investment cycle for some and elementary brutalities for the many millions who lost their homes. Next I examine the global potential for such instruments and focus on some other countries that have experienced similar expulsions, even though in each country there is a different specific explanation.

What matters to my analysis is that these diverse countries are beginning to share a deeper underlying dynamic that cuts across familiar divisions even as it gets filtered through the thick specifics of each situation. Conceptually we tend to remain captives of existing and inherited distinctions among different countries, different national banking systems, and so on. This has consequences: our focus on familiar, often long-standing distinctions serves to hide or make less legible the fact that a similar dynamic can underlie diverse cases. Local or national developments and trends can be building blocks of a global trend that transcends the familiar separations. The chapter concludes with a discussion of the intersection of complexity and brutality as it is filtered through national political economies, veiling the making of a deeper global political economy. While the latter is partial in its specificity, it cuts across many of the familiar divisions of nation-states, economic sectors, and markets.

WHEN LOCAL HOUSING BECOMES A GLOBAL FINANCIAL INSTRUMENT

Beyond its social and political role, housing has long been a critical economic sector in all developed societies and has made major contributions to economic growth. There have historically been three ways in which it played this economic role: as part of the construction sector, as part of the real estate market, and as part of the banking sector in the form of mortgages. In all three sectors it has at times been a vector for innovations. For instance, solar energy has largely been applied to housing rather than to offices or factories. Mass construction has used housing as a key channel to develop new techniques and formats, and the industrial production of prefabricated buildings has similarly focused on housing to work out the kinks. Finally, mortgages have been one of the key sources of income and innovations for traditional-style banking. The thirty-year mortgage, now a worldwide standard, was actually a major innovation for credit markets. Japan and then China instituted, respectively, ninety- and seventy-year mortgages to deal with a rapidly growing demand for housing finance in a situation where three generations were necessary to cover the cost of housing in a boom period—the 1980s in Japan and the 2000s in China.

The securitizing of mortgages, which took off in the 1980s, added yet another role for housing in the economy. Securitizing home mortgages can create growth in an economy. But it also opens up the mortgage market to speculation, making it vulnerable to risk and loss. This is acceptable if the owner of the mortgaged property decides to speculate and is fully informed of the risks. But it is not acceptable if the decision to enter a risky arrangement is made without such knowing consent. Even knowing consent may not be enough at a time when contracts are long and impenetrable and the culture pervading the financial and investment industry is not characterized by openness and transparency. It is worth recalling the notorious bankruptcy of Orange County, a municipal government in California: what the local government thought was a loan turned out to be a highly speculative investment, bankrupting the county and its pension funds. A similar crisis happened late in 2012 when dozens of municipal governments in Italy confronted a budget crisis because what they thought were straightforward bank loans turned out to be credit default swaps—one of the riskiest and most speculative types of investment.

The securitizing of home mortgages has a similar effect: it transforms what might look like a traditional mortgage into part of a speculative investment instrument to be sold and bought in speculative markets. But it follows a different pathway and represents yet another financial innovation capable of extreme destruction. It inserts a new channel for using housing as an asset that is to be represented by a contract (the mortgage) and can be sliced into smaller components and mixed with other types of debt for sale in the high finance circuit. In the case of the particular type of subprime mortgage developed in the United States in the 2000s, the contract representing the mortgage was spliced and then each bit mixed with high-grade debt to generate an "asset-backed security" to be sold to financial investors. All that mattered to succeed in such selling was, in the last instance, a signed contract between bank and homebuyer representing an asset—the modest house. The actual value of the underlying asset (the house) did not matter, nor did the mortgage itself or the value of interest payments. The financial instrument was constructed so as to delink the instrument from those values. What mattered was that the instrument could function as an asset-backed security in the investment circuit, even if the instrument contained merely a small slice of a very low-cost asset (playing the role of material asset) and was mostly made up of other types of debt. The challenge was to delink the actual value of that asset (house) from the contract that was to be used in the high-finance circuit. It meant developing a series of complex steps, numbering up to fifteen, so that the fact of the actual value of the home and the mortgage payments did not matter. That is, the asset-backed security had to be "liberated" from the burden of the actual value of the asset, which was mostly very modest. The result was an enormously complex and opaque instrument.

Such delinking made the creditworthiness of mortgage holders irrelevant to the potential for profit. The result was to put modest households in a high-risk situation, with salespeople pushing to get the contract signed. What mattered was the mere existence of the signed contract, or, more precisely, the accumulation of large numbers of such signed contracts. This innovation opened up the world of lower-middle-income households to the high circuits of finance, creating what could potentially be a global market comprising billions of households. Later in this chapter I briefly examine the potential for this new financial instrument to spread to major developing regions of the world.[3]

This is not the first time the financial sector has used housing to develop an instrument for investors. The first residential-mortgage-backed securities were produced in the late 1970s. The concept, a good one in many ways, was to generate another source for funding mortgages besides the traditional one, which was basically bank deposits in their many variants. In their benign early form, mortgage-backed securities served to lower interest rates on mortgages and to stabilize the loan supply: that is, they allowed banks to continue lending even during downturns.

But that earlier incarnation of subprime mortgages was a state project. The one developed in the United States at the beginning of the twenty-first century and now spreading internationally is built by and for the financial sector. It is not about helping households to get housing but rather is intended to build a financial instrument, an asset-backed security, for use in financial circuits. Two features make this innovation different. One is the extent to which these mortgages function purely as financial instruments, in that they can be bought and promptly sold. Ownership of the instrument may just last for a matter of hours. Thus, when an investor has sold the instrument, what happens to the house itself is irrelevant; indeed, the firms or bank divisions that suffered sharp losses were largely those specialized subprime lenders or divisions within banks that did retain ownership of the debt. Further, as already described, since these mortgages have been divided, spliced, and distributed across diverse investment packages, there is no single component in such a package that actually represents the whole house. In contrast, the owner loses the entire house and all the value she has invested in it if she is unable to meet the mortgage payments for a few months—no matter who owns the instrument and the slice of her house inside that instrument.

The second difference from traditional mortgages is that the source of profit for the investor is not the payment of the mortgage itself but the sale of the financial package that bundles hundreds or thousands of mortgage slices. This particular feature of the instrument enables lenders to make a profit from the vast potential market represented by modest-income households. The billions of these households across the world can become a major target when the source of profit is not the payment of the mortgage itself but the sale of the financial bundle. What counts for the lender is not the creditworthiness of the borrower but the sheer number of mortgages sold to (often pushed onto) households. This particular feature might be fine if the target for such mortgages is wealthy speculators, but it becomes alarming when less well-off households are the target.

The asymmetry between the world of investors (only some will be affected) and the world of homeowners (once they default, they will lose the house no matter what investor happens to own the instrument at the time) creates a massive distortion in the housing market and the housing finance market. While homeowners unable to meet their mortgage obligations cannot escape the negative consequences of default, most investors can, because they buy these mortgages in order to sell them; there were many winners among investors and only a few losers in the years before the crisis broke in August 2007. Thus, investors could relate in a positive way to even the so-called subprime mortgages (poor-quality instruments), and this indifference in itself was bad for potential homeowners. We see here yet another sharp asymmetry in the position of the diverse players enacting an innovation.

Finally, the current period makes legible a third asymmetry. At a time of massive concentration of financial resources in a limited number of superfirms, any that own a large share of the subprime mortgages when a mortgage default crisis hits get stuck with massive losses. In an earlier period, ownership of mortgages was widely distributed among a huge number of banks and credit unions, and hence losses were more widely distributed as well. The fact that several large, powerful firms wrongly felt that they could manage high-risk instruments further raised their losses. Ruthless practices, the capacity of firms to dominate markets, and the growing inter-connectedness of the markets have made these superfirms vulnera-ble to their own power, in a sort of network effect.[4] One notorious example is that of now defunct Lehman Brothers, whose value still has not been established by the team of top-level experts assembled for the company's bankruptcy proceedings.

It is easy to persuade modest-income households to take out risky mortgages in a country such as the United States, where owning a house has been constructed into a high priority, unlike, for instance, Germany. Presented with the possibility (which turned out to be mostly a deception) of owning a house, modest-income people will put whatever savings they have into a down payment, and future earnings into monthly payments. The small savings or future earnings of modest-income households or the prior ownership of a modest house were used to enable customers to enter into a contract. And, as we have seen, to the lender it was the contract that mattered, not the house itself or the mortgage payments, for the contract was necessary to develop a financial instrument that could profit investors.

By 2004, the strategy was so successful with investors that mort-gage sellers did not even ask for full credit reports or a down pay-ment, just a signature on the contract. In a financial world over-whelmed by speculative capital, speed and numbers mattered, so the premium was on selling subprime mortgages to as many households as possible, including those who qualified for a regular mortgage that would have afforded them more protections but would have taken much longer to process. The negative effects on households, on neighborhoods, and on cities received no consider-ation. It is interesting to note that the same innovation that oper-ated in the securitization of mortgages, in which a negative for some can actually translate into a categorical positive for a larger system, can be seen in the case of outsourced jobs as well. Out-sourcing involves complex and costly logistics, but it is worth it to gain those cents on each work hour because it translates into additional value for a firm's shares in the financial markets, and hence additional profits for shareholders and executives.

Furthermore, within the logic of finance, it is also possible to make a good profit by betting against the success of an innovation—that is, to profit by predicting failure. This type of profit making happened as well with subprime mortgages and a series of other financial innovations, notably credit default swaps. In fact, it was the far larger market of swaps that sparked the September 2008 financial crisis: anxious investors trying to cash in their credit default swaps beginning in 2007 made visible the fact that this $60 trillion market lacked the actual funds to meet its obligations. In short, the so-called subprime crisis was not due to irresponsible households taking on mortgages they could not afford, as is still commonly asserted in the United States and the rest of the world. Rather, the mounting foreclosures signaled to those investors who had bought credit default swaps, that it was time to cash in their "insurance," but the money was not there, because the foreclosures had also devalued the swaps.

Multiple conditions, including the decline in housing prices, led to extremely negative outcomes for households, including foreclosure.[5] From 2005 to 2010, out of more than 13.3 million mortgage

TABLE 3.1: U.S. Home Foreclosures, 2006–2010

Year	Foreclosure notices (in millions)
2006	1.2
2007	2.2
2008	3.1
2009	3.9
2010	2.9
Total	13.3

Data source: RealtyTrac 2012b.

foreclosure notices, 9.3 million ended in evictions, affecting perhaps as many as 35 million people. In 2008, an average of 10,000 U.S. households a day lost their homes. Not all foreclosures lead to eviction, of course, or at least not promptly, and some households may have been sent more than one foreclosure notice. But the available evidence shows that by 2010, more than 7 million of these households were no longer in the foreclosed home. There are still an estimated 4 million households that could be in trouble until 2014. This is a brutal form of primitive accumulation achieved through an enormously complex sequence of instruments using vast talent pools in finance, law, accounting, and mathematics.

For millions of people with modest incomes, the impact was catastrophic. New York City offers an example in microcosm. Table 3.2 shows how white residents of New York, who have a far higher average income than all other groups in the city, were much less likely to have subprime mortgages than all other groups. By 2006, when the numbers of subprime mortgages had risen sharply, just 9.1 percent of all mortgages taken in by whites were subprime, compared to 13.6 percent for Asian Americans, 28.6 percent for Hispanic Americans, and 40.7 percent for African Americans. The table also shows that all groups, regardless of incidence, experienced high growth rates in subprime borrowing from 2002 to 2006. If we consider the most acute period, from 2002 to 2005, subprime borrow-

TABLE 3.2: Subprime Lending by Race in New York City, 2002–2006

	2002	2003	2004	2005	2006
White	4.6%	6.2%	7.2%	11.2%	9.1%
Black	13.4%	20.5%	35.2%	47.1%	40.7%
Hispanic	11.9%	18.1%	27.6%	39.3%	28.6%
Asian	4.2%	6.2%	9.4%	18.3%	13.6%

Source: Furman Center 2007.

ing more than doubled for whites, tripled for Asians and Hispanics, and quadrupled for blacks. A further breakdown by neighborhood in New York City shows that the ten worst-hit neighborhoods were poor: between 34 and 47 percent of residents who took mortgages got subprime mortgages.

The costs extend to whole metropolitan areas through the loss of property tax income for municipal governments. Table 3.3 shows the ten U.S. metro areas with the largest estimated losses of real gross municipal product (GMP) for 2008 due to the mortgage crisis and associated consequences, as measured by Global Insight.[6] The total economic loss of these ten metro areas is estimated at over $45 billion for the year 2008. In that year New York lost more than $10 billion in GMP, Los Angeles $8.3 billion, and Dallas, Washington, and Chicago each about $4 billion.

The subprime mortgage instrument developed in these years is just one example of how financial institutions can achieve major additions to financial value while disregarding negative social outcomes and even negative outcomes for the national economy. This disregard is entirely legal, notwithstanding its pernicious effects.

THE POTENTIAL FOR GLOBAL SPREAD

Given its features, this type of subprime mortgage can travel globally, and could in principle reach at least a billion or more modest-income households across the world.[7] Indeed, it already has traveled, and defaults outside the United States are rising fast. Hungary, for example, has already seen more than a million defaults on subprime mortgages.

One critical measure for gauging the potential growth of residential mortgage capital is the incidence of mortgaged homes in an economy. Figures 3.1 and 3.2 show the ratio of residential mortgage debt to GDP in diverse countries in Europe and in Asia, respectively. The mostly low incidence of this type of debt points to considerable potential for the selling of subprime mortgages.

TABLE 3.3: U.S. Metro Areas with Largest Losses of GMP, 2006

Rank	Metro area	Revised real GMP growth (%)	Loss in real GMP growth (%)	Loss of GMP (million $)
1	New York–Northern New Jersey–Long Island, NY/PA	2.13	0.65	10,372
2	Los Angeles–Long Beach–Santa Ana, CA	1.67	0.95	8,302
3	Dallas–Fort Worth–Arlington, TX	3.26	0.83	4,022
4	Washington, DC–Arlington–Alexandria, VA/MD/WV/DC	2.79	0.60	3,957
5	Chicago-Naperville-Joliet, IL/IN/WI	2.23	0.56	3,906
6	San Francisco–Oakland–Fremont, CA	1.88	1.07	3,607
7	Detroit-Warren-Livonia, MI	1.30	0.97	3,203
8	Boston-Cambridge-Quincy, MA	2.16	0.99	3,022
9	Philadelphia-Camden-Wilmington, DE/NJ/PA/MD	1.85	0.63	2,597
10	Riverside–San Bernadino–Ontario, CA	3.51	1.05	2,372

Source: Global Insight 2007, table 2.

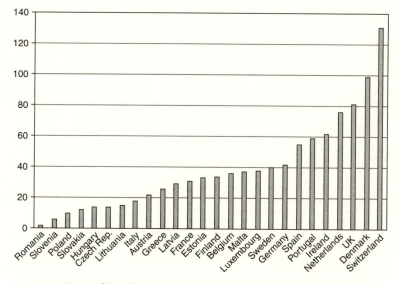

FIGURE 3.1 Ratio of Residential Mortgage Debt to GDP in Europe, 2006

Data source: Miles and Pillonca 2008, figure 1.

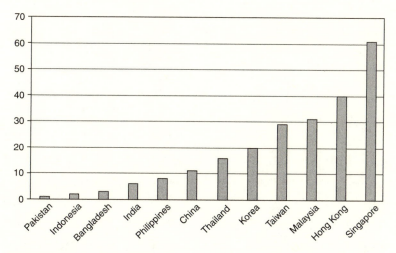

FIGURE 3.2 Ratio of Residential Mortgage Debt to GDP in Emerging Asia, 2001–2005

Data source: Warnock and Warnock 2008, table 2.

A second critical measure is the ratio of overall household credit (that is to say, debt) to household disposable income in the rapidly changing 2000–2005 period (see Table 3.4 and Figure 3.3). In some countries this ratio increased sharply: for instance, in the Czech Republic it grew from 8.5 percent in 2000 to 27.1 percent in 2005 and in Hungary from 11.2 percent to 39.3 percent, while in South Korea it rose from 33 percent to 68.9 percent. This growth is also evident in India, where the initial level was low, 4.7 percent in 2000, but had doubled to 9.7 percent by 2004. In mature market

TABLE 3.4: Ratio of Household Credit to Personal Disposable Income, 2000–2005

	2000	2001	2002	2003	2004	2005
Emerging Markets						
Czech Republic	8.5	10.1	12.9	16.4	21.3	27.1
Hungary	11.2	14.4	20.9	29.5	33.9	39.3
Poland	10.1	10.3	10.9	12.6	14.5	18.2
India	4.7	5.4	6.4	7.4	9.7	
Korea	33.0	43.9	57.3	62.6	64.5	68.9
Philippines	1.7	4.6	5.5	5.5	5.6	
Taiwan	75.1	72.7	76.0	83.0	95.5	
Thailand	26.0	25.6	28.6	34.3	36.4	
Mature Markets						
Australia	83.3	86.7	95.6	109.0	119.0	124.5
France	57.8	57.5	58.2	59.8	64.2	69.2
Germany	70.4	70.1	69.1	70.3	70.5	70.0
Italy	25.0	25.8	27.0	28.7	31.8	34.8
Japan	73.6	75.7	77.6	77.3	77.9	77.8
Spain	65.2	70.4	76.9	86.4	98.8	112.7
United States	104.0	105.1	110.8	118.2	126.0	132.7

Data source: IMF 2006.

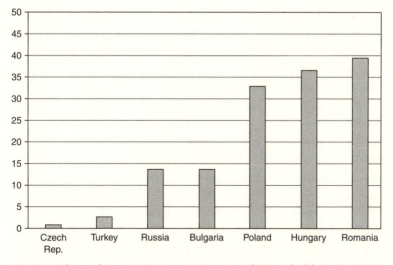

FIGURE 3.3 Share of Foreign Currency Dominated Household Credit, 2005
Data source: IMF 2006.

economies, this ratio is much higher but grew at a far lower rate than in emerging markets. For instance, in Japan it grew from 73.6 percent to 77.8 percent between 2000 and 2005, and in the United States from 104 percent to 132.7 percent. Spain had one of the highest increases, from 65 percent in 2000 to 112.7 percent in 2005, as did Australia, growing from 83.3 percent to 124 percent. Finally, who owns this household debt also can make a difference. If a small local bank owns it, there is a good chance that the proceeds (e.g. interest payments by local households on that debt), will recirculate in the locality. If a foreign bank owns it, such recirculation is unlikely.

THE OTHER GLOBAL HOUSING MARKET:
SUPERPRIME FOR THE VERY RICH

The internationalizing of housing markets has taken on yet another novel format: a global superprime housing market for the very rich.

It is an invented or made market, where setting a very high base price allows it to avoid regular market dynamics, and then makes its specialness part of the cost to buyers. The basic concept is probably as old as wealth. But the developments of the past decade mark a distinctive phase. In a growing number of global cities, extremely rich foreigners have bought a significant number of luxury houses; in some cities this entails buying several smaller units to combine into one larger mansion. Among the main destinations for the superrich are Monaco, London, Paris, New York, Moscow, Singapore, Hong Kong, Shanghai, and Dubai. It is worth noting that Shanghai was the only city to show a marked decrease in the percentage of foreign buyers during the period of the economic crisis, from 2007 to 2012, when it showed a decline of 24 percentage points, while Hong Kong had the highest increase (23 percent), albeit mostly from China's mainland. In the other cities, the number of foreign buyers remained the same or increased.

As Table 3.5 shows, the minimum price of a house for it to be included in the superprime market varies considerably, from $6.4 million in Shanghai to $18.9 million in Monaco. The demographics of the market, specifically the incidence of foreign buyers, seem to play a role in the price. Thus, to take an extreme case, 100 percent of the market for superprime housing in Dubai consists of foreigners, compared to 10 percent in the cheaper market of Shanghai. As for nationalities, Russians have been the main foreign buyers in London, Paris, and Monaco. British buyers have been strong in Monaco, Paris, New York, and Singapore. Africans seem to be purchasing superprime real estate exclusively in Dubai. There is in some cases a regionalism in the choices. Housing in Singapore is predominately purchased by other Asians and Australians; in Hong Kong, mostly by mainland Chinese; in Paris, Monaco, and Moscow, mainly by local Europeans and citizens of the CIS. London, Dubai, and New York City seem to attract foreign buyers from all around the globe.

TABLE 3.5: Foreign Buyers in the Superprime Housing Market, 2007–2012

City	Country of origin of foreign buyers	Minimum price to qualify as superprime (in millions of $)	% foreign (of all buyers)	
			2007	2012
Monaco	Russia, CIS,[a] United Kingdom, Italy, Switzerland	18.9	100	100
Paris	Russia, CIS,[a] Italy, France, Germany, United Kingdom, United States	8.8	90	95
London	Russia, France, South Africa, Italy, India, United Arab Emirates, Greece, Australia, United States, Canada	15.9	75	85
Dubai	Kenya, Somalia, Tanzania, Saudi Arabia, Russia, India, Iran	8.0	45	60
New York	United Kingdom, France, Italy, Spain, China, Singapore, Australia, Brazil, Argentina, Canada	10.0	50	50
Shanghai	Hong Kong, Taiwan, United States, Canada, Japan, Malaysia, Germany, France	6.4	34	10
Singapore	Indonesia, China, Malaysia, India, Australia, United Kingdom	8.3	24	31
Hong Kong	China	15.4	12	35
Moscow	CIS[a]	7.8	10	10

Data source: Powley and Warwick-Ching 2012.
Note: a. CIS refers to Commonwealth of Independent States, which includes the following countries: Armenia, Azerbaijan, Belarus, Kazakhstan, Kyrgyzstan, Moldova, Russia, Tajikistan, and Uzbekistan.

FINANCE: UNABLE TO GOVERN ITS OWN POWER?

Financial assets have grown far more rapidly than the overall economy of developed countries, as measured by GDP. This would not necessarily be bad, especially if the growing financial capital is transformed into large-scale projects for public benefit. But in the period that began in the 1980s, this accrual of benefit to the public was rare; among the exceptions were, for example, large-scale greening and environmentally sound projects in a range of cities, from London's Olympic Park to Rio's expansion of its mass-transport system. Mostly, finance focused on developing more speculative instruments and investments. Historically, this seems to be part of the logic of finance: As it grows and gains power, it does not use its power well. Giovanni Arrighi has argued that when speculative finance becomes dominant in a historic period, it signals the decay of that period.[8]

In the United States, the home of many organizational and financial innovations, the value of financial assets by 2006—before the economic crisis—was 450 percent the value of GDP.[9] In the European Union, the corresponding figure was 356 percent, with the United Kingdom well above the EU average at 440 percent. More generally, the number of countries where financial assets exceeded the value of the country's GDP more than doubled, from thirty-three in 1990 to seventy-two in 2006.

These numbers signal that the period beginning in the late 1980s and continuing to the present constitutes an extreme phase. But is it anomalous? I argue that it is not. Furthermore, this phase is not created by exogenous factors, as the notion of crisis suggests. Recurrent crises are characteristic of this particular type of financial system. Even after the first crises of this phase occurred, in the 1980s, the U.S. government gave the financial industry the instruments to continue its leveraging stampede, as is illustrated in the savings and loan crisis and the New York stock market crash of 1987. In the United States, perhaps the most extreme case, there have been five major bailouts, starting with the 1987 stock market crisis. Each time, taxpayers' money was used to pump liquidity into the financial system, and the financial industry used it to leverage, aiming at more speculation and gain. It did not use it to pay off its debt because this industry is about debt.

The financializing of a growing number of economic sectors since the 1980s has become both a sign of the power of this financial logic and the sign that it is exhausting its growth potential in the current phase, insofar as finance needs to use and invade other economic sectors in order to grow. Once it has subjected much of the economy to its logic, it reaches some type of limit, and the downward curve is likely to set in. One acute illustration of this is the development of instruments by some financial firms that allow them simultaneously to bet on growth in a sector and bet against that sector. This clearly is not made public, but every now and then we gain an insight into how it might work. In one recent case, Goldman Sachs designed derivatives for the Greek government that facilitated Greece's entry into the EU and then developed instruments for another client that would deliver profits if Greece's government went bankrupt. This generated considerable outrage in Greece and in the EU.

The current crisis contains features suggesting that financialized capitalism has reached the limits of its own logic for this phase. Finance has been extremely successful at extracting value from many an economic sector and from chains of derivative on derivative in an often long sequence. However, when everything in a sector has become financialized in a long chain that consists basically of finance building instruments on finance, then there is no longer value to extract. At that point the sector needs new, nonfinancialized sectors to build on. In this context, two of the last frontiers for financial extraction are housing for the modest-income household, of which there are a billion or more worldwide, and bailouts through tax-payers' money (real, old-fashioned—not financialized—money).[10]

Credit default swaps, yet another recent innovation, are a critical factor in the current financial crisis. Their rapid growth was partly due to the fact that they were sold as a sort of insurance, which was valuable to many investors in a worrisome hypergrowth market. The second factor that fed the growth of this market was a familiar condition in any speculative market: some investors saw the economy as nearing crisis and others saw it as still having a few years of rapid growth. In short, there were eager buyers of swaps and there were eager sellers, and a market was thus made. From under $1 trillion in 2001, swaps reached a value of $62 trillion by 2007, more than the $55 trillion of global GDP in 2007. But by September 2008 they had led to massive losses. The critical factor creating instability for the financial sector was not that millions of people with subprime mortgages were facing foreclosures, because the overall value of foreclosures was relatively small for global financiers. It was not knowing what might next turn out to be a toxic asset, since vast numbers of small slices of these mortgages had been bundled with high-grade debt in order to sell these instruments as backed by an actual material asset. The complexity of these investment instruments made it almost impossible to trace that tiny toxic component. What was a housing crisis for millions of people was only a crisis of confidence among investors. Yet it was enough to make that powerful system tremble. In other words, this type of financial system has more of the social in it than is suggested by the technical complexity of its instruments and electronic platforms.[11]

The language of crisis remains ambiguous. A first point is that what we call "crisis" has enormous variability. Since the 1980s, there have been several financial crises. Some are well known, such as the 1987 New York stock market crash and the 1997 Asian meltdown. Others have received less attention, such as the financial crises that occurred in more than seventy countries during the

1980s and 1990s as they deregulated their financial systems. These are usually referred to as "adjustment crises," the language of "adjustment" suggesting that these are positive changes inasmuch as they move a country toward economic development.

Typically, the term "financial crisis" is used to describe an event that has a deleterious effect on the leading sectors of finance rather than on a country's institutions and people. Adjustment crises involved a far larger region of the globe than did the financial crises of 1987 and 1997. Yet the miseries the adjustment crises inflicted on middle-income people in the countries where they occurred, and the resulting destruction of often well-functioning national economic sectors, have largely been invisible to the global eye. These adjustment crises in individual countries intersected with global interests only when there were strong financial links with global firms and investors, as was the case with the 1994 crisis in Mexico and the 2001 crisis in Argentina.

A second point arises from data that present the period after the 1997 Asian financial crisis as a fairly stable one—until the current financial crisis. One element of this representation is that after a country goes through an adjustment crisis, what follows can be measured as "stability" and even prosperity according to conventional indicators. Except for the dot-com bust and the Argentine sovereign default, the post-1997 period was one of considerable financial stability for the leading financial markets and firms. But behind this "stability" lay the savage sorting of winners and losers that has already been described. It is easier to track winners than to track the often slow descent into poverty of households, small firms, and government agencies (such as those concerned with health and education) that are not part of the new glamour sectors of finance and trade. The postadjustment losers became relatively invisible globally over the last twenty years. Every now and then they became visible, as when members of the traditional middle class in Argentina engaged in food riots in Buenos Aires and elsewhere in the mid-1990s, breaking into food shops just to get food—something that was previously unheard of in Argentina and took many by surprise. Such rare events also make visible the very incomplete character of postadjustment stability and the new "prosperity" praised by global regulators and media.

Thus, we need to disaggregate the often-touted fact that in 2006 and 2007 most countries had a GDP growth rate of 4 percent a year or more, a rate much higher than that of previous decades. Behind that measure lies the making of extreme forms of wealth and poverty and the destruction of well-established middle classes. In contrast, a 4 percent GDP growth rate in the Keynesian years described the growth of a massive middle class.

Also left out of this macro-level picture of relative stability in the decade after the Asian financial crisis is the critical fact that crisis is a structural feature of deregulated, interconnected, and electronic financial markets. Two points are worth mentioning in this regard. One is the sharp growth in the extent to which nonfinancial economic sectors were financialized, leading to the overall growth of financial assets as a share of sector value. That is to say, if crisis is a structural feature of current financial markets, then the more nonfinancial economic sectors experience financialization, the more susceptible they become to a financial crisis, regardless of their product. As a result, the potential for instability even in strong economic sectors is high, particularly in countries with sophisticated financial systems and high levels of financialization, such as the United States and the United Kingdom. Germany, which has weathered the financial crisis much better than the United States and the United Kingdom, has a manufacturing economy and a fairly low level of financialization—before the 2007 crisis hit, the value of financial assets in Germany was only 175 percent of GDP, compared with 450 percent in the United States.

Let me illustrate with an example from the current crisis and another from the 1997 Asian crisis. When the current crisis hit the

United States in 2007, many healthy firms, with good capitalization, strong demand for their goods and services, and good profit levels, were brought low. Large U.S. corporations, from Coca-Cola and Pepsi to IBM and Microsoft, were doing fine in terms of capital reserves, profits, market presence, and so on, but the financial crisis still hit them, directly via devalued stock and other financial holdings and indirectly through the impact of the crisis on consumer demand and credit access. Highly financialized sectors such as the housing market and commercial property market suffered directly and immediately. In many countries that underwent adjustment crises in earlier years, too, basically healthy nonfinancial firms were negatively affected. These adjustments were aimed at securing the conditions for globally linked financial markets, but they ruined many firms in the nonfinancial sector as well as small domestic banks.

We saw this also in the 1997 Asian financial crisis. Thousands of healthy manufacturing firms were destroyed in South Korea—firms whose products were in strong demand in national and foreign markets and that had the workforces and the machines to fill worldwide orders but which had to close because credit dried up and they were prevented from paying the up-front costs of production. The result was the unemployment of more than a million factory workers.[12]

The critical event that brought the financial system to a momentary standstill in 2008 was the classic bursting of a speculative bubble: the $62 trillion credit default swap crisis that exploded in September 2008, a full year after the subprime mortgage crisis of August 2007. By 2008, the decrease in house prices, the high rate of mortgage foreclosures, the decline in global trade, and the growth of unemployment all alerted investors that something was not right. This in turn led those who had bought credit default swaps as a sort of insurance (see Figure 3.4 for the rapid growth in the value of such swaps between 2001 and 2007) to want to cash in.

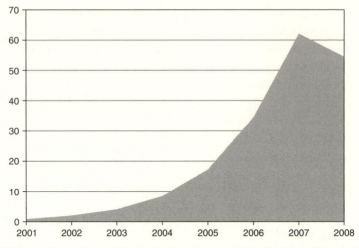

FIGURE 3.4 Rising Value of Credit Default Swaps, 2001–2008 (in trillions of $)
Source: Varchaver and Benner 2008, based on data from ISDA.

But credit default swaps were not really insurance; they were derivatives, meaning that the sellers of the swaps did not have the capital required to back these instruments up, which would have been required had they really constituted insurance. The sellers had expected neither the downturn nor the desire of buyers to cash in. This catapulted much of the financial sector into crisis. However, not everybody lost; investors such as George Soros made large profits by going against the trend. Credit default swaps are part of what is referred to as the shadow banking system. According to some analysts, the shadow banking system accounted for 70 percent of banking at the time that the crisis exploded.

The shadow banking system is not informal, illegal, or clandestine. It is in the open, but it thrives on the opaqueness of investments. This opaqueness facilitates the recoding of instruments (a derivative recoded as insurance), which permits practices that are now, after the fact, viewed as bordering on the illegal. For instance, it is now clear that credit default swaps were sold as a type of insurance. From the perspective of the financial system, this makes a significant difference, for had they constituted insurance, the law would require that they be backed by capital reserves and be subject to considerable regulation. Turning them into derivatives was de facto deregulation and eliminated the requirement for adequate capital reserves. Credit default swaps would not have grown so fast and reached such extreme values if they had needed to meet capital reserve requirements, which would have reduced much of the impact of the September 2008 crisis. Because they were derivatives, however, they could have an almost vertical growth curve.

A key component of the shadow banking system is so-called Dark Pools. A dark pool may refer to a wide variety of private, off-exchange Alternative Trading Systems (ATS) that share a key component: they do not display order size or price until after a trade has been completed. In a traditional public securities exchange, an electronic "order book" displays the volume of a particular stock available to be bought or sold at a certain price: these buy orders and sell orders are then matched algorithmically on a first-come-first-served basis. In dark pools, such information stays hidden until buy and sell orders are matched against each other, at which point the ATS is expected to report to a trade reporting facility any transaction of exchange-listed equities or options within ten seconds.[13]

Initially, dark pools appealed to institutional investors such as pension funds and mutual funds that need to periodically make large transactions in a single security. In a public exchange with an open order book, the presence of a large order can immediately move the price of a stock (for example, if ABC Co. has an average trading volume of 1 million shares a day, and there is an entry placed in the order book to buy 500,000 shares, it's an easy bet that ABC stock is going to go up, and the price that the purchaser will have to pay likely to be higher by the time the transaction is completed). To combat this, large investors had brokers "work" trades, breaking large blocks of stock into smaller transactions carried out on an extended period of time. This solution was never entirely effective: it increased price volatility and transaction time, and market participants could still detect a general upsurge of demand. The introduction of computerized high-frequency trading (HFT) made the situation much worse for institutional investors; algorithmic trading models could reliably detect even the most patiently distributed orders.[14] Dark pools, first offered by financial giants such as Credit Suisse and Goldman Sachs, offered a refuge for investors who wanted to make transactions without immediately losing value. Today, dark pool trading represents about 13 percent of all stock market action[15] and their numbers are increasing (see Figure 3.5).

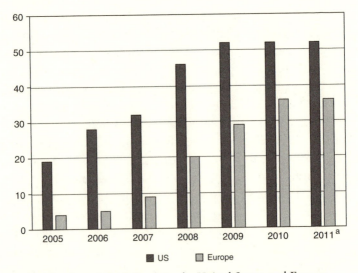

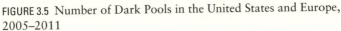

FIGURE 3.5 Number of Dark Pools in the United States and Europe, 2005–2011

Source: Economist 2011b, referencing data from TABB Group.

Note: a. Through August

The potential for abuse within dark pools is massive. The 10-second reporting delay for ATS transactions is an eternity in the modern stock market: in 2010, the major financial exchanges averaged 215,162 quotes per second and 28,375 trades.[16] In this environment, the opacity provided by dark pools may distort markets. Further, the same opacity has enabled an extreme potential for abuse: large banks that run their own dark pools are suspected of giving unequal access to their own traders, and dark pool operators have been penalized for running the same HFT strategies within their exchanges and sharing confidential trade information with investors (Citigroup, in a recent case, received trade information from a dark pool it helped fund).[17]

In short, the so-called 2008 crisis contained several distinct crises. One was the subprime crisis experienced by the people who obtained these mortgages and lost out. A second crisis emerged from the fact that the millions of home foreclosures were a signal that something was wrong. But in itself, this crisis could not have brought down the financial system. It led to a crisis of confidence in the investor community. This, in turn, led those who had bought swaps as insurance against what they saw as the end of the growth cycle to want to cash in those swaps. And it was this that engendered the major crisis because the sellers of swaps were not ready for such a massive sudden disbursement. The decision by several governments to bail out banks with taxpayers' money, with no guarantees from banks that they would recirculate bailout funds in the economy, led to further declines in growth and rising poverty of citizens and governments. It pushed already overindebted governments and households over the edge. And this is the crisis that lingers on and has led to the current austerity politics examined in Chapter 2. In contrast, global finance has gone back to super-profits after a brief but sharp fall in 2008.

We all need debt, whether we are a firm, a household, or a country. But do we need this level of debt? More important, do we need such complex instruments to finance basic needs for firms and households? No. Many of these needs can be met with traditional banking loans. We need finance because it "creates" capital, and can enable large-scale projects that we need—to clean toxic dumps, green our energy sources, address the vast needs of the destitute in poor and rich countries. In this latest growth cycle finance never did. It opted for financialization—of consumer loans and home mortgages, of student loans and pensions, of municipal government debt, and more. Finance was aggressive, invasive, and self-interested, and rather than being regulated firmly, it was too often left to risk our money for its own gain.

Changing Our Understanding of Growth and Prosperity

One important difference between the current crisis and other post-1980 crises is the order of magnitude that speculative instruments made possible. A second important difference involves the larger economic landscape: we now recognize clearly that we need to act quickly to curb financial excess, because existing international treaties and national laws are not sufficient. A third difference is the wider recognition that the growing extremes of wealth and poverty have become problematic. We now know that the profits secured by the richer segments of society do not "trickle down." And we know that epidemics resulting from poverty and inadequate health care will in time also reach the rich.

The extreme character of the current crisis and the fact that we have recognized other major crises—most important among these being climate change—create an opening for the establishment of novel criteria for economic benefit. Yes, we need financial institutions: finance has the capacity to make and efficiently distribute capital. However, financial capital has been used during the past decades for extremely speculative investments that largely served to enrich the already wealthy and has often wound up destroying healthy firms, even if more often that not this was unintended. Instead, we must use that new capital for large-scale investments in public goods, to develop manufacturing sectors, to green our economies, and more.

This combination of goals creates an opportunity to reorient financial capital to meet a broad range of needs. As an example, financial capital helped lift countless people in China out of poverty in recent years. But it did so via investments in manufacturing, infrastructure, and other material economies. Using financial capital to expand material economic sectors and to green our economies is distributive—the opposite of using financial capital to make more financial capital, which leads to massive concentrations of wealth and power. In principle, a serious effort to use financial capital to develop the material economy is an opportunity to green those investments—to encourage the development and use of technologies and practices that do not harm the environment.

The greater our capacity to produce wealth has become over the last twenty years (and finance has played a critical role here), the more radical the condition of poverty has become. It used to be that being poor meant owning or working a plot of land that did not produce much. Today the 2 billion people living in extreme poverty own nothing but their bodies. The fact is that we have the capacity to feed everybody on the globe, but feeding the poor is not the priority of the most powerful economic actors, so we have more hunger than ever before, and hunger is now growing in rich countries as well, notably the United States. Most of us have heard about the abusive conditions under which diamonds are extracted and how those profits get rerouted to armed warfare rather than to development. Fewer know about the circumstances surrounding the mining of rare earth elements, key metals needed for electronic components (notably cell phones), for green batteries, and more. These metals are often mined by unprotected workers who use their naked hands to extract the minerals, live in extreme poverty, and die too young from poisoning to have been able to pass on the news of their abuse to the wider world. Finally, there is the well-established fact that discovering oil in a poor country becomes the formula for the creation of even more poverty and a small elite of the superrich.

We need to change the logics through which we define genuine prosperity. The triple crisis we confront should become an opportunity to reorient our enormous capacities to make capital and to produce what is urgently needed in both the Global South and the Global North.

CHAPTER 4

Dead Land, Dead Water

The biosphere's capacities to renew land, water, and air are remarkable. But they are predicated on specific temporalities and life cycles that our technical, chemical, and organizational innovations are rapidly outpacing. Industrialized economies have long done damage to the biosphere, but in at least some of these cases, and with time on its side, the biosphere has brought land and water back to life. Existing data show that in specific zones these sorts of recoveries have failed, however. We now have vast stretches of land and water that are dead—land overwhelmed by the relentless use of chemicals and water dead from lack of oxygen due to pollution of all sorts. The surge of foreign land acquisitions by governments and firms examined in Chapter 2 is one of many sources of this destruction. But the purchases are also partly a response to the crisis: more land and water need to be acquired to replace what has died. And if we take finance as a capability, following the analysis in Chapter 3, we can see more grist for its mill in the most foundational elements—not only the commodification of land and water, but also the further financializing of the resulting commodities.

The trends described in this chapter point to accelerated histories and geographies of destruction on a scale our planet has not seen before, making substantive the notion of the Anthropocene, the age marked by major human impact on the environment. Many of these destructions of the quality of land, water, and air have hit poor communities particularly hard, producing an estimated 800 million displaced people worldwide. But none of us is immune, as other destructions can reach us all, spread by massive transformations in the atmosphere.

Here I examine extreme conditions. As in the other chapters of this book, this is a partial view that rests on the assumption that extreme conditions makes visible trends that are more difficult to apprehend in their milder versions. Most of the land and most of the water on our planet are still alive. But much of it is fragile. Scattered evidence in news media signals that the extent of this fragility may not be widely understood or recognized. For instance, polls suggest that few in the United States seem to know that more than a third of that country's land, including much of the cherished fertile Midwest, is actually stressed according to scientific measures. Or that the six major gyres that help keep our ocean currents going have now become massive trash zones, full of circling garbage that leads to the asphyxiation of marine life. Or that we have at least 400 clinically dead coastal ocean zones. We *made* this fragility and these deaths.

We can think of such dead land and dead water as holes in the tissue of the biosphere. I conceive of these holes as sites marked by the expulsion of biospheric elements from their life space, and as the surface expression of deeper subterranean trends that are cutting across the world, regardless of the local politico-economic organization or mode of environmental destruction. The mix of conditions examined in previous chapters and in this chapter all contribute to these expulsions. Massive demand for land and water, growing poverty, the eviction of fauna and flora in order to develop plantations and mines, together reposition vast stretches of land as nothing more than sites for extraction. In each place there is a specific genealogy that explains the outcome. But from a conceptual distance all these different genealogies of destruction become visible as a sort of generic condition: a global multisited array of dead patches of land and water in the tissue of the biosphere.

This multisited space of devastation tells a story about biospheric destruction that is much more than a tale of the individual, specific ways in which countries and sectors are destructive. I briefly invoke a diversity of sites in this chapter to serve the conceptual effort of detecting forces that transcend the familiar divisions of our geopolitical systems, economic sectors, and regulations. We often overemphasize these familiar differentiations when it comes to biosphere destruction, blaming the specific for problems that are generic. I use cases from countries with different forms of political and economic organization to signal that while environmental destruction may take on specific shapes and contents in each country, and may be worse in some than in others, the similarities in destructive capacities are what really matter in my analysis. A mine that pollutes in Russia looks different from a mine that pollutes in the United States, but both are polluting above the threshold of the sustainable.

This chapter tries to show the nature and scale of our problems in three major parts: land, water, and global scale-up. The first examines evidence on the degradation of land, attempting to get a global view of sites that are effectively dead. It includes a series of brief incursions into specific sites, from the Dominican Republic to Peru and from Russia to the United States, marked by acute land toxicity. The second examines water scarcities created by humans, and the increasing number of water bodies that pollution has starved of oxygen. I include a number of cases from around the world that illustrate the specifics of scarcity and oxygen depletion. Each of these extreme conditions carries multiple implications for life that depends on the presence of clean land, air, and water. The third part examines some of the most extreme outcomes and scale-ups generated by these practices: the melting of the permafrost, rising temperatures, and massive floods.

LAND

Not all land degradation is created equal, not all is caused by human action, and not all is accompanied by increased erosion or salinity.

There are multiple causes of land degradation, just as there are many types of land. Erosion, desertification, and overuse through monocultures, as in plantations, are critical causes of agricultural land destruction. Climate change has brought heat waves of a kind rarely seen before, affecting agricultural areas across the world and increasingly including places that have been successful food producers for a very long time. These heat waves and their consequences are probably the key source of land degradation in agricultural regions. Mining and industrial waste degrade land in a very different way. Here I will focus mostly on the degradations caused by mining and industry, after a brief examination of the current state of agricultural land.

At its most general, land degradation can be defined as "a long-term loss of ecosystem function and productivity caused by disturbances from which land cannot recover unaided."[1] It is difficult to measure accurately on a large scale. The few studies that have attempted to map the global process estimate that about 40 percent of the world's agricultural land is seriously degraded. The worst-affected regions are Central America, where 75 percent of agricultural land is infertile; Africa, where a fifth of the soil is degraded; and Asia, where 11 percent has become unsuitable for farming. A recent global examination of land by the World Bank cites the findings of several scientists that "if the world warms by 2°C—warming which may be reached in 20 to 30 years—it will cause widespread food shortages, unprecedented heat-waves, and more intense cyclones. . . . Today, our world is 0.8°C above pre-industrial levels of the 18th century. We could see a 2°C world in the space of one generation." The area of land affected by drought has increased over the past fifty years, and has done so somewhat faster than projected by climate models. For instance, the 2012 drought in the United States affected about 80 percent of agricultural land, making it the most severe drought since the 1950s. In sub-Saharan Africa, with "warming of less than 2°C by the 2050s, total crop production could be reduced by 10 percent. For higher levels of warming there are indications that yields may decrease by around 15–20 percent across all crops and regions" of sub-Saharan Africa. A warming of 3°C is estimated to reduce savannas from "a quarter at present to approximately one-seventh of total current land area."

Some more detail about the evolution of land degradation can be found in two major earlier studies executed between 1997 and 2008 and covering just about all countries in the world.[2] The Global Assessment of Human-Induced Soil Degradation produced a map of degradation between 1950 and 1997 based on expert opinion guided by standardized qualitative guidelines; this methodology is considered to have limited replicability, and such maps will be accurate for a relatively brief period of time given ongoing degradation. But it captures the condition of one particular period.

The second, by Bai, Dent, Olsson, and Schaepman, used twenty-three years' worth of data from the remotely sensed Normalized Difference Vegetation Index, generated mostly by satellite observation of green vegetation.[3] The index measures the amount of light spectrum absorbed by photosynthesis, adjusted for rain use efficiency, to create a proxy for net primary productivity that can be tracked over time. Overall, researchers estimate (with diverse adjustments for particular variables) that 24 percent of global land area suffered degradation between 1981 and 2003. In addition to the overall findings, these results have been validated empirically in several very diverse places—northern China, Kenya, and Bangladesh.

Over the past few years, heat waves have become the main source of agricultural land degradation, with all this entails for the global food supply, particularly for the poor.[4] Based on studies of specific heat waves around the world, the World Bank finds that the past decade has seen extreme heat waves with major societal impacts. Other researchers report that "these events were highly unusual with monthly and seasonal temperatures typically more than 3 standard deviations (sigma) warmer than the local mean temperature—so-called 3-sigma events. Without climate change, such 3-sigma events would be expected to occur only once in several hundreds of years."[5]

Heat waves can lead to a variety of problems.[6] A decline in precipitation, for instance, is the major issue in some areas. Extreme cases include southern Africa, where annual precipitation "is projected to decrease by up to 30 percent under 4°C warming . . . and parts of southern and west Africa [will see] decreases in groundwater recharge rates of 50–70 percent." Worldwide, warming of 1.2°C–1.9°C by 2050 would increase the proportion of the population that is undernourished by 25–90 percent compared to the present. In South Asia, such an increase would require a doubling of food imports to meet per capita calorie demand. "Decreasing food availability is related to significant health problems for affected populations, including childhood stunting, which is projected to increase by 35 percent compared to a scenario without climate change by 2050."

The facts about these increased temperatures and their causes have been convincingly established. On the facts, the Fourth Assessment Report of the Intergovernmental Panel on Climate Change (IPCC) found that the rise in global mean temperature and warming of the climate system were "unequivocal." Furthermore, "most of the observed increase in global average temperature since the mid-20th century is very likely due to the observed increase in anthropogenic greenhouse gas concentrations." Recent work reinforces this conclusion. Global mean warming is now approximately 0.8°C above preindustrial levels. Further, in the absence of human activity during the past fifty years "the sum of solar and volcanic forces would likely have produced cooling, not warming."[7]

Recent studies have shown that extreme summer temperatures can now largely be attributed to climatic warming since the 1960s.[8] In the 1960s, summertime heat extremes (more than three standard deviations warmer than the mean of the climate) were practically absent, affecting less than 1 percent of the earth's surface. The affected area increased to 4–5 percent by 2006–2008, and by 2009–2011 such extremes occurred on 6–13 percent of the land surface. Now such extremely hot outliers typically cover about 10 percent of the land area.

Industrial Waste: Its Variable Mechanisms

Beyond the gradual degradation of agricultural land, there are processes that cause extreme destruction to land of all sorts. Mining and manufacturing are the most obvious culprits in much of the world. Their capacity to kill land is enormous; it is particularly hard for land to recover from the type of degradation they create. Consider, for instance, that much of the estimated 1 billion tonnes of industrial waste produced by OECD countries in 2001 still lives with us more than ten years later. And industry produces more waste than that produced by agriculture, forestry, and power production *combined.*[9]

In sufficient concentrations, industrial waste, including heavy metals and greenhouse gases, can render an environment so toxic that plants cease to grow and even people become sterile. Some heavy metals (a misnomer, as this category includes some elements that are neither heavy nor metals) are vital to human health in controlled amounts, such as iron and zinc. Others, such as mercury and lead, are toxic at any level. However, the output of waste generated by modern industry is so massive it can render even a benign substance such as carbon dioxide toxic.

I present here a range of concentrated situations that make visible the worst types of poisoning and destruction of people and land. But we should remember that the real problem is the vast accumulation of less extreme cases that pile up with less negative publicity day after day.

Norilsk, Russia

The city of Norilsk, Russia, was founded in 1935 as Norillag, a Soviet labor camp that came to serve one of the largest mining operations in the Soviet Union.[10] The prisoner population grew steadily from 10,000 in 1936 to 90,000 in 1953, at which time the Norilsk camp held more than a third of the Soviet Union's total prisoner population. It has ever since remained a massive vector for environmental destruction, poisoning land, water, and air. Important for my argument is that it has done so under a series of highly varied political and economic regimes, from the Soviet Union of the 1930s to that of the 1960s, through the privatization of the 1980s, and back to state control after 2000.

Located north of the Arctic Circle in Siberia, Norilsk is home to the world's largest nickel smelting complex; it also produces significant amounts of platinum, palladium, and cobalt. The publicly traded MMC Norilsk Nickel is Russia's leading producer of non-ferrous and platinum-group metals. It controls one-third of the world's nickel deposits and accounts for 20 percent of global nickel production, 50 percent of palladium, 20 percent of platinum, 10 percent of cobalt, and 3 percent of the world's copper output. Intensive metal production has continued to rely largely on outdated technology. The Blacksmith Institute estimates that in 2007 almost 1,000 tons of copper and nickel compounds were released into the air annually, along with 2 million tons of sulfur dioxide; in 1999, elevated copper and nickel concentrations were found in soils up to a 60-kilometer radius around Norilsk. Norilsk has become a toxic city, "where the snow is black, the air tastes of sulfur and the life expectancy for factory workers is 10 years below the Russian average," which is already low.

The local population has been severely affected by pollution: heavy metals suppress the immune system, and overall illness rates in the Norilsk industrial zone are 27.6 percent higher than in control areas with identical climate and geography. Respiratory diseases among children occurred 150 percent more often than average in Russian cities. Lung cancer rates among men have been found to be elevated, and children in Norilsk are almost twice as likely to develop some kind of cancer than other Russian children. Women in the industrial zone give birth to children with an average weight of 3,000 grams, as compared to an average weight of 3,430 grams in unpolluted areas, and pregnancies are more likely to be complicated. In 2007 15,000 residents of the Norilsk industrial zone signed a letter to the Russian State Duma, expressing their concern over the impact of pollution on health: "The presence in atmospheric pollution of heavy metals leads to a drop in the immunity of city residents, which is so vital in our climactic conditions . . . we are falling sick and dying."[11]

The deposits of nickel and copper ore in Siberia's Taimyr Peninsula have been known since the 1600s. But industrial production was not undertaken until 1935, when the Council of People's Commissars of the Soviet Union passed a resolution titled "On Building the Norilsk Combine" and placed the project under the control of the NKVD security service. The project was considered of the highest priority and overseen directly by the head of the gulag system to ensure a workforce in that remote area. The demands of rapid industrialization and militarization touched off by World War II could not be met with forced labor alone. In 1941 the labor camp became integrated and 3,734 free laborers joined the workforce; by 1949 20,930 free laborers composed nearly a third of the production force. By 1953, when Norilsk was granted township status and removed from the direct control of the NKVD, the metallurgical combine was producing 35 percent of the Soviet Union's nickel, 12 percent of its copper, 30 percent of its cobalt, and 90 percent of its platinum-group metals.[12]

The transition from Soviet state ownership and command production to capitalist private ownership and market productions did not substantially decrease the velocity with which land, air, and water were destroyed. Between the fall of the Soviet Union in 1989 and 2003, Norilsk's production of sulfur dioxide increased as a proportion of Russia's total output. The Soviet-era infrastructure, built between 1930 and the late 1970s with absolutely no consideration of ecological impact, is still the backbone of the plant. Private ownership groups have shifted emphasis from raw production to economic efficiency and profitability, but they have maintained the policy of not bothering with massive toxicity. It is considered an inevitable by-product of industrial production. In a 2005 interview in Golovnina, Norilsk's deputy director general, Zhak Rozenberg, said:

> We were set up at a time when ... there was no ecological ideology, when the Soviet Union had an entirely different agenda. ... As a global company we certainly have to accept global standards. That's why we are introducing international technology at our facilities. But one can't force us to drop everything else and achieve that overnight ... Ecological problems are not ecological problems as such. They come as a result of unsatisfactory technology. We are looking for ways of improving that technology which would allow us—and that's a dream—to produce so little [sulfur] dioxide as to be harmless for the environment. ... Ecological and economic projects have to be harmonized. Otherwise we might as well return to the stone age, sit by a crystal clear river all day, eat absolutely ecologically clean fish, and that would be it.

To bring some perspective, it is worth adding that what may sound like an extreme statement, the sort that could only come from a company with brutal roots in a totalitarian regime and a mining workforce originating in forced labor camps, is echoed in the United States when it comes to mining of all sorts, as the case of the Zortman-Landusky mining operation (discussed in the next section) illustrates. Russia and the United States have very different histories and forms of economic organization. But let's recall just one familiar case: in the United States, 40 percent of damaging emissions today are from dirty coal plants—no minor share, since the United States accounts for 14 percent of global emissions.[13]

Zortman-Landusky, United States

The trajectory of the U.S. mining firm Zortman-Landusky evokes a similar set of abuses across different periods and geographies. The political economies are different from those in Russia, yet they too enabled a set of major abuses over time, and through different incarnations of this firm.

In 1974, Frank Duval founded the Pegasus Gold Corporation. At the heart of the venture was a proprietary mining technique called cyanide heap leaching, capable of extracting trace amounts of gold from spent ore at sites that were no longer productive for conventional mining. Pegasus Gold debuted this technique at previously abandoned gold and silver mines on the Fort Belknap Reservation in Montana. The company ran the mines profitably for nearly thirty years before falling gold prices and mounting ecological liabilities led to a bankruptcy and corporate reorganization, leaving the State of Montana with more than $30 million in environmental reclamation costs for "perpetual" water treatment. This sort of severe ecological degradation and the discharge of associated costs through corporate restructuring is the rule, rather than the exception, for this kind of resource extraction: Frank Duval went on from the Pegasus Gold catastrophe to operate many other mines, including Superfund sites. He was at no point liable for environmental damage.

The Zortman-Landusky gold deposits were discovered in the late nineteenth century on reservation lands of the Assiniboine and Gros Ventre peoples in Montana's Little Rocky Mountains. In

1895, faced with imminent starvation, the tribes signed the Grinnell Agreement to sell the land to the U.S. government. Mining activity grew rapidly until the 1920s, when yields began decreasing steadily; most claims were abandoned by 1959. Pegasus Gold began operating at the site in 1977. Its technique of cyanide heap leaching proved to be incredibly successful. The process is usually conducted on ore with a gold concentration of up to 11.3 grams of gold per ton. It can be used to process huge quantities of spent or low-quality ore to profitably produce a relatively small amount of gold: in 1989 at Carlin Trend mine in Nevada, about 105,000 kg of gold were recovered from cyanide-leaching 129.8 million tonnes of ore. The scale on which Pegasus Gold operated is astounding. A 1994 U.S. Environmental Protection Agency (EPA) report noted that in 1994 it processed "75,000 tons of ore a day . . . [while] heaps and tailings cover[ed] 175 acres and contain[ed] 60 million tons of material."[14]

In the heap-leaching process, ore is deposited in stages, or "lifts," onto a clay, asphalt, or plastic liner. It is then treated with a solution as strong as 454 g of sodium cyanide per ton of water, powerful enough to dissolve microscopic traces of gold. The cyanide solution then seeps down the mountainside until it collects in pools at the bottom of the heap of ore, having dissolved and bonded with gold as it flows through the ore. After it is collected in the "pregnant pools" at the bottom (so called because the solution has absorbed gold), the solution is pumped through a special processing center to reclaim the gold.

Cyanide is regularly used in a variety of industrial processes, and it is considered safe to use because it rapidly degrades and does not bioaccumulate. However, cyanide is a powerful asphyxiate (so called because it easily replaces oxygen in many chemical reactions), highly poisonous, and highly reactive. Cyanide spillage was a chronic problem at Zortman-Landusky. In 1982, 2,953 liters of cyanide-laced water leaked from a containment pond, and in a separate accident a ruptured pipe leaked 196,841 liters of cyanide solution. Eight different cyanide spills occurred between 1983 and 1984, and in 1986 the company, lacking a disposal permit, released 75 million liters of cyanide solution when a containment pond threatened to overflow. Following some spills, the local water showed elevated levels of cyanide and could not be used, and wildlife die-offs occurred.

Cyanide compounds and acidic mine drainage water have severely impacted the water supply of the Fort Belknap Reservation. Just as cyanide releases gold from ore, it can free toxic metals such as cadmium, selenium, lead, and mercury. If not properly contained, the tons of solution applied to ore heaps can form a toxic slurry of active cyanide, heavy metals, and sulfuric acid that can continue to drain into the local water table for centuries. Acidic drainage water became a major problem: in 2001, three years after the mine stopped operating, water from the Swift Gulch tributary to the Little Bighorn River had a pH of 3.7, roughly the same acidity as apple juice or wine. Members of the local community and environmental organizations eventually filed suit under the Clean Water Act, and Pegasus Gold was ordered to post a bond for $36 million in 1996. After paying out more than $5 million in executive bonuses, and despite having taken $300 million worth of gold out of the mines, Pegasus declared bankruptcy in 1998 and left the state of Montana with cleanup costs of $33 million beyond the settlement. After bankruptcy, the company reformed as Apollo Gold and continued to operate Pegasus's profitable holdings with many of the same directors and executives in place.[15]

Founder Frank Duval had left the company earlier, in 1987, after he had accepted sanctions from the Securities and Exchange Commission (SEC). This, the third action against Duval by the SEC, was for failing to disclose a financial stake he held in a company that Pegasus Gold had bought. This is a violation of antifraud provisions and numerous reporting requirements of the 1934 Securities Exchange Act. Duval quickly became involved in a series of mine reclamation projects that had similarities with Zortman-Landusky: he sought out either exhausted mines or claims that had proved technically difficult, promised great results from untested technology, and left a large mess for the state and federal governments after discharging responsibility through bankruptcy.

After leaving Pegasus, Duval launched Bunker Hill Mining and restarted silver production at a section of the Crescent Mine, a seventy-two-year-old mine that had been idle for four years. Duval and his partners were able to raise $10 million on the Vancouver and Toronto stock exchanges, reported profitable quarters in Q3 1989 and Q1 1990, and promptly declared bankruptcy in January 1991. The mine was located in a previously existing Superfund site, Idaho's Silver Valley, but Bunker Hill Mining did not invest significantly in environmental remediation. Indeed, it did not even pay taxes or its employees: at the time of bankruptcy, Bunker Hill Mining had never paid property tax, owed Shoshone County approximately $2 million, and owed workers back wages of $90,000. The company sought bankruptcy protection only weeks after issuing a strong quarterly earnings report, leading to allegations of fraud and misleading investors.[16]

Duval also owns and oversees one of the most toxic mining sites in the United States, Midnite Mine in Ford, Washington, a major uranium mine located on the Spokane Indian Reservation. In 2006, the Office of Environmental Cleanup reported that Midnite Mines Inc. controlled a 49 percent interest in Dawn Mining, the operating company of the Midnite Mine; the other 51 percent was controlled by giant mining conglomerate Newmont Mining through its wholly owned subsidiary Newmont USA Limited. Production at the mine stopped in 1981, when uranium prices dropped sharply: sensing an opportunity to pick up a potentially valuable asset on the cheap,

Duval bought a majority position of Midnite Mines Inc. and became president and CEO in 1984.

Unfortunately for Duval, the Washington Department of Health decided the mine was a threat to public safety and terminated Dawn Mining's lease in 1991. The company was then, due to its licensing agreement, required to reclaim the site, which contained 33 million tons of radioactive mine tailings distributed over about 40 hectares of exposed uranium ore, and radioactive mine seepage into the Spokane River. At this point, Dawn Mining declared that it did not have "sufficient funds to pay for the reclamation plan it proposed, for any alternate plan, or for the closure of its mill," as reported by its owner, Newmont Mining. Dawn proposed instead turning the Midnite Mine site into a radioactive waste facility, importing low-level radioactive refuse from around the country and using the fees generated to clean up the site. This proposal was soundly rejected. In 2000, the Midnite Mine officially became a Superfund site. And in 2001, Duval's Sterling Mining received permission to develop a mine in Montana that overlaps with both the Cabinet Mountain Wilderness Area and the Kootenai National Forest.[17]

As they did in these cases, corporate structures and bankruptcy laws work together to severely limit the power of local claims. Well-structured subsidiaries function to limit losses to the amount that a parent company invested in such auxiliaries but place no such ceiling on profits. Despite the fact that Newmont was a very wealthy multinational and, as the majority shareholder, had appointed board members, shared office space, and guaranteed loans for Dawn Mining, Newmont had a strong legal argument that it was not liable for its subsidiary. Newmont dug in its heels for a drawn-out legal battle. However, Boston Common Asset Management filed a shareholder resolution criticizing Newmont's disclosure of environmental liability, increasing pressure on the company. Moreover, with annual net income of $2.2 billion in 2011 and $1.9 billion in 2010, the $153 million called for in the settlement with the

EPA amounted to a mere 7 percent of 2011 earnings. For whatever the comparison is worth, the U.S. Department of the Interior's contribution of $42 million would make up 21 percent of the total site funding: if Newmont had been forced to pay 21 percent of its 2011 profit, it would have had to pay $462 million. One of Duval's mining companies had gone broke yet again, but it was structured in such a way that he could abandon it with neither difficulty nor liability.

In what is a many-decades-long sequence of violations and exits, Frank Duval did not use his personal assets to pay fines, but simply let a company go bankrupt and start a new one.

Times Beach, Missouri

The 480-acre Times Beach site is located 27 kilometers west of St. Louis. In 1970, the incorporated city was home to about 1,200 people, including the residents of several mobile home parks. City funds were insufficient to pave local roads, and dust from unpaved roads was considered a constant problem. In 1972 and 1973, the Russell Bliss waste-oil company was contracted to spray oil on city roads as a means of dust abatement. Former residents recall the roads immediately turning purple, terrible odors, and significant wildlife die-offs. The EPA eventually determined that the waste oil was severely contaminated with dioxins, a group of persistent environmental pollutants that, according to the World Health Organization, "are highly toxic and can cause reproductive and developmental problems, damage the immune system, interfere with hormones and also cause cancer." The town was flooded by the nearby Meramec River while the EPA was in the process of conducting tests, and the toxic dioxins were distributed over the entire city. In 1982, the EPA recommended that all residents be permanently relocated. The Federal Emergency Management Agency took over the site and the relocation process, and by the end of 1986, Times Beach was a ghost town.[18]

Sumgayit, Azerbaijan

Sumgayit is located 30 kilometers north of Azerbaijan's capital, Baku, on the Caspian coast. The city, once a model development of the Soviet industrial economy, housed factories manufacturing industrial and agricultural chemicals, including synthetic rubber, chlorine, aluminum, detergents, and pesticides. During the Soviet heyday, between 70,000 and 120,000 tons of emissions were released into the air annually; in the 1990s, the still functioning factories produced an estimated 600 million cubic meters of polluted water annually. Today, with only 10–15 percent of the old factories still in production, annual water pollution has been reduced to about 100 cubic meters. Untreated industrial sludge and sewage, contaminated with mercury and by-products of the chlor-alkali industry, are still dumped haphazardly.

The city once had the Soviet Union's highest rates of infant mortality and cancer, and contemporary cancer rates remain elevated at 22–51 percent above the national averages. People who live in the city or work in the remaining factories have been exposed to severe toxins for decades. And this exposure will continue due to a lack of infrastructure for pollution control, the preponderance of outdated technology, and the low emphasis on occupational safety.[19]

LEAD CONTAMINATION

Lead, a common industrial material, is extremely toxic. Exposure to lead can cause damage to the kidneys, the nervous system, and the brain, as well as induce seizures, coma, and death. Additionally, lead can be stored in bone tissue for decades and can be a threat to unborn children long after a mother's exposure. It is a very stable element and degrades little over time; 90 percent of lead dust in surface soil will still be present seventy years after contamination, according to the Illinois Department of Public Health. Blacksmith

Institute estimates that in 2011, nearly 18 million people world-wide were exposed to harmful levels of lead.[20] Figure 4.1 shows a global overview of known lead pollution.

Any process that involves lead can be dangerous. Lead smelting, the extraction of lead from mined ore or its recovery from recycled materials through a hot air combustion process, can release large amounts of lead dust and sulfur into the air, if not properly treated, and generates significant amounts of toxic slag leftovers. Informal battery recycling is another key vector for lead pollution. Used lead-acid batteries (particularly car batteries) are imported in bulk into developing countries, where they are broken up manually and the lead is extracted for resale. Much of this work is done in the home or at informal factories without safety equipment, and the risk of exposure to lead particulate and battery acid is high. Among the workers involved in battery recycling are children.[21]

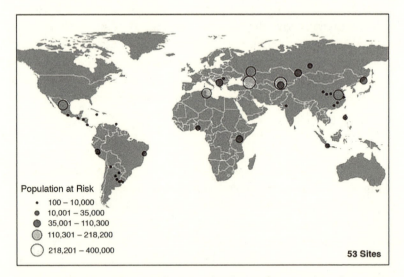

FIGURE 4.1 Population at Risk from Lead Pollution from Lead Smelters, 2012
Source: Blacksmith Institute 2011d.

Haina, Dominican Republic

Bajos de Haina is located on the coast of the Dominican Republic, about 32 km from the capital, Santo Domingo. Initially an industrial zone home to several battery recyclers and gasoline refineries, it is today inhabited by more than 80,000 people, the majority of whom are affected by the legacy of industrial pollution. The last battery recycler was closed in 1997, after local activists attracted the attention of an organization called the Friends of Lead Free Children.

The MetaloXa Company operated a battery recycling and lead smelting plant in Haina from 1979 to 1997. When Stephen Null, director of Friends of Lead Free Children, visited the plant in 1996, he found the 45-hectare industrial lot covered in 30-foot piles of used batteries and a lead smelter, operating twenty-four hours a day, surrounded by homes. Initial testing of plant employees found that many had a blood lead level over 300 µg/dL, more than twice the amount of exposure necessary to trigger brain swelling and cause serious damage. After expanded testing showed that 91 percent of children had lead poisoning (the average blood level was more than seven times the internationally recognized 10 µg/dL threshold), the plant was forced to shut down. MetaloXa moved its smelting operation in 1997, and in 1999 the Dominican government announced that the site had been cleaned up; however, lead levels in children remained dangerously high and soil samples recovered by researchers still registered nearly 50 percent lead. This is an extremely high level. Indeed, it is the most heavily lead-polluted site known in the world, with lead soils as high as 463,970 ppm.[22] Null found that the company's "cleanup," apparently given the go-ahead by the government, amounted to burying the remaining batteries at the site and installing a metal door to keep people out. Excavation of the battery plant in 2008 and 2009 removed nearly 6,000 cubic meters of toxic material. The Blacksmith Institute reports that average blood levels of lead declined from 71 µg/dL in 1997 to 28 µg/dL in 2009; but these 2009 levels of lead remain nearly three times higher than the accepted threshold for lead poisoning in children.[23]

La Oroya, Peru

La Oroya is a mining town of more than 30,000 people in the central highlands of Peru. It is home to what was the highest-elevation standard-gauge railroad in the world from 1893, when the Lima-Huancavelica line was completed, until the Qinghai-Tibet Railway was inaugurated in 2006. Mining expanded in 1922 when the U.S.-owned Cerro de Pasco Copper Corporation built a smelting and refinery complex it described as "especially designed to process the polymetallic ore typical of the central Andes." The mining complex was nationalized in 1974 by the military dictatorship of General Velasco Alvara and administered by the Peruvian government until it was privatized and purchased at auction by the Doe Run Company in 1997. Under the new ownership, annual production capacity reached 77,000 tons of copper, 134,000 tons of lead, 50,000 tons of zinc, 1.15 million kg (37 million troy ounces) of silver, and 2,000 kg (64,000 troy ounces) of gold.[24]

Serious public health problems emerged soon after the transaction was completed. In 1999, the Peruvian Ministry of Health found that 99.1 percent of the children in La Oroya suffered from lead poisoning and that 20 percent of those cases were critical. Further testing by the St. Louis University School of Public Health found elevated levels of other heavy metal pollutants in the blood of residents: cadmium levels registered at three times the U.S. average, antimony levels were thirty times the U.S. average, and arsenic levels were twice that of the control site. La Oroya was confirmed to be one of the most toxic sites in the

Western Hemisphere. The pressure on Doe Run became enormous, and despite spending more than $316 million on environmental upgrades (roughly triple the amount agreed on with the Peruvian Ministry of Energy and Mines), heavy metal emissions remained toxically high; a 2005 study showed that 97 percent of children under the age of six had elevated levels of lead in their blood.[25]

In 2009, in the wake of declines in commodity prices and continued environmental problems, Doe Run Peru halted production. A year later, with no date for the restart of production, 3,500 employees held protests and blocked access to a critical highway. Although acutely aware of the environmental and health problems that plagued their community due to the mining complex, employees could no longer make do without work. Most people in La Oroya, facing a choice between wages and toxicity, want the smelter reopened after the installation of adequate environmental controls. Currently, creditors are running the mining complex as part of an operational liquidation and are in the process of selling off assets. It is unknown when the plant will return to full capacity, or under what environmental protocol.[26]

Chromium Contamination

Chromium, like lead, is present in large amounts during some industrial processes. Also like lead, concentrated chromium by-products are highly toxic. Hexavalent chromium causes asthma, diarrhea, intestinal bleeding, and kidney and liver damage, and it is a powerful carcinogen. It is estimated that high levels of chromium threaten the health of 1.8 million people across the globe.

The leather tanning industry is a large producer of industrial chromium by-products. Low- and middle-income countries have successfully entered the tanning industry: since 1970 their share of the global heavy leather industry has grown from 26 percent to 56 percent and their share of the light leather industry from 35 percent to 56 percent. Globally, the tannery business has expanded among disadvantaged communities. These are likely to be without sufficient regulatory or industrial infrastructure. Further, the organization of the industry at the local level in developing countries creates synergies that can vastly intensify the effects of pollution. In such regions, tannery industries frequently consist of clusters of small and medium-sized enterprises (SMEs) that concentrate in marginal sections of urban areas to gain access to, among other things, large pools of unskilled laborers willing to take on dirty, toxic work that in many cultures is stigmatized.

Ready access to high-quality water is also a factor in the location of these clusters because the tanning process involves repeatedly soaking hides in chemical baths and then wringing out the wastewater. Many of the small businesses lack access to adequate treatment facilities and cannot afford to either store or process the toxic effluvium. Often the waste is simply released into the street. The location of these businesses near a quality water source means that chromium and other by-products quickly make their way into the water supply, while the clustering of SMEs produces a concentration of pollutants that can overwhelm the natural environment's buffers and result in bioactive chemical levels.

Further, these businesses are located in marginalized neighborhoods largely separated from the residences of the affluent or influential; the people most exposed to these toxins are the stigmatized tannery workers and their families. The amounts of waste generated by these tannery clusters can be immense: a large agglomeration in Bangladesh included roughly 200 tanneries and produced an estimated 7.7 million liters of wastewater and 88 million tons of solid waste a year, according to the Blacksmith Institute.[27] Figure 4.2

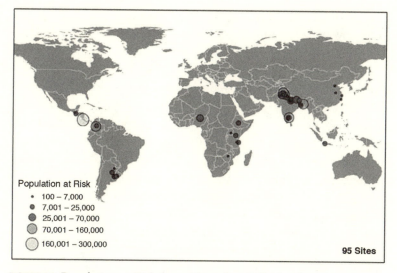

FIGURE 4.2 Population at Risk from Chromium Pollution from Tanneries, 2011
Source: Blacksmith Institute 2011f.

provides a global overview of major sites registering chromium pollution from tanneries.

Ranipet, India

During the 1970s, the government of the Indian state of Tamil Nadu sought to shift industry out of heavily urban areas and increase employment in the rural hinterland. To accomplish this, the state offered significant subsidies and incentives for industrialists to set up in designated "backwards areas." The town of Ranipet, located on the banks of the Palar River 20 kilometers from the industrial city of Vellore, was seen as having the water resources necessary for the notoriously water-intensive and polluting leather tanning industry, and quickly developed as a center for the industry. However, the growth of the industry overwhelmed the water supply, and the town now suffers from acute pollution from tannery waste, including hexavalent chromium and azodyes.

Today, Ranipet is home to more than 50,000 people and is still a center of the leather goods industry. There is a preponderance of small leather producers operating facilities without the economies of scale necessary to afford proper waste disposal systems. Added to the general lack of awareness of environmental issues, the result over four decades is contaminated groundwater. In 2001 the town's 60 tanneries employed 10,000 people to produce 100,000 kilograms of leather products daily. But there were only seven individual effluent treatment plants and one public treatment plant to process the industry's waste. By 2009, there were an additional 180 tanneries, but still only one public waste treatment plant. This sharp expansion is partly explained by the fact that Ranipet is not an isolated town; it is an industrial suburb located about 20 kilometers from the city of Vellore. This city has the largest leather export industry in India—a district the size of Oregon, it has 5 million people, of whom 2.5 million, including children, work in some aspect of the leather trade.

It is safe to assume that that there has been a massive increase in waste and that the majority of it is improperly disposed of. In 2009, the town government estimated that more than half of all solid waste went uncollected, and that none of the solid waste that was collected was disposed of properly. The state pollution control board estimates that a single factory producing tanning compounds would have accumulated more than 1.5 million tons of improperly stored solid waste after two decades of operation. Farmers complain that 80 percent of their crops fail and that irrigation water causes rashes and blisters on their skin. Most concerning is that the unabated pollution of the Palar River now threatens the water supplies of larger cities downstream, including that of the 3.5 million people in Vellore.[28]

MINING/RESOURCE EXTRACTION

Hard rock mining and extraction industries play a significant role in wide-ranging territorial degradation and in the making of dead land. Researchers estimate that for the 2000s "at least ten billion tons per year on a dry basis of fine particle waste [not including liquid refuse] is produced by this industry worldwide. Arguably then the minerals industry is the largest producer of waste in the world." Other sources report that in the United States, mining is "less than one tenth of one percent of gross domestic product" but produces pollution and consumes energy at disproportionately higher levels. In 2001 it was estimated that mining in OECD countries produced 550 million tons of solid waste. Because most significant mining operations are located in the developing world, the total amount of global mining waste is likely to dwarf the OECD numbers.

Throughout most of the world, standard industry waste management practice is "to recycle solid waste as fill back into the mine and to pump low-concentration liquid waste products known as 'tailings' into gigantic manmade reservoirs." Both the tailings and solid waste produced by mining can seriously damage local environments. Metal ores generally have significant levels of heavy metals that are chemically similar to the target material and arranged in similar formulations (oxides or sulfites, for example); when ores are processed to remove the target mineral, large amounts of undesirable heavy metals are also released into the environment. For instance, the National Wildlife Federation finds that 40 percent of the watersheds in the western United States are contaminated by pollution from hard rock mines. The pollution lasts long after the mine closes down: a typical hard rock mine may exhaust profitable material in five to fifteen years, but contaminants can continue to leach into the environment at accelerated rates for hundreds of years. Standard hard rock mining by-products can have disastrous effects if not properly handled. The tailings are full of heavy metal toxins, and crushed rubble used as fill or gravel in and around the mine (or dumped directly into the local water, whatever the case may be) is capable of oxidizing to produce highly acidic runoff.

Nor does low-tech mining spare the environment. For instance, artisanal gold mines are generally informal and rather small-scale operations. Sediment from gold-rich soils is collected from either pit or surface mining operations, usually with little more than a shovel. The sediment is then treated directly with mercury, which bonds to gold ore. After the mercury-gold amalgam has been isolated from the debris, it is heated and the mercury vaporizes, leaving behind pure gold. This low-tech mining creates negligible amounts of rock waste or traditional mine effluvium; however, it is estimated that this method is responsible for one-third of the global annual release of mercury into the environment, while the chemicals used for processing are likely to be mishandled, spilled, or accidentally ingested.[29]

Hydraulic Fracturing

Hydraulic fracturing, or "fracking," refers to the process of injecting water, chemicals, and silica sand into impermeable rock at high pressure in order to release hydrocarbons (usually natural gas) for fuel. The process uses vast amounts of water and introduces mining chemicals and hydrocarbons into local water tables. Its extreme water usage and poisonous emissions make it highly destructive of the environment. It is worth noting that we are beginning to see bans on fracking because of its damaging consequences: hydraulic fracturing has been banned in France, South Africa, and the provinces of New South Wales in Australia and Quebec in Canada due to environmental and health concerns.[30]

A typical fracking site uses between 4 million to 20 million liters of water over its lifetime. All told, fracking and other types of mining accounted for between 1 and 2 percent of the United States' non-thermoelectric water consumption in the early 2000s. But fracking has expanded rapidly since then. In one Colorado county, fracking accounts for between one-third and two-thirds of total water consumption: "A report in March from the Colorado Oil & Gas Conservation Commission (COGCC), which regulates energy development in the state, said that water used for fracking in Colorado totaled about 13,900 acre feet in 2010, and is expected to rise 35 percent to about 18,700 acre feet in 2015."

Perhaps the major threat posed by fracking, however, is the type of damage it does to water supplies. The water used in fracking frequently becomes mixed with hydrocarbons or mining debris and chemicals. Chemicals used in a fracking site include ammonia and boric acid, sulfuric acid, trimethyloctadecylammonium chloride, and potassium chloride. Furthermore, 10 to 40 percent of all water used in fracking flows back to the surface, where it is either segregated in toxic waste ponds or seeps back into the water table. Water pollution also occurs when natural gas released from impermeable rock seeps into water wells and reservoirs.

These impacts are set to grow and to affect more and more areas of the world as the practice of fracking increases. It should be noted that much of the information provided by the industry itself presents hydraulic fracturing as a well-established, traditional method. But this is misleading. Despite industry claims of sixty years of experience, the specific type of fracking used today is relatively new. These recently developed methods of hydraulic fracturing incorporate a horizontal drilling technique that uses more water and produces more natural gas. It also creates water pressure fifty to a hundred times greater than found in earlier wells.[31]

Radioactivity
A recently released report by Melissa Belcher and Marvin Renikoff for the FreshWater Accountability Project in Ohio examined the effects of fracking in context of the known radioactive properties

of the Marcellus Shale stratum. This is an area of natural gas production that stretches from West Virginia to eastern Ohio and southern New York, with high concentrations of radium, uranium, and thorium isotopes that emit radiation as much as thirty times greater than standard background emissions. This raises two important questions: how much radiation is released to the surface during fracking, and how is the industry disposing of radioactive waste? In 2013, the New York State Department of Environmental Conservation found that flow-back water from wells contained radioactivity "as high as 267 times the limit for discharge into the environment and thousands of times the limit for drinking water." It takes massive amounts of water to drill the Marcellus Shale: between approximately 7.5 and 30 million liters of water are used in each fracking event, and wells may need to be fracked multiple times over their life span. Between 65 percent and 95 percent of this water is usually returned to the surface during drilling, raising serious concerns about how this radioactive wastewater is treated.

Drilling a standard natural gas well in the Marcellus produces, on average, about 117 cubic meters of radioactive debris: it is estimated that Pennsylvania alone has produced more than 1 million cubic meters of such waste. While most landfills in Pennsylvania are not equipped with radiation alarms, those that are reported that detectors went off a total of 1,325 times in 2012, with more than 1,000 of those alarms caused by drilling waste. Drilling waste transported to Ohio for disposal has been found to contain levels of radium thirty-six times the regulatory limit. Improper disposal of such material would be a major cost savings for drilling companies: the prices for proper disposal of radioactive waste can be as much as $12,350 per cubic meter.[32]

Water Table
Given its rapid growth over the last few years, fracking increasingly presents a threat to the water tables, in terms of both consumption

and pollution. We have already discussed the amount of water used per well, and mentioned that a single well may be fracked multiple times. Also, more than 750 different chemicals can be mixed into the water for fracking, including benzene, napthalene, diesel fuel, hydrogen chloride, and ethylene glycol. Toxic chemicals and substances have been found to be many times higher than the EPA allows. Hurdle reports on a lawsuit against Atlas Energy:

> Baseline tests on [the plaintiff's] water a year before drilling began were "perfect." . . . [After drilling began,] water tests found arsenic at 2,600 times acceptable levels, benzene at 44 times above limits and naphthalene five times the federal standard. Soil samples detected mercury and selenium above official limits, as well as ethylbenzene, a chemical used in drilling, and trichloroethene, a naturally occurring but toxic chemical that can be brought to the surface by gas drilling. The chemicals can cause many serious illnesses including damage to the immune, nervous and respiratory systems, according to the Endocrine Disruption Exchange, a researcher of the health effects of chemicals used in drilling.

A study published in 2013 found that natural gas components such as methane and propane occur at elevated levels near natural gas wells. Methane concentrations in drinking water wells less than one kilometer from extraction sites were on average six times higher than the level found in water wells farther from natural gas sites. Ethane in drinking wells close to gas wells was twenty-three times the level found in drinking wells farther away from natural gas wells, and propane was found only in drinking wells near natural gas wells.

Earthquakes
Recent reports have raised concern over the potential for fracking to trigger earthquakes in areas where they have not been witnessed in the past. Researchers for the U.S. Geological Survey have tied

increased earthquake activity in the central United States to fracking, and another study reports that seismic activity in Oklahoma
increased elevenfold between the period 2008–2011 and the period
1976–2007. Research indicates that the number of earthquakes in
the North American midcontinent was on average 21 between
1970 and 2000 but increased to 50 earthquakes in 2009, 87 in
2010, and 134 in 2011. That rise in earthquake numbers is almost
certainly caused by human activity, specifically the reinjection of
wastewater into disposal wells: increased water pressure in heavily
used disposal wells has acted to separate previously stable faults.
Evidence also suggests that the size of earthquakes associated with
fracking may be larger than previously believed. A series of earthquakes in Oklahoma between 2010 and 2011 ranged between 5.0
and 5.7 on the Richter scale, after vulnerable faults were disturbed
by high-pressure wastewater disposal.

Earthquakes have also been reported in areas of the United Kingdom and the Netherlands where fracking is present. In 2011, shale
gas developer Cuadrilla Resources found that it was "highly probable" that fracking caused a series of minor earthquakes ranging
from magnitude 1.5 to 2.3 in Lancashire, England. In the Netherlands, the number of earthquakes near fracking sites has increased
from twenty annually before 2011 to eighteen in the first month
and a half of 2013.[33]

Mountaintop Removal Mining

In traditional subsurface or "deep" coal mining, coal is removed
from its substrate, altering internal geology but leaving most of the
surface ecology intact. Mountaintop removal mining, as the name
suggests, is the process of removing a mountain from the coal bed
to expose the coal for extraction. The scale is enormous: in the largest mountaintop removal operation, enough of the mountain was
removed to expose an area greater than 65 square kilometers. Not

only does this process destroy the local surface ecology, but the mineral refuse leaches into the water table, where it has significant downstream effects. The radical ecological transformation caused by the removal means that even after mining operations have ceased, many indigenous plants and animals may not be able to return, possibly outcompeted by invasive species.

This process, known formally as mountaintop mining with valley fills, is a type of high-tech surface mining. The process begins by clearing vegetation and removing topsoil, at which point explosives are used to break up rock and expose coal. The volume of waste created by this process is greater than that of the mountain removed, because the rubble is less dense than solid rock. This waste is then pushed into neighboring valleys, therewith often covering the headwaters of streams. The coal residues, rock salts, and trace metals combine to form the chemical equivalent of a giant leaking battery, which, along with toxins such as selenium, seriously affects downstream ecologies. Small species that form the lowest rungs of the aquatic food chain, such as mayflies, are especially vulnerable, and their absence is felt by the entire ecosystem. People are also vulnerable: studies indicate that proximity to this sort of mining is related to increases in cancer, birth defects, and cardiovascular problems.

Blowing up mountains to expose coal is an exercise in economies of scale: it creates bigger mines, with fewer employees needed and hence lower operating costs. According to a 2012 report by the U.S. Energy Information Administration, coal mine productivity rates in central Appalachia (which has been mined consistently for more than a century) decreased 45 percent between 2000 and 2010, putting pressure on producers to reach for extreme solutions and on local communities dependent on mining to accept them. The Bureau of Labor Statistics reports that as more coal is extracted by increasingly destructive methods, the benefits for miners and communities shrink: employment in the U.S. coal industry has declined by more than 50 percent over the past twenty-seven years, from 177,800 in July 1985 to 80,600 in July 2012., But the amount of coal extracted annually has increased over the same period, from 883.6 million tons in 1985 to 1,084.4 million tons in 2010. Such a situation is untenable.[34]

Ok Tedi Mine in Papua New Guinea

The Ok Tedi mining operation in Papua New Guinea exemplifies the damage mining by-products can wreak on the environment if they are not properly handled. The mine was opened in 1984 and controlled by a cadre of multinational financial interests. Initial plans for containing waste, although farsighted by industry standards in the 1970s, did not adequately account for the highly acidic potential of the local substrate or the region's history of landslide activity. Completely overlooked was the possible impact of the mine on indigenous farmers at the foot of the mountain. In 1983, three years after the mine opened, it was decided that the waste management plan would have to be completely rethought: the project's hydroelectric dam and one of its tailings reservoirs was canceled. The state, without technical counsel and in violation of its own national development laws, certified a temporary plan to let mining go forward without a formal waste reclamation program. The mine began discharging tailings directly into the watershed.

By 1984, the mine was generating 20,000 tons of rubble per day. "From 1981 through 1998 the total waste produced by the Ok Tedi Mine that entered the watershed, by the company's own reporting, which is not likely to be an underestimate, was 884 million [tons], increasing the solid wastes to 8 times the background load." The sediments raised riverbeds and triggered extreme flooding. The fine silt of acidic rock and heavy metal particulate left broad sterile strips along the riverbanks after a flood: "By 2002, 1461 sq km of vegetation had been impacted. . . . The riparian environment was altered, with the loss of fish habitat and dramatically declining

numbers and diversity of fish." The tailings contained levels of copper safe for human consumption, but dangerous to aquatic life. "By
the 1990s the lower Ok Tedi [River] had silted up so much that it
regularly overflowed its banks and deposited a layer of sterile sand
on top of levees that had previously been the most productive garden sites for people living along the river. Side branches and channels became choked with sediment, killing sago stands and up to
480 square kilometers of forest, while the water's constant turbidity
drove local fish stocks away." Sago palms, the staple of the lowland
community's diet, saw declines in growth rate and nutrition value.
Neither the government nor the ownership group had studied the
mine's potential effect on the region's staple crop.

In 1988, tribal villagers filed suit against Broken Hill Proprietary,
at the time the world's largest mining conglomerate. The parties
reached a settlement in 2004 that would award compensation to
local residents; the mine was supposed to continue producing until
2010, when it was scheduled to run out of recoverable ore, but as
of March 2013 it was still operating.[35]

Atomredmetzoloto Mines in Chita, Russia

The Siberian city of Chita is located near what may be Russia's
richest mineral deposits, an area that has been a center of gold and
uranium mining since the 1960s. Today it produces the vast majority
of the country's uranium, with the Krasnokamensk mine producing
50 percent of the 15,000 tons Russia consumes annually. The mine
has produced a minimum of 5 million tons of uranium waste and tailings annually for the last thirty years, making it the largest continuous
producer of uranium waste in the world. Today, the state-controlled
Atomredmetzoloto (ARMZ) mining company owns and operates
the mine.

The 400,000 people who live in and around Chita are severely
affected by the waste. In the Balei area alone, hundreds of houses
have been found to have radiation levels more than ten times the

permissible level, and almost a thousand homes have been shown to have radiation levels above international safety standards. The toll on human health has been extreme: in some areas, as many as 95 percent of children have chronic diseases or disabilities, and children are frequently born with severe mutations such as missing limbs or retardation. Rates of Down syndrome are four times the national average. Currently, there are no public plans for environmental remediation: the Russian government does not acknowledge that a problem exists.[36]

THE POWER TO POISON LAND, WATER, AND AIR

Nuclear Accidents, Deadly Gases

While mining and industrial waste certainly have the capacity to poison the environment, it is worth isolating nuclear waste as uniquely dangerous in several respects, not least because it can be carried by air and water over enormous distances and because of its long life. Poison gas, though it has a shorter life, can be no less dangerous in the short term and continues to be produced lawfully and in large quantities for industrial use. These two contaminants pose risks that not even the rich can escape, unlike most hazards associated with mining and industrial waste. They have mostly been far more tightly regulated than mining and the types of manufacturing described earlier in this chapter. But neglect and accidents do occur. The following cases tell a large story that needs little explaining.

Chernobyl, Ukraine

The explosion of a high-power channel nuclear reactor (known by the acronym RBMK) at the Chernobyl power complex on April 26, 1986, remains the worst nuclear accident to date. It released 5.2 million terabecquerels of radioactive emissions (one becquerel is equivalent to one event of atomic decay per second)—a hundred times more radiation than was released by the atomic bombs dropped on Hiroshima. The meltdown was caused by faulty plant design and serious operational mistakes. During a routine test of the system's operational capability at low power, the reactor became unstable because it was not receiving enough cooling water. Operators had disabled important plant functions, including the automatic shut-down system, and when the situation became unstable they were forced to try alternative measures to stop the reaction. During the attempt, they triggered a massive power spike, setting off a steam explosion that displaced the 1,000-ton protective steel cover plate and sent radioactive steam and fission products into the atmosphere. A second explosion followed seconds later, ejecting pieces of fuel from the reactor core. RBMK reactors were designed without the concrete and steel containment dome that surround most nuclear plants, so there was no mechanism to contain radiation once the reactor was compromised.

The reactor burned for the next ten days, releasing at least 5 per-cent of the reactor's 192 tons of radioactive fuel into the environ-ment. Vast stretches of territory were degraded: 150,000 square kilometers of land in Ukraine, Belarus, and Russia were soon classi-fied as contaminated (radiation levels above 38,000 becquerels per square meter), primarily by isotopes of cesium, strontium, and iodine. The mandatory evacuation area was eventually enlarged to 4,300 square kilometers, and 336,000 people had to be permanently reset-tled. Twenty-six years after the accident, the government of Ukraine bans human habitation within a 30-kilometer radius of the plant.

The accident's toll on human life is an issue of debate. At the site of the accident, two workers died in the initial explosion, and twenty-eight more died within the next three months after being exposed to 20 sieverts of radiation. The impacts of radiation expo-sure are not always easy to determine: individuals who are exposed to elevated levels of radiation may or may not develop health prob-lems such as cancer, but if they do, it is difficult to determine whether it was induced by radiation exposure or something else, such as smoking. The World Health Organization reports that a total of 4,000 people will eventually die as a result of the accident and that the total increase in cancer incidence will be 3 percent; however, the organization concluded that the most significant public health issue resulting from the crisis is the widespread decline in psychological health and economic well-being among those forced to abruptly relocate from contaminated areas. The WHO especially notes people's intense anxiety about the health effects they anticipate but may never experience

On the other hand, scholars at the New York Academy of Science claim that the International Atomic Energy Agency and World Health Organization, among others, "have largely downplayed or ignored many of the findings reported in the Eastern European scientific literature and consequently have erred by not including these assessments," and calculate that more than 985,000 people have died as a result of the Chernobyl accident.

In any case, a great deal of radioactive material remains inside the remnants of the reactor, protected by a steel and concrete sarcophagus built as a temporary measure in the immediate aftermath of the crisis. That containment vessel is decaying rapidly, and the site continues to leak radiation. A new protective structure, designed to last a hundred years, is scheduled to be installed in 2015.[37]

Hanford, Washington

In 1943, the U.S. government used the War Powers Act to seize 1,450 square kilometers of land near the Columbia River in southern Washington State, displacing all 1,200 people who lived in the agricultural communities of Hanford, White Bluffs, and Richland.[38] The military, concerned that Nazi Germany was ahead of the United States in the race for the atomic bomb, had decided to accelerate the research and development of plutonium weaponry. Hanford became the site of the world's first large-scale plutonium production plant. Today, it contains approximately two-thirds of the country's highly radioactive waste.

Plutonium is created during fission, when uranium-238 absorbs a neutron to become uranium-239, which then twice undergoes beta decay, first into neptunium-239 and then into plutonium-239. To harvest the fissionable plutonium from nuclear reactors, spent fuel rods are dissolved in acid, from which the plutonium is precipitated out to separate it from the other fission by-products. Before it was decommissioned in 1987, the Hanford complex processed an estimated 120,000 kilograms of plutonium. The vast majority of this highly radioactive material remains in situ: only 11,655 kilograms have been disposed of or removed, leaving enough plutonium buried at the site to build 1,800 copies of the "Fat Man" bomb that destroyed Nagasaki.

Today, the site is a slow-motion tragedy: more than about 189 million liters of high-level radioactive and chemical waste are stored in 177 tanks, many of them leaking, buried about 19 kilometers from the Columbia River. About 3.8 million liters have escaped. A 2008 report by the Department of Ecology of the State of Washington noted that toxic substances had already entered the water table and might be as few as seven years from entering the water of the river at a point upriver from cities inhabited by 1 million people and farms with a combined value of $6.4 billion. The Department of Energy, which runs the site, currently has no plans to intercept the toxins before they enter the water supply, nor does it have any plans to clean up the solid waste at the site. In fact, the department has petitioned the federal government to move *more* nuclear waste to Hanford from other nuclear sites, in effect declaring Hanford a lost cause.

Fukushima Daiichi, Japan
Areas near the Fukushima Daiichi nuclear power plant, crippled by an earthquake and tsunami in 2011, may be off-limits for decades,

according to the Japanese government. In 2011, Japanese officials told community leaders that areas emitting 100 millisieverts of radiation per year would not be safe for a decade, and areas with 200 millisieverts would be uninhabitable for twice that time. Currently, people are banned from entering within 20 kilometers of the plant.

The amount of damage at Fukushima is not yet known, but it will be largely determined by the proportion of long-lived isotopes in the radioactive steam that escaped the plant during the initial damage. Radioactive cesium-137, with a half-life of 30.2 years, is likely to be the most noxious toxin (in terms of amount emitted and length of half-life), as was also the case at Chernobyl. About 50,000 people were ordered to evacuate after the disaster, and many farmers and fishermen lost their livelihoods.[39]

Chemical Explosion in Bhopal, India
Bhopal is the capital of the state of Madhya Pradesh, India. It experienced the worst-ever industrial disaster in 1984 when a Union Carbide pesticide plant in the city released 45 tons of a cyanide-derivative gas into a nearby slum. The leak killed 3,800 people as they slept, and some of the 558,125 who were exposed died later from injuries.

The plant was sold in 1994 to a consortium of Indian banks and the Indian government, which had previously owned 49 percent of the plant. The toxic compounds that were stored in the factory were never adequately removed, and it is believed that 450 tons of waste still contaminates the 4.5 hectares factory site. The pesticide chemicals and residues are now thought to be the cause of the unusually high number of birth defects (cleft palates, mental retardation, missing eyeballs) in the city, which in 2011 had a population of 2,368,145, an increase of 28.46 percent over a decade earlier. The government has agreed to truck in drinking water to Bhopal because of local complaints about drinking water, but the deliveries are irregular and many poor people still drink the local water.[40]

The World's Oceans

Dead Zones

The acidity level of surface ocean waters has been rising since industrialization and is projected to become significantly higher as oceans continue to absorb carbon dioxide. Based on multiple scientific studies, the World Bank reports that "estimates of future carbon dioxide levels, based on business as usual emission scenarios, indicate that by the end of this century the surface waters of the ocean could be nearly 150 percent more acidic, resulting in pH levels that the oceans have not experienced for more than 20 million years."[41]

Perhaps the most brutal instance of the destruction or degradation of water bodies is the existence of an estimated 400 dead zones in the world's oceans, comprising an area of more than 245,000 square kilometers. A range of human practices, including agricultural pollution, play a key role in this, one of the most extreme forms of environmental degradation. The zones are suffering from hypoxia, a lack of the oxygen necessary to sustain life, and do not experience the water-column turnover necessary to replenish oxygen levels.

Hypoxia and the resulting eutrophic state are the by-product of fertilizer runoff from commercial agriculture into the ocean. The shallow, sun-heated bodies of fresh water that carry runoff to the ocean are both warmer and less dense (due to their lack of salinity) than the deep ocean saltwater. As they enter the ocean, they create a fertilizer-rich top layer that does not mix with water below it. The fertilizer in the top layer triggers a bloom of algae, especially toxic cyanobacteria poisonous to many fish. As the fish and algae die, they sink to the bottom of the water column, where their decomposition consumes oxygen. When the levels of oxygen below the top eutrophic layer are depleted to the point that they can no longer sustain life, they become what are known as dead zones. These dead zones last until water columns become adequately disturbed to replenish the oxygen in the lower strata of the ocean. It is estimated that dead zones around the globe have eliminated between 343,000 and 734,000 tonnes of biomass. As formerly rich waters become dead zones, fisheries wither and coastal populations face reduced sources of livelihood.

Rising Sea Levels

The rise in sea levels is another major outcome of climate warming, and has been occurring faster than we once thought likely. The World Bank reports that "a rise of as much as 50 cm by the 2050s may be unavoidable as a result of past emissions" according to experts. It will be particularly sharp in some areas of the world, most especially parts of Asia. Water levels at the Southeast Asian coastline are projected to be "10–15 percent higher than the global mean by the end of the 21st century relative to 1986–2005." Manila, Jakarta, Ho Chi Minh City, and Bangkok are likely to experience a rise in sea levels of more than 50 cm above current levels by about 2060, and 100 cm by 2090.

This carries major implications for the local populations and local economies. For instance, the Mekong Delta accounts for about 50 percent of Vietnam's total agricultural production and a considerable share of the country's rice exports, so that "a sea-level rise of 30 cm, which could occur as early as 2040, could result in the loss of about 12 percent of crop production . . . relative to current levels." Making these problems even worse, annual rainfall is projected to increase by up to 30 percent if the world's temperature rises 4°C. For instance, Bangkok would experience up to 40 percent sea level increases if sea levels globally rise by about 15 centimeters above present levels, something that could occur by the 2030s. And the city could experience a sea level increase of up to 70 percent if sea levels rise globally by 88 centimeters, which could occur by the 2080s if there is up to 4°C warming.

At the same time, in other parts of the world, higher temperature will be experienced as more drought. This includes Asia's northwest, a key food-producing area, which is projected to get ever drier. Finally, we can expect sharper differences in precipitation across the seasons, "with a decrease of up to 30 percent during the dry season and a 30 percent increase during the wet season under a 4°C world."

The dualizing pattern of desertification in some regions and floods in others could appear in many different parts of the world. "Under 2°C warming, the existing differences in water availability across [sub-Saharan Africa] are likely to become more pronounced. For example, average annual rainfall is projected to increase mainly in the Horn of Africa (with both positive and negative impacts), while parts of Southern and West Africa may see 50–70 percent decreases in rainfall and groundwater recharge rates. Under 4°C warming, annual precipitation in Southern Africa may decrease by up to 30 percent, while East Africa is projected by many models to be wetter than today, leading to an overall decrease in the risk of drought."[42]

Larger countries experience climate change through a range of patterns. In the case of the United States, there has been an accelerated rise of water levels in some areas and drought in others. The year 2012, the latest for which there are data available, was the worst in recorded history for extreme weather events, according to the National Oceanic and Atmospheric Administration. Eleven major events—including tornadoes, wildfires, droughts, and hurricanes—together generated a collective bill of over $110 billion, ranging from crop losses due to drought in the Midwest to flood damage on the East Coast due to Hurricane Sandy (at $60 billion, the single biggest cost). In the summer of 2013, drought affected approximately 50.1 percent of the contiguous United States.[43]

Trash Gyres

The confluence of major ocean currents at five points around the globe creates massive whirlpools, or gyres. These are the North Atlantic Gyre, South Atlantic Gyre, North Pacific Gyre, South Pacific Gyre, and Indian Ocean Gyre (see Figure 4.3). The effluvium of the ocean collects in these gyres like debris circling around a drain: anything floating at sea long enough will eventually come to one of these five collection points. These gyres are central nodes in the vast networks of ocean currents, long known to merchants and sailors. However, as plastics used around the world find their way into the ocean, the gyres have come to resemble nothing so much as landfills. Roughly 300 million tons of plastic are produced every year around the globe, 7 million tons of which end up in the oceans. Plastic does not decompose, but rather photodegrades: when exposed to sun and water it breaks down to its constituent molecules, but no further. Vari-

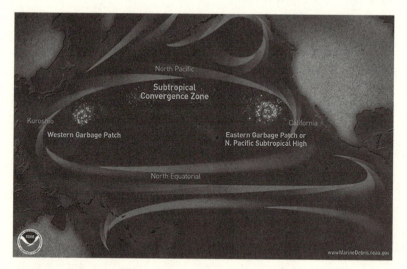

FIGURE 4.3 North Pacific Gyre (Now Also Known as the Great Pacific Garbage Patch), 2010

Source: NOAA n.d.

ous molecules of plastic and other noxious chemicals such as DDT or PCBs remain suspended in the water, forming something akin to a toxic stew. Chemicals from the plastics leach into aquatic plants and animals and become concentrated at the top of the food chain. Evidence suggests the amount of plastic dissolved in the oceans doubled between 1999 and 2009.[44]

Water Grabs

As we saw earlier in the chapter, in their turn to fracking, mining companies are becoming some of the most intensive consumers of water in the developed world, both directly and indirectly through the poisoning of supplies. More quietly, soda companies and water bottlers have also been rapidly increasing their consumption of water. Together these diverse actors have exhausted whole underground water supplies in several parts of the world. To compensate for water shortages, Nestlé and other water companies are now constructing huge pipelines and using supertankers and giant sealed water bags to move water long distances for commercial purposes. And as water demand for drinking alone is predicted to increase 50 percent by 2030, some journalists and scholars warn that water is likely to become "the new oil." But water has not received as much attention as food, even though levels of need are increasingly similar. The estimate is that 870 million people currently suffer from malnutrition, and 780 million people do not have access to safe drinking water, according to the World Food Program and UNICEF. Water grabs are rapidly adding to water scarcity for the poor in growing areas of the world.[45]

Nestlé's Controversial Operations around the World

Nestlé is the leading water bottling company in the world today. It owns eight international brands of bottled water, of which Perrier is the best-known. The industry grew quickly before the recession, expanding at an annual rate of 7.6 percent between 2002 and 2007. The recession put even more pressure on the business: as North American water sales declined 13 percent between 2007 and 2009, Nestlé aggressively fought for access to new water rights and new environmental regulations.[46]

In a 2005 interview, Nestlé's chairman, Peter Brabeck-Letmathe, expressed Nestlé's logic when it comes to water use. Access to water, "the most important raw material," should not be considered a human right:

> It is a question of whether we should privatize the normal water supply for the population. And there are two different opinions on the matter. The one option, which I think is extreme, is represented by the NGOs, who bang on about declaring water a public right. That means that as a human being you should have a right to water. That's an extreme solution. The other view says that water is a foodstuff like any other, and like any other foodstuff it should have a market value. Personally, I believe it's better to give a foodstuff a value so that we're all aware that it has its price, and then that one should take specific measures for the part of the population that has no access to this water and there are many different possibilities there.[47]

The idea that human beings shouldn't be entitled to water caused a great deal of negative publicity, and Brabeck-Letmathe went back on his statement in several new interviews as the fallout became clear. One of those later interviews on the subject, however, strengthened and further illuminated the idea that everything must have a market value and be managed within a market structure, an idea with worrying consequences for the poorest. In a 2012 interview he explained an approach to saving water that would ensures that water would remain under constant threat and constantly exploited:

The 25 liters we need as a minimum as a person in order to live decently . . . this is a human right. But I don't think it's a human right to fill up my swimming pool, to wash my cars . . . or even to water the garden, I don't think this is a human right. And if we do not understand that the [amount of] water which is a human right is the smallest part of the water which we are using, and . . . we are using in the United States about 400 liters per day. So this 380 liters, I don't think it's a human right, and this should have a price. Why? Because if you do not put a price, we will not make the investments which are necessary in order to use the most precious of the resources that we have in a more responsible manner. . . . If we do not give a value to the water, those investments are not going to be made, because no one has an interest to invest because you do not have an economical return.[48]

Nestlé has been criticized most harshly for its overpumping of water in the United States. This can be explained on two grounds. First, the U.S. legal system leaves water especially vulnerable to overexploitation. "The common law of groundwater offers some protection from injury by large well pumps but almost no protection of the public interest in conservation or environmental protection. The common law of groundwater is a law of capture. Groundwater use is a 'natural' right incident to surface ownership. Groundwater law was formulated at a time when the mechanics of aquifers were not well understood and high-capacity pumps had not yet been developed."[49] Second, U.S. citizens have the material and legal resources to sue big corporations such as Nestlé. It is not coincidental that India's battle against Coca-Cola was fought by a U.S.-based NGO, the India Resource Center.

Nestlé's pattern of appropriation has been clear. It looks for sources of water in areas unaccustomed to negotiating contracts with multinational companies, notably small rural communities. They bring a promise that the water plant will create new jobs and that it will invest in philanthropic causes. Citizens, local associations, and environmental groups that have initiated legal action to protect local water resources have found their task difficult given the vastly superior resources of the company, from money to lawyers to politicians' support.

Nestlé in the United States

In North America today, Nestlé's consumption of water for bottling is emerging as a controversial issue. It is estimated that in 2003 (one year for which there is available data) Nestlé Waters withdrew a total of about 7 trillion liters for its bottled water production in the United States alone. In particular, serious concerns have been raised about Nestlé's water takings in areas that are prone to drought conditions. Here are some of the cases fought against Nestlé.[50]

FLORIDA: OVERPUMPING IN DROUGHT-STRICKEN AREAS

The Crystal Springs Recreation Preserve, located 30 miles from Tampa, bills itself as a "525-acre sanctuary devoted to environmental education and dedicated to the preservation of Florida's natural environment." However, in 1996, Bob Thomas, owner of the property and president of the preserve's board, closed the park to public access after reaching an agreement to sell water to Nestlé, and began petitioning local government for a drastic expansion of his water rights. During a severe drought in Florida in 2000–2001, Thomas asked for an increase in water extraction from about 1.1 million liters per day to 6.8 million liters per day. This increase was denied because of concern that it would deplete local water supplies, but Thomas has been cited multiple times for exceeding his water quota by as many as 5,000 gallons per day.

In Madison County, Nestlé was able to secure access to pump unlimited amounts of water from a spring located in a state park for only $230. No royalties or additional fees were secured by the state. The case triggered some controversy, as Florida was in a bitter dispute with its neighboring states over a regionwide water shortage while Nestlé was extracting hundreds of millions of gallons virtually for free. Referring to Nestlé's corporate taxes, company spokesman Jim McClellen asserted that Florida got a great deal: "You're talking about millions and millions of dollars in tax benefit . . . a very good deal for the state of Florida."[51]

TEXAS: THE RULE OF CAPTURE

In Henderson County, Texas, Nestlé's Great Spring Waters of America faced charges for pumping excessive volumes of groundwater for its Ozarka bottling plant. In March 1996, the company began to extract 350,000 liters of water per day from Rohr Springs in Big Rock. Days after the pumping began, local wells went dry. Families who lost their water filed a lawsuit, arguing that the pumping constituted a violation of their private property rights. In a ruling that surprised many observers, a lower court upheld a Texas law known as the "rule of capture," which gives land owners the right to all the groundwater on their property, and ruled that Nestlé was in no way liable. The rule of capture is based on English common law and dates back to when Texas was an independent republic. This anachronistic law states that "ground water is the private property of the owner of the overlying land" and they "have the right to capture the ground water beneath their land." In 1998 the Texas Supreme Court reaffirmed the decision, and the law is still in place.[52]

MICHIGAN: UNREASONABLE USE OF WATER

In 2000, Nestlé's Ice Mountain Spring Water was granted a permit to pump about 1,500 liters of water per minute from Mecosta County, Michigan. In 2001, the company sought to increase the amount of water it was allowed to withdraw so that it could expand its plant. Local voters opposed by two to one a ballot measure authorizing the plant's expansion, and in 2002 a local judge ruled that while Nestlé had the right to pump water on a "reasonable use" basis, the company's water withdrawal had harmed, or was likely to harm, community residents and the environment. Nestlé appealed, and legal action continued until 2009, at which point it settled out of court to secure reduced water rights. The company's nine-year legal battle is indicative of the lengths it will go to secure sources of water.[53]

Nestlé Outside the United States
Here follow a few cases involving what is one of the most global of companies.

NESTLÉ IN BRAZIL
The Serra da Mantiqueira region of Brazil is famous for its Circuito das Aguas, springs with high mineral content thought to have medicinal properties. It is also the source of Nestlé's Pure Life water brand. After Nestlé set up production in the late 1990s, overpumping led to the drying up of local springs. Residents filed suit in 2001 and were able to stop Nestlé from extracting more water in 2006, because demineralization is illegal under Brazilian law. Nestlé's actions, however, will continue to affect the quality of water in the region for a long time to come, as it took hundreds of years of exposure to rock aquifers for the water Nestlé has taken to become highly mineralized. Corporate Watch reports that it now seems that Nestlé has exhausted the supply of the locally prized mineral water.[54]

NESTLÉ IN CANADA
Nestlé Waters Canada and its precursors, Aberfoyle Springs and Aberfoyle Fisheries, have had a permit to take water from a well on property located in the village of Aberfoyle in the Guelph region since 1984. Nestlé submitted an application for a five-year renewal of the current water taking, without an increase in either rate or amount, to Ontario's Ministry of the Environment on March 30,

2007. Nestlé pumps 3.6 million liters of water a day from the local sub-watershed. This triggered controversy, as the city of Guelph was at the time asking its citizens to conserve water. But the permit was renewed. The reason was lack of evidence that the water extraction was harmful; however, no tests were conducted to determine the extent of damage.[55]

Other Firms and Their Cases

Augustin Ranch in New Mexico
In May and June 2010, more than 900 people protested an application to extract water, submitted to the New Mexico State Engineer's Office. The request came from a New York City–based corporation, Augustin Ranch LLC, which owns land near Datil at the north end of the Augustin Plains, in south-central New Mexico.[56] The corporation submitted the original application to the Engineer's Office in the fall of 2007 and is now trying to expand its operations.

It is worth getting into the details to make visible what this type of development entails. The new plan calls for drilling thirty-seven wells to a depth of about 900 meters in order to pump out about 64 trillion liters of water a year from the Augustin Plains aquifer. It also plans to expand the area of exploitation to any points within Socorro, Catron, Sierra, Valencia, Bernalillo, Sandoval, and Santa Fe counties that are in the Rio Grande Basin. The amended application states the water could be used for broad, unspecific purposes. Activists say it would probably be sold and piped over to the Rio Grande to make up for shortfalls caused by overconsumption upstream.

Coca-Cola's Water
The Indian state of Karmala is an internationally important exporter of spice and rubber and a major hub of agricultural production.

It covers almost 40,000 square kilometers of land in southwest India, on the coast of the Indian Ocean. In 2000, a Coca-Cola subsidiary called Hindustan Coca-Cola Beverages started operating a bottling plant in the village of Plachimada, with a permit to extract 510,000 liters of water per day from wells and boreholes. As reported by Right to Water and Sanitation, for every 3.75 liters of water harvested, the factory produced 1 liter of product such as mineral water, Coca-Cola, Fanta, and Thumbs-Up. The rest was released as wastewater. By 2003, there was no potable water left within 10 kilometers of the plant, and crop failure had led to 10,000 laborers being put out of work. That same year, Coca-Cola blamed the exhaustion of the water table on a decline in rainfall.

In 2002, farmers began daily protests at the factory, complaining that irrigation wells had suddenly run dry and that chemicals had fouled what water remained. Testing by the Centre for Science and Environment in New Delhi showed that Coca-Cola's bottled products in India contained pesticides in excess of the European Common Council's consumer standards; furthermore, chemicals released by the plant entered the water supply, causing burns and blisters on the skin. The village refused to renew the plant's permit in 2003, and after a series of court cases, the plant was forced to stop operating in 2004. In 2010, the Coca-Cola Company was fined $48 million.[57]

Using Public Waterways to Discharge Poisons

Dzerzhinsk, Russia

During the cold war Dzerzhinsk was a secret industrial city, the production site of the Soviet Union's chemical weapons. The chemical factories are now running at less than 30 percent capacity. They have stunted the city's economy and they have left 136,000 kilograms of solid waste from when they still manufactured large quantities of sarin and VX gas. About a quarter of the population works in the chemical plants that dispose of untreated waste in manmade swamps in the forests around the city, many of which are ringed with white circles of chlorine compound.

Today the plants manufacture civilian goods rather than weapons. But the Blacksmith Institute reports that some 180 highly toxic chemicals (including phenol and dioxins) are found in the local groundwater, at concentrations measuring up to 17 million times the accepted health limits. Life expectancy among residents is average according to city officials, but some international organizations claim that it is well below average (forty-two years for men and forty-seven years for women) and that babies have a severely increased risk of birth defects. UN specialists have tested the breast milk of local women and found toxic levels of dioxin. No current plans are in place to clean up Dzerzhinsk; while some ideas do exist, they have been considered too expensive to implement. Officials suggest that the problem has been exaggerated, despite the fact that Dzerzhinsk has been named the world's most polluted city by the *Guinness Book of World Records*.[58]

Sukinda Mines, India
Chromium, a trace mineral and elemental metal already discussed, is used in a wide variety of industrial processes, including steelmaking, plating operations, textile dying, and leather tanning. There is great demand for the metal and its compounds across the world. But it is produced in just a few locations. In 2008 global consumption reached 31.86 million tonnes of chromium and chromium compounds, more than 70 percent of which were produced in South Africa, Kazakhstan, and India.

India's share of the global output (16.0 percent) was generated almost entirely in the Sukinda mining district, where more than 90 percent of the country's reserves are located. In 2008, more than ten open-pit mines were operating in the district, none of them following adequate waste removal or environmental plans and with no state regulation or environmental legislation in place. The form of chromium present in Sukinda, hexavalent chromium, is highly carcinogenic and toxic to the human body. Compounding the risk is the fact that the mining area is on the banks of the Brahmani River, the only source of water for the 2.6 million residents in the Sukinda Valley, most of whom live near the mines. Surface water in the region has been measured as containing 3.4 milligrams of chromium per liter, far surpassing the U.S. limit of 0.1 milligram per liter; 60 percent of all drinking water is tainted. Widespread chromium poisoning is present in the population: more than 80 percent of deaths in the mining area and the nearby industrial zone are the result of chromium poisoning. The government and the industry are aware of the problems, but they consider solutions to be too expensive, the local government stating: "It is unique, it is gigantic and it is beyond the means and purview of the [State Pollution Control] Board to solve the problem."[59]

GLOBAL SCALE-UP

There was a time when the environmental damage we produced remained somewhat localized, confined to specific places. That time is gone. Today, nonindustrial areas, such as Greenland and the Antarctic, experience the industrial pollution generated in the United States and in Russia, to mention just two countries. Damage produced in particular sites now scales up, driven by the vastness of destruction, and becomes a planetary problem that drifts back down to hit even those places that did not contribute to the damage.

Greenhouse gases (including carbon dioxide, methane, nitrous oxide, and particulate matter such as black carbon) are key causes of climate change.[60] Diverse measures arrive at an estimate that human activity has generated 350 billion tonnes of carbon since 1959; 55 percent of this has been taken up by the oceans and land, and the rest has been left in the atmosphere. In 2009 alone, global carbon dioxide emissions totaled 30 billion tonnes. By 2011, annual emissions had increased by 5.3 percent to 31.6 billion tonnes. And by early 2013, the level of carbon dioxide in the atmosphere surpassed the critical level of 400 parts per million. This is a level not seen on earth since the Pliocene era 3 million years ago.

Under current conditions, global CO_2 emissions (including emissions related to deforestation) will reach 41 billion tonnes per year in 2020. The EPA estimates that industrial emissions account for 50 percent of greenhouse gases emitted in the United States, and industry is almost certainly responsible for an even higher proportion of China's huge and growing emissions. At this scale, and with the relationship of carbon dioxide to climate change, industrial pollution is a driver of massive global problems.

One major effect is rising land temperature (see Figure 4.4). The numbers for the current warming phase are extreme compared

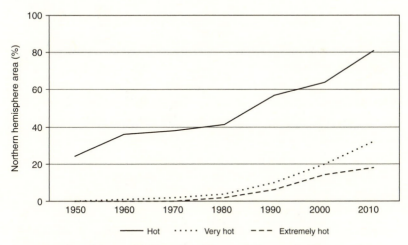

FIGURE 4.4 Land Area with Hot, Very Hot, and Extremely Hot Temperatures, 1960–2010

Data source: World Bank 2012, figure 18.

to the available historical records. May 2012 was "the 327th consecutive month in which the temperature of the entire globe exceeded the 20th-century average," writes Bill McKibben. The spring of 2012 was the hottest ever, and marked the biggest difference with the average seasonal temperature recorded for any season. In the United States, the month of June 2012 broke 3,215 heat records across the country, and May 2012 was the warmest May in the country's recorded history. There are debates and disagreements about the precise rate, timing, and level of increase. But very diverse types of studies all document this upward trend. (See Figure 4.5.)[61]

Climate change has already started to affect global agricultural output (see Figure 4.6). The Club of Rome predicts that climate change will cause an increase of 2°C in average temperature by the year 2052 and a 2.8°C rise in average temperature by 2080. An increase of that magnitude is predicted to "reduce yields across two-thirds of the

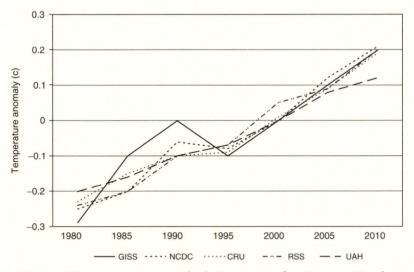

FIGURE 4.5 Temperature Data: Multiple Sources Confirm Warming Trend, 1980–2010

Data source: World Bank 2012, figure 3.

FIGURE 4.6 Insufficient Water Supply: Impacts on Agricultural Productivity, 2009

Source: Gonzalez-Valero 2009, p. 4.

maize-growing region of Africa, even in the absence of drought"; crop losses for maize could reach 20 percent by midcentury.[62]

Not all droughts (or floods) can be attributed to this type of climate change, as I indicated earlier in this chapter. For instance, what is referred to as the "Dust Bowl" in the United States—a dry plain extending from the central United States into Canada, with Oklahoma and Texas as its center—predates anthropogenic climate change. Seager et al. write that one difference today is that the impact of greenhouse gases on the climate has caused the Chihuahuan Desert to expand, or, in Mingfang's words "We're essentially moving the desert further north." There is research on climate change suggesting that by the year 2020, the American Southwest will face permanent drought.[63]

In Asia, the Aral Sea is one instance of a shockingly dried-out lake (see Figure 4.7). Like the Dust Bowl in the United States, climate

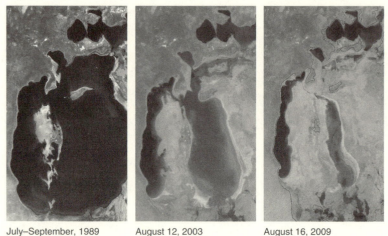

July–September, 1989   August 12, 2003   August 16, 2009

FIGURE 4.7 The Aral Sea, 1989, 2003, and 2009
Source: NASA n.d.

change is not the sole cause of the drying. But the scale and velocity of water loss may be partly due to the global scale-up of climate change and its blowback to sites only indirectly implicated. Not unlike the United States at the time, Soviet-era irrigation projects are known to have been wildly inefficient. One example is that of the world's largest irrigation canal, the Qaraqum Canal, which diverted 13 cubic kilometers of water from the Aral Sea for years; as much as 50 percent of this water was lost en route due to poor engineering. On top of these inefficiencies, climate-change-induced drought and desertification sharply increased the stress on the Aral Sea. The end result is that what was once the world's fourth-largest body of fresh water has been reduced to less than 10 percent of its original volume.[64]

The other major planetary transformation arising from direct and indirect effects of greenhouse gases is the rise of ocean levels (see Figure 4.8) and their acidity. Between 443 billion and 629 billion tons of meltwater are added to the world's oceans each year, which

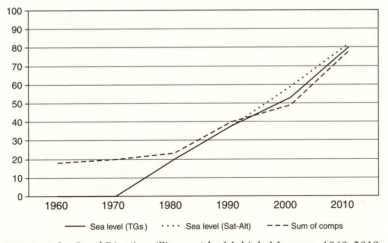

FIGURE 4.8 Sea-Level Rise (in millimeters) by Multiple Measures, 1960–2010

Data source: World Bank 2012, figure 6B.

Note: TGs (tidal gauges), Sat-Alt (satellite observations), sum of comps (sum of components: water released into the oceans from diverse sources, including glaciers and ice caps).

raises sea level by about 1.5 millimeters a year. This is in addition to the 2-millimeter yearly rise caused by expansion of the warming ocean. It's true, of course, that not all ice-bound areas are melting. Some glaciers are seeing as much ice added to higher-elevation points as melts away from the base; this may occur because thaw at the periphery evaporates into the air and then recondenses and freezes at the colder, less humid peaks. Further, for a variety of meteorological reasons, parts of the Antarctic, as well as particular glaciers elsewhere, are not losing ice due to melting; this is partly explained by the fact that ice forms more easily over land than over the ocean. However, the extent of ice melt is indeed alarming.[65]

Every now and then the major effects of environmental destruction become visible to a larger public. In 2012, 57 percent of Greenland's ice sheet melted between July 8 and July 12. This reduced ice coverage to 3 percent of its maximum, stunning scientists, terrifying climate watchers, and mobilizing the media into reporting it.

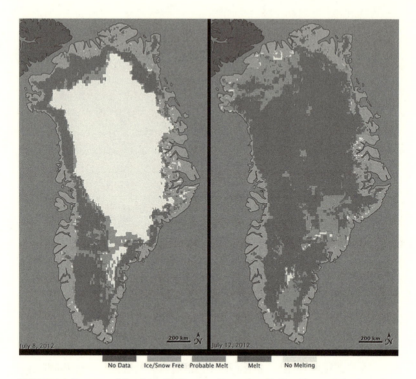

No Data · Ice/Snow Free · Probable Melt · Melt · No Melting

FIGURE 4.9 Extent of Surface Melt over Greenland's Ice Sheet, July 8 and July 12, 2012

Source: Viñas 2012.

Figure 4.9 shows the extent of this melt in satellite images from NASA's Earth Observatory. This ice melt could be part of an annual warming trend. But the evidence suggests that the fact of massive loss of ice and permafrost are becoming permanent.

The melting of ice at this scale becomes a major factor in raising sea levels. The interaction between water temperature and ice melt arises from the fact that ice reflects more solar energy than water: this insulates the ocean beneath the ice from the sun. When the ice melts, that insulation thins or disappears, and the ocean water warms, which in turn melts more ice, and so on in a chain of warming water, melting ice, and rising ocean levels. At present, the losses of ice are shared roughly equally between Greenland and Antarctica. If the present acceleration continues, ice sheet melting alone could contribute up to 56 centimeters to sea level rise by 2100.[66]

A distinct type of melt is the thawing of permafrost in the Arctic Circle. This too is caused by anthropogenic climate change. In 2008, the permafrost under the town of Newtok, Alaska, began to thaw and the buildings started to sink. The Bering Sea ate away at what had become a permeable coastline. The 320-person community of Yup'ik Inuit, whose forebears had lived in the same location for two thousand years, was forced to leave. Of Alaska's 213 Alaska Native villages, 184 have been seriously affected by erosion and flooding; six of them have been deemed to be in need of immediate help.

Permafrost thaw creates a feedback loop that accelerates the type of climate change we are observing. As permafrost thaws, the trapped organic matter begins to decay and to release methane and carbon dioxide. Permafrost thaw is especially dangerous because it is likely to produce methane (CH_4), which has a much stronger warming effect than carbon dioxide. Scientists generally agree that between 9 percent and 15 percent of the top three levels of permafrost will melt by 2040; this is expected to increase to between 47 percent and 61 percent by 2100. The estimated carbon release from permafrost degradation is 30 billion to 63 billion tons of carbon by 2040, 232 billion to 380 billion tons by 2100, and 549 billion to 865 billion tons by 2300.[67]

Current efforts by many governments to stem this kind of climate change are not going to be enough. Even if we implement existing agreed-upon standards, we would still not secure the planet's sustainability. Figure 4.10 shows two future patterns: one under current conditions and the second if we implemented all current agreements

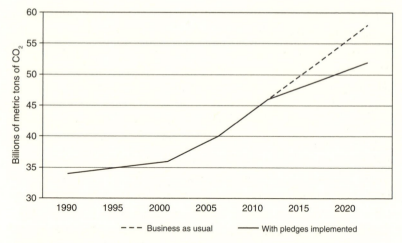

FIGURE 4.10 Annual Greenhouse Gas Emissions[a] with Full Implementation of Agreements, 2010–2020
Note: a. Total greenhouse gases emissions including deforestation related emissions.
Data source: World Bank 2012, figure 2B.

to reduce environmental damage. It would make a difference, but one far too small to alter the basic trajectory. Existing agreements to address environmental destruction operate at a level and through formats that fail to address the deeper dynamics causing the climate change. These dynamics cut across the existing boundaries and divisions of the interstate system.

CONCLUSION. BEYOND NATIONAL DIFFERENCES: A GLOBAL CONDITION

The guiding conceptual effort throughout this examination of concrete cases across our planet was to make visible the recurrence of environmentally destructive modes no matter how diverse the political economies in play. Together and over time, we have generated a planetary condition that reaches far beyond the specific sources of destruction and the specific forms of politico-economic organization within which they take place. It is a condition that hovers in spaces that range from the stratosphere to deep ocean gyres.

There is a profound disjuncture between this planetary condition and its sources, on one hand, and the dominant logics shaping governmental responses and much policy, on the other. Destroyed air, land, and water become a generic condition, a facticity disembedded from the geopolitical landscape of countries and mainstream policies. States mostly focus on benefiting from today's basic consensus policy approach to climate change, which is carbon trading. The effort is not to reduce destruction but to maximize a state's advantage in the right to destroy: governments push to augment their "lawful" quota either to augment their right to pollute or to augment what they can sell to governments that want to pollute more. Leaderships of all sorts appear to find it impossible to address the fact of planetary destruction and prefer to scale down their efforts to the lowest common denominators, which makes the task seemingly more manageable.

Do the cases discussed suggest that some forms of political and economic organization prevent some of this destruction? Yes, but to a surprising extent the differences are minor compared to the scale of destruction. Those organizational differences fall mostly beneath the consequential levels for reducing destruction at the global scale; they matter more for the place than for the overall planetary condition. Do newer technologies prevent more destruction than older ones? Some of the newest, most complex technologies being deployed are not much better than older, far more elementary modes of producing. They are only different: fracking or removing an entire mountaintop versus digging a coal mine. It all points to the limits of our current dominant approach, with its emphasis on the differences among countries, and the common proposition that more advanced modes of producing will allow us to reduce environmental destruction.

Deeper and conceptually invisible dynamics are cutting across very diverse countries and places. I see at work a global systematicity, no matter its thick localized instantiations. It is deeper than the diverse geopolitical formations and economies we have built on our planet. Globally, across these differences, segments of the biosphere are being expelled from their life space—they become dead land and dead water. What then is the biosphere? It is as if it does not belong on our planet, no matter that it accounts for a good share of the planet and that the biosphere is us.

Is there a parallel to be made with the modes that expulsion can take in the very different domains examined in preceding chapters? Yes, there is. It is the ambiguous status of the biosphere in our political economies, not unlike today's ambiguous politico-economic status of a majority of citizens in the majority of our nation-states. Too many citizens and too much of the biosphere are used and abused without regard to their health or prosperity.

Conclusion

At the Systemic Edge

The point of inquiry in this book is the systemic edge. The key dynamic at this edge is expulsion from the diverse systems in play—economic, social, biospheric. This edge is foundationally different from the geographic border in the interstate system. The focus on the edge comes from the core hypothesis organizing this book: that the move from Keynesianism to the global, era of privatizations, deregulation, and open borders for some, entailed a switch from dynamics that brought people in to dynamics that push people out. Such a switch from incorporation to expulsion might also be emerging in China and India; China, especially, has seen a massive incorporation of people into monetized economies, but now is also experiencing sharpening inequality, new forms of economic concentration at the top, and corporate bullying.

Each major domain has its own distinctive systemic edge—this edge is constituted differently for the economy than it is for the biosphere and the social. One of the organizing assumptions in this book is that the systemic edge is the site where general conditions take extreme forms precisely because it is the site for expulsion or incorporation. Further, the extreme character of conditions at the edge makes visible larger trends that are less extreme and hence more difficult to capture. I conceive of these larger trends as conceptually subterranean because we cannot easily make them visible

211

through our current categories of meaning. Thus the importance of positioning my inquiry at the systemic edge.

To illustrate with reference to an earlier era, there was a period when on the surface, from a bird's-eye view, England looked like an overwhelmingly rural economy. But in fact industrial capitalism was already the dominant logic of the political economy. The sheep on the land were now feeding the machines in city factories. Both sheep and machines were at the systemic edge: they were moving into a new urban industrial era even though the larger visual order was that of a rural economy.

Today, I see new systemic logics arising from the decaying political economy of the twentieth century. This decay began in the 1980s. By then the strong welfare states and workers' syndicalisms established in much of the West, including in several Latin American countries, either had been devastated or were under severe pressure. To some extent state projects with people-oriented welfare programs had also been strong features in other parts of the world, including, in their own ways, communist countries and those with varieties of socialist nationalism, as illustrated by Nasser's welfare state policies in Egypt, systems developed in several postindependence African countries, and India's brand of state socialism. In these countries too, decay began in the 1980s and 1990s.

To talk of this decay is not to romanticize the twentieth century, a period marked by devastating war, genocide, starvation, and extreme ideologies of both left and right. But the world that we began to build in the wake of devastation, starting in the West in particular after World War II, was driven by a logic of inclusion, by concerted efforts to bring the poor and the marginalized into the political and economic mainstream. The Keynesian, egalitarian, and nation-based assumptions underlying this project of building the just society began to crumble toward century's end. We have been slow in understanding and labeling the powers and dynamics that have emerged from the dust.

What I argue here is that we have fallen under the sway of a dangerously narrow conception of economic growth. Growth was of course crucial to the project of the welfare state. But it was also a means of advancing the public interest, of increasing a prosperity in which many would share, even if some far more than others. Today, by contrast, our institutions and assumptions are increasingly geared to serve corporate economic growth. This is the new systemic logic. Perhaps not all, but enough corporations have sought to free themselves from constraints, including those of local public interest, that interfere with their pursuit of profit. Anything or anybody, whether a law or a civic effort, that gets in the way of profit risks being pushed aside—expelled. This switch in economic logics is one major systemic trend not fully captured in current explanations.

As we have seen, corporations have remarkable new tools at their disposal: advanced mathematics and communications, machines that can literally move mountains, global freedoms of movement and maneuver that allow them to ignore or intimidate national governments, and increasingly international institutions that force compliance with their agenda across the world. Western governments, central bankers, the IMF, and kindred international institutions now speak of the need to reduce excess government debt, excess social welfare programs, excess regulation. This is the language of today's key order-making institutions in the West and increasingly elsewhere. It carries the implicit promise that if we could reduce these excesses we would get back to normal, back to the easier days of the postwar era. But this promise disguises the extent to which that world is truly gone—and the extent to which, whatever national governments might say, too many corporate economic actors do not want it back. They want a world in which governments spend far less on social services or on the needs of neighborhood economies or small firms, and much more on the deregulations and infrastructures that corporate economic sectors want.

This is de facto a project of shrinking the space of a country's economy, though not the economic profitability of the corporate sector. In its simple brutality, the transformation of Greece illustrates this well: the massive and rapid expulsion of the modest and not so modest middle classes from jobs, social and medical services, and increasingly their homes. This "economic cleansing" has been so effective that by January 2013, the European Central Bank could announce that the Greek economy was on the path to recovery and Moody's could raise the credit rating of Greek government debt. What was not said was that this recovery rested on about one-third of the Greek workforce being expelled not just from jobs but also from basic services. It depended on decisions that caused a sharp growth in hunger, in the number of children abandoned in churches by parents too poor to feed them, and in suicide rates. This sort of process is taking place in many European countries, from Spain and Portugal to the Netherlands, though not so drastically nor with such a strong command role by the European Central Bank. Even countries with growing employment, such as the United States, have in fact shrunken the space of their economies, as is evident when we include the sharp rise in the numbers of the long-term unemployed and of the incarcerated.

I want to emphasize again that this shift away from a phase of increasing social and economic inclusion for the average person has also taken place in areas that are now seen as hopeless, whose better times have been forgotten by many observers as if their hopelessness were an intrinsic condition. In sub-Saharan Africa, beneath today's wars and dismembered societies lies an earlier period of mass manufacturing, growth of the middle classes, thriving market towns and capital cities, government-developed infrastructures, and functioning health care and school systems. Before it broke down, Somalia was a fairly prosperous, fairly well-run (even if autocratic) country with a well-educated middle class. Or consider Russia. In years past, communist regimes in the Soviet Union and eastern Europe had welfare states that took care of their citizens.

But today the huge numbers of homeless people, the abandoned elderly, and the very poor without access to social services are a new development.

One of the intentions of this book was to make visible the crossing into the space of the expelled—to capture the visible site or moment of expulsion, before we forget. The villagers and small farmers evicted from their land due to the development of palm plantations soon materialize as slum dwellers in vast megacities, completing the erasure of their past as small farmers. Government employees in Greece cut out of their jobs in the name of EU demands to reduce the debt soon become part of the mass of unemployed, no longer recognized as erstwhile government employees. Stretches of dead land, poisoned by toxic emissions from factories or mines, are expelled from working land and forgotten.

The organizing hypothesis is that beneath the specifics of each of the major domains examined in this book lie emergent systemic trends. Despite their enormously diverse visual and social orders, from the empowerment of the global corporation to the enfeeblement of local democracy, they are shaped by a few very basic dynamics of liberated profit seeking and indifference to the environment.

This also means that empirical research and conceptual recoding must happen together—they need each other. Visually it may look "Russian" or "American," but are these geographical markers of an earlier era still helpful in understanding the character of our epoch? My argument is not that the destructive forces I discuss are all interconnected. Rather, it is that these destructive forces cut across our conceptual boundaries—the terms and categories we use to think about the economy, the polity, the diversity of nation-states and ideologies from communism to capitalism. But they do so in ways that are invisible to our conceptual eye. In that sense, then, I describe them as conceptually subterranean. Complexity is part of the condition here. The more complex a system is, the harder it is to understand, the harder it is to pinpoint accountability, and the harder it is for anyone in the system to feel accountable. When destructive

forces do pop up and become visible, the problem is one of interpretation. The tools we have to interpret them are not up to date, so
we fall into our familiar categories: we talk about governments that
are not fiscally responsible, households that take on more debt than
they can handle, capital allocations that are inefficient because
there is too much regulation, and so on. I do not deny that these
can be real problems—there is excellent empirical scholarship that
documents this, and I use and partly depend on it. But my effort in
this book was to explore whether there are other dynamics at work
as well, dynamics that cut across these familiar and well-established
conceptual/historical boundaries. In a way, the land grab empirics of
Chapter 2 are one concrete instance of a much larger and more elusive
type of grab. In that sense, the chapter makes accessible a larger history that does not always take on such a literal form as one's land plot,
the source of one's livelihood, one's history, and one's social being.

Inside capitalism itself we can characterize the relation of emergent forms of capitalism to more traditional capitalisms as marked
by expulsions but also as erasure by incorporation. Describing our
current epoch as characterized by the expansion of market economies is far too vague and partial a description, since large corporate firms control much of most markets. Manufacturing firms, plantations, or mines owned by traditional capitalists with roots in a
single nation are increasingly destroyed or bought up by the more
powerful global firms. Even sectors where profits per unit are minimal can today be corporatized because scale—the vast number of
units involved—will make up for low per-unit profits. The relationship between today's advanced capitalism and more traditional
forms of market capitalism can, at the limit, be characterized as one
of increasingly primitive accumulation: complexity and technical
progress serve causes of brute simplicity.

Each of the chapters covered a particular mix of expulsions at
the systemic edge. I conceive of such expulsions as the material moment of a more elusive and complex dynamic—the conceptually

invisible subterranean trends that cut across the familiar meanings and concepts through which we explain our economies and societies. These material outcomes are partly determined by specific and often complex instruments, even for elementary expulsions. Eventually expulsions and the instruments that enable them become part of an interconnected, often mutually reinforcing trajectory that moves us farther and farther away from our preceding age of incorporation and middle class growth. We could say that each chapter captured one of these trajectories.

Chapter 1 examined and conceptualized the reconstitution of "the economy" in well-established highly developed countries as a shrunken space with relatively fewer firms, fewer workers, and fewer consumer households, all indicators of a system geared toward expelling what does not fit its evolving logic. Government deficits in the developed world have risen sharply, partly due to large corporate tax avoidance and excess appropriation for dubious projects that range from wars and bank bailouts to the grabs by predatory elites. Most of the governments in the Americas and Europe, and in the immediate postcolonial period of the 1960s in much of Africa, could not do today what they did during the massive reconstruction and infrastructure developments of the 1950s and 1960s because they are now too indebted. The exceptions are several Asian countries, Brazil, and a few others where governmental capacity to encourage and directly undertake development is in full force. It is an important question whether they will avoid the drift toward the mode of expulsion we face in the West. The indications are that they will not. At the opposite end of the spectrum from newly indebted governments lie the sharply expanded wealth and profits of large corporations, a third element of that evolving logic.

This evolving logic in the Global North has a parallel in the Global South with the IMF and World Bank restructuring programs put into effect in numerous countries there during the 1980s and 1990s, briefly discussed in Chapter 2. In both cases the outcome is a tightening of the meaning of "economy" and the expulsion of what does not fit. Greece, Spain, Portugal, the United States, and a few other Western developed countries are but the most extreme cases of the Global North. They make visible what is perhaps more intermediated in the United Kingdom, the Netherlands, and other rich and highly developed countries. But the general dynamic is one of shrinking the space of the economy, no matter the hardships. The aim is always to achieve a fine-running economy. Again, Greece is now regarded by the European Central Bank as being on its way to recovery—after expelling up to 30 percent of what was once part of its economy. Similar statements were made about diverse African countries once they cut their health, social, and infrastructure "costs" and devoted a significant, often larger share of state revenues to paying the interest on their debt.

We can conceive of this shrinking as a weakening and degrading of the project of the liberal welfare state, broadly understood. With all its shortcomings and the unequal structural power of its various branches and agencies, a working liberal state can secure a measure of socioeconomic redistribution. It can do so partly by enabling the disadvantaged to fight for their rights and for social justice. It worked when powerful sectors needed more and more workers and couldn't simply import cheap labor or move production overseas But when the mechanisms for accumulating profit shift from expanded mass manufacturing and public infrastructure development to financial innovations and the post-1980s corporate format, the ground for making claims of justice crumbles and it becomes a systemic edge. That is what is happening today in growing parts of the world. The claimants are at the systemic edge, and they can easily wind up on the other side, expelled. We saw the slide of more and more urban households and small businesses to the systemic edge in the Global South, in good part through the IMF and World Bank restructuring programs launched in the 1980s, and we see it beginning in the 2000s in rural areas through the sharp rise in land acquisitions by foreign governments and firms. We are seeing it in the

Global North, with Greece merely a simple and accelerated case of this restructuring—which is only more intermediated and hence slower in other countries.

The global geography of extraction that has long been part of economic development has gone well beyond its traditional association with plantations and mines, even as these are also expanding. It extends to extracting the gains workers fought for during much of the twentieth century, the land from beneath small farmers, and the modest homes from many who trustingly put down their savings. The mechanisms for these extractions are often far more complex than the outcomes, which are often quite elementary.

Chapters 1, 2, and 3 all bring to the fore this tension between complex instruments and often brutally elementary outcomes. Nowhere is this tension more evident and powerful than in finance, with the case of subprime mortgages a key example discussed in Chapter 3. It took up to fifteen complex steps to transform such subprime mortgages into a financial project aimed at satisfying the needs of the high-finance world. What was in its origins a state project enabling modest-income households to own a house was transformed into a financial project designed to enable increased profit. Such a permutation from state to financial project was no easy task. It took advanced mathematicians, brilliant lawyers and accountants, and complicated financial instruments impenetrable even to many of the traders (who simply used the software). These instruments are such that they can circulate well beyond the United States (the Silicon Valley of financial innovations), where they were invented and where they resulted in more than 13 million households being foreclosed on. We are beginning to see unusually high numbers of foreclosures in other countries, notably Hungary and Spain, discussed in Chapter 1. The global potential of these instruments to create devastation is enormous. Beyond finance, this tension between complex instruments and brutally elementary outcomes is present in other economic sectors as well. Examples are new types of mining, such as hydraulic fracturing (discussed in Chapter 4), and the often long chains of steps involved in buying land in a foreign sovereign country (discussed in Chapter 2).

What I sought to extract from all these cases is what I see as a foundational juxtaposition in our present ways of constituting economic space: a deployment of complex forms of knowledge and creativity that too often bring with them, besides robust profits, astoundingly elementary brutalities. One question this engenders is whether what we still understand as diverse and discrete economic sectors are merely the aboveground manifestations of what are actually a few major transformative technical and organizational capabilities that underlie all these surface differentiations. Are there a few logics that drive what on the surface becomes present as enormously diverse worlds—the world of fracking, the world of finance, the world of the logistics for outsourcing? Does all this visible specialized variability come down to a few less visible logics that can swallow up and reposition diverse types of specialized knowledge into a few organizing logics? Yes—I see this in the economy and in the ways some of the most powerful actors in the economy use people, governments, and the world's resources to ensure corporate economic growth with an absolute minimum of global restraints and as few local responsibilities as possible. I say this about the space of the corporate economy, not about spaces such as universities, where differentiation is part of the traditions of teaching and learning that can (still) coexist with the reshaping of economic space I have examined in this book. Even so, bits and pieces of technical, engineering, biological, economic, and other forms of academic knowledge are increasingly repositioned to service dominant and domineering logics organizing economic space.

This is clearly an extreme formulation, but that is what it looks like from the systemic edge. The most powerful form of such an organizing logic is captured analytically in the concept of predatory formations I introduced in Chapter 1; it captures some of the major instances examined in the four core empirical chapters of the book.

Such formations are assemblages of powerful actors, markets, technologies, and governments. They are far more than simply the richest individuals or the richest firms or the most powerful governments. These formations incorporate only elements of any of these worlds. The logics that drive them are not easily subject to existing governance mechanisms. In many ways not even the most powerful individuals and firms can control or direct these assemblages—too many bits break out of these diverse institutional worlds and come together to shape powerful new dynamics that cannot be reduced to any of the source institutions—not the economy, not the law, not capital. The historical record suggests that such formations are not new. But what might be different today is the complexity of key components. One major instance involves the advanced financial innovations that can cut across a variety of economic sectors and subject them to their own logic, no matter the content, from intangible debts to massive buildings. A second major instance is the global scale-up of our environmental destruction, which boomerangs back across the world and affects places and flows that never contributed to that destruction—with perhaps the most extreme case the Arctic's permafrost, now threatened by climate change.

This possibility helps explain what is at the heart of this book: that there are larger dynamics that cut across older forms of differentiation and thereby can generate expulsions across different worlds. This is putting it rather starkly for the sake of clarity, and it is not to deny that we have still made progress in certain areas, as in the extension of minority rights. But I do find that it is the direction in which we are going in far too many places, whether in the United States, South Africa, Russia, China, and more.

Today's systemic edge is a space of expulsions, in contrast to the Keynesian epoch where the systemic edge was a space of incorporation, not because it was an ideal period but because the constitutive systematicities were about mass production and mass consumption. Today's are not.

What is in play in all these processes is the question of membership and constitutive participation. I examined diverse modes and domains in order to remind us of a larger life space that is itself at threat. I did this by focusing on a series of thick microspaces. Each is an extreme condition, indeed so extreme that it allows us to see a capacity for destruction that most of us still do not necessarily apprehend or experience in our daily lives. More conceptually, I sought to grasp the existence of larger transversal trends that point to planetary conditions—expulsions of people, economies, life spaces. Our divisions of countries and sectors still are useful to explain much that happens, but they do not help us address larger emergent planetary conditions.

I want to conclude with a question: what are the spaces of the expelled? These are invisible to the standard measures of our modern states and economies. But they should be made conceptually visible. When dynamics of expulsion proliferate, whether in the shape of the shrunken economy of Greece, the predatory elites of Angola, or the growth of the long-term unemployed or the incarcerated in for-profit prisons in the United States, the space of the expelled expands and becomes increasingly differentiated. It is not simply a dark hole. It is present. Also the spaces of the expelled need to be conceptualized. I make a similar argument about the proliferation of stretches of dead land and dead water due to our toxic modes of development. These are also present. Thus, in a conceptual move aimed at making dead land present, I argue it should be conceived of as an informal jurisdiction. More generally, the spaces of the expelled cry out for conceptual recognition. They are many, they are growing, and they are diversifying. They are conceptually subterranean conditions that need to be brought aboveground. They are, potentially, the new spaces for making—making local economies, new histories, and new modes of membership.

REFERENCES

NOTES

ACKNOWLEDGMENTS

INDEX

References

Aabø, Ellen, and Thomas Kring. 2012. "The Political Economy of Large-Scale Agricultural Land Acquisitions: Implications for Food Security and Livelihoods/Employment Creation in Rural Mozambique." Working paper no. 2012-004. United Nations Development Program, New York.

Aalbers, Manuel B. *Subprime Cities: The Political Economy of Mortgage Markets.* Chichester, West Sussex: Wiley-Blackwell, 2012.

Abel, Heather. 1997. "The Rise and Fall of a Gold Mining Company." *High Country News.* December 22.

Alderman, Liz. 2013. "Greece Shuts Broadcaster in Bid to Show Resolve." *New York Times.* June 12.

Alexander, Michelle. 2010. *The New Jim Crow: Mass Incarceration in the Age of Colorblindness.* New York: The New Press.

Allegretto, Sylvia. 2011. "The State of Working America's Wealth, 2011: Through Volatility and Turmoil, the Gap Widens." Briefing paper 292. Economic Policy Institute, Washington, DC.

Alvarenga, Carlos. 2013. "HFT Update: The Rise of the 'Dark Pool.'" *Reconomics* [blog].

American Civil Liberties Union. 2011. "Combating Mass Incarceration—The Facts" [infographic]. June 17. www.aclu.org/combating-mass-incarceration-facts-0.

Amin, Ash. 2012. *Land of Strangers.* Cambridge, UK: Polity.

Amin, Ash, and Nigel Thrift. 2013. *Arts of the Political: New Openings for the Left.* Durham, NC: Duke University Press.

Amin, Samir. 2010. "Exiting the Crisis of Capitalism or Capitalism in Crisis?" *Globalizations* 7, no. 1 (April 27): 261–273.

Anseeuw, Ward, Mathieu Boche, Thomas Breu, Markus Giger, Jann Lay, Peter Messerli, and Kerstin Nolte. 2012. *Transnational Land Deals for Agriculture in the Global South.* Rome: International Land Coalition.

Anseeuw, Ward, Lily Alden Wily, Lorenzo Cotula, and Michael Taylor. 2012. *Land Rights and the Rush for Land: Findings of the Global Commercial Pressures on Land Research Project.* Rome: International Land Coalition.

Arestis, Philip, Rogério Sobreira, and José Luís Oreiro. 2011. *The Financial Crisis: Origins and Implications.* Houndmills, Basingstoke: Palgrave Macmillan.

ARMZ Uranium Holding Co. 2012. "Priargunsky Industrial Mining and Chemical Union." www.armz.ru/eng/companies/subsidiaries /ppgho.

Arrighi, Giovanni. 1994. "The Three Hegemonies of Historical Capitalism." In *The Long Twentieth Century: Money, Power, and the Origins of Our Times,* 27–84. London: Verso.

Asian Human Rights Commission. 2012. "Indonesia: Police Shoot and Injure Five Farmers in Riau during Land Rights Protests." March 27. www.humanrights.asia/news/urgent-appeals/AHRC-UAC-051-2012. Accessed June 30, 2013.

Associated Press. 1991. "Bunker Hill Mining Files for Bankruptcy Protection." *Moscow-Pullman Daily News.* January 18.

———. 2007. "'Most Polluted' Town Sees a Ray of Hope." NBCNews .com. June 20.

———. 2010. "Peru to Seek Bids for First Private Prison." Associated Press. April 1.

Atinc, Tamar M., Abhijt Banerjee, Francisco H. G. Ferreira, Peter Lanjouw, Marta Menendez, Berk Ozler, Giovanna Prennushi, Vijayendra Rao, James Robinson, Michael Walton, and Michael Woolcock. 2006. *World Development Report 2006: Equity and Development.* Washington, DC: World Bank.

Atkinson, Anthony B., Thomas Piketty, and Emmanuel Saez. 2011. "Top Incomes in the Long Run of History." *Journal of Economic Literature* 49, no. 1 (March): 3–71.

Aurora Lights. 2013. "What Is Mountaintop Removal?" http://aurora lights.org/map_project/theme.php?theme=mtr&article=primary. Accessed January 2, 2013.

Austin, James, and Garry Coventry. 2001. *Emerging Issues on Privatized Prisons.* Washington, DC: U.S. Department of Justice, Office of Justice Programs.

Badkar, Mamta. 2012. "Here Comes the 2012 Tidal Wave of Foreclosures." *Business Insider.* March 15.

Bai, Z. G., D. L. Dent, L. Olsson, and M. E. Schaepman. 2008. "Proxy Global Assessment of Land Degradation." *Soil Use and Management* 24, no. 3 (July 24): 223–234.

Bakalidou, Sophia. 2013. "Press Release: Index Of Wages Of The Whole Economy." *Hellenic Statistical Authority.* http://www.statistics.gr /portal/page/portal/ESYE/BUCKET/A0199/PressReleases/A0199 _DKT08_DT_QQ_03_2013_01_F_EN.pdf. Accessed January 1, 2014.

Ballantyne, A. P., C. B. Alden, J. B. Miller, P. P. Tans, and J. W. C. White. 2012. "Increase in Observed Net Carbon Dioxide Uptake by Land and Oceans during the Past 50 Years." *Nature* 488, no. 7409: 70–72.

Banai, Adam, Julia Kiraly, and Marton Nagy. 2011. "Home High Above and Home Deep Down: Lending in Hungary." Research working paper 5836, World Bank.

Bank for International Settlements. 2012. "Semiannual OTC Derivatives Statistics at End-June 2012." www.bis.org/statistics/otcder/dt1920a .pdf. Accessed July 17, 2013.

Barriopedro, David, Eric M. Fischer, Jürg Luterbacher, Ricardo M. Trigo, and Ricardo Garcia-Herrera. 2011. "The Hot Summer of 2010: Redrawing the Temperature Record Map of Europe." *Science* 332, no. 6026: 220–224.

BBC News. 2007. "Toxic Truth of Secretive Siberian City." BBC News. April 5.

———. 2011. "How Does Fukushima Differ from Chernobyl?" BBC News Asia-Pacific. Accessed January 3, 2013. www.bbc.co.uk/news /world-asia-pacific-13050228.

———. 2012. "Greece's Economy Shrinks Further." BBC Business News. November 14.

Behrman, Julia, Ruth Meinzen-Dick, and Agnes Quisumbing. 2011. "The Gender Implications of Large-Scale Land Deals." IFPRI Policy Brief. April 17. http://www.ifpri.org/sites/default/files/publications/bp017.pdf.

Belcher, Melissa, and Marvin Renikoff. 2013. "Hydraulic Fracturing: Radiological Concerns for Ohio." FreshWater Accountability Project Ohio. http://catskillcitizens.org/learnmore/OHIO_FACT_SHEET _6–10-13.pdf. Accessed June 26, 2013.

Belton, Catherine. 2006. "For Russia, Dependence on 'a Man-Made Disaster.'" *New York Times.* January 12.

Bensasson, Marcus. 2013. "Greek Economy Shrank in First Quarter as Investment Fell." Bloomberg.com. June 7.

Bergmann, Karyn S. 2004. "Bankruptcy, Limited Liability and CERCLA: Closing the Loophole and Parting the Veil." Center for Health and Homeland Security, University of Maryland School of Law.

Bertola, Luis, and Jose Antonio Ocampo. 2013. *The Economic Development of Latin America since Independence.* Oxford: Oxford University Press.

"Bhopal Census 2011 Highlights." 2011. Census 2011: Population Census India. May 19. www.census2011.co.in/news/747-bhopal-census-2011-highlights.html.

Bhuiyan, M. A., N. I. Suruvi, S. B. Dampare, M. A. Islam, S. B. Quraishi, S. Ganyaglo, and S. Suzuki. 2011. "Investigation of the Possible Sources of Heavy Metal Contamination in Lagoon and Canal Water in the Tannery Industrial Area in Dhaka, Bangladesh." *Environmental Monitoring and Assessment* 175, nos. 1–4 (April): 633–649.

Bice, Sara. 2013. "Ok Tedi Immunity Gone, with Implications beyond BHP." *The Conversation.* http://theconversation.com/ok-tedi-immunity-gone-with-implications-beyond-bhp-19188. Accessed January 4, 2014.

Biello, David. 2013. "400 PPM: Carbon Dioxide in the Atmosphere Reaches Prehistoric Levels." "Observations" blog. *Scientific American.* May 19.

Bivens, Josh. 2011. *Failure by Design: The Story behind America's Broken Economy.* Washington, DC: Economic Policy Institute.

———. 2013. "Using Standard Models to Benchmark the Costs of Globalization for American Workers without a College Degree." Briefing paper no. 354. Economic Policy Institute, Washington, DC.

Blackman, Allen, and Arne Kildegaard. 2003. "Clean Technological Change in Developing-Country Industrial Clusters: Mexican Leather Tanning." Discussion paper 03-12. Resources for the Future, Washington, DC.

Blacksmith Institute. 2007. "The World's Worst Polluted Places: The Top Ten of the Dirty Thirty." www.blacksmithinstitute.org. Accessed January 3, 2013.

———. 2011a. "Artisanal Gold Mining." www.worstpolluted.org/projects_reports/display/. Accessed November 23, 2013.

———. 2011b. "Chromium." www.worstpolluted.org/projects_reports/display/80. Accessed November 23, 2013.

———. 2011c. "Lead-Acid Battery Recycling." www.worstpolluted.org /projects_reports/display/90. Accessed November 23, 2013.

———. 2011d. "Lead Smelting." www.worstpolluted.org/projects_reports /display/86. Accessed November 23, 2013.

———. 2011e. "Mining and Ore Processing." www.worstpolluted.org /projects_reports/display/84. Accessed November 23, 2013.

———. 2011f. "Tannery Operations." www.worstpolluted.org/projects _reports/display/88. Accessed November 23, 2013.

———. 2011g. "The World's Top Ten Pollution Problems 2011." www .worstpolluted.org/2011-report.html. Accessed November 23, 2013.

———. 2013a. "Norilsk, Russia." www.worstpolluted.org/projects _reports/display/43. Accessed January 3, 2013.

———. 2013b. "Top Ten Most Polluted Places 2007: Sumgayit, Azerbaijan." www.worstpolluted.org/projects_reports/display/27. Accessed January 3, 2013.

———. 2013c. "World Bank and Blacksmith Institute Partner to Take Care of 'Orphaned' Toxic Polluted Sites." www.blacksmithinstitute .org/legacy-pollution-sites.html.

———. 2013d. "Dzerzinsk, Russia." www.worstpolluted.org/projects _reports/display/42.

———. 2013e. "Sukinda, India." www.worstpolluted.org/projects_reports /display/36. Accessed January 3, 2013.

———. 2013f. "Blacksmith's Work in Haina." www.blacksmithinstitute .org/haina.html. Accessed January 3, 2013.

Blackstone, Brian, Stelios Bouras, and Cassell Bryan-Low. 2012. "Europe's Growth Woes Worsen." *Wall Street Journal.* February 15.

Blair, David. 2012. "Greece Sinks to Its Knees." *Telegraph.* February 26.

Blomfield, Adrian. 2007. "Doom and Gloom in Dzerzhinsk." *Telegraph.* November 5.

Bolaños, Alejandro. 2012. "Las Rentas Empresariales Superan Por Primera Vez a Las Salariales en España." *El País.* http://economia .elpais.com/economia/2012/02/16/actualidad/1329424061_546148 .html. Accessed January 1, 2014.

Bolton, Patrick, Frederic Samama, and Joseph E. Stiglitz, eds. 2011. *Sovereign Wealth Funds and Long-Term Investing.* New York: Columbia University Press.

Borodkin, Leonid, and Simon Ertz. 2004. "Coercion versus Motivation: Forced Labor in Norilsk." In Paul R. Gregory and Valery Lazarev, eds., *The Economics of Forced Labor: The Soviet Gulag*. Stanford, CA: Hoover Institution Press.

Borras, Saturnino M. Jr., and Jennifer C. Franco. 2012. "Global Land Grabbing and Trajectories of Agrarian Change: A Preliminary Analysis." *Journal of Agrarian Change* 12, no. 1: 34–59.

Borras, Saturnino M. Jr., Jennifer C. Franco, Cristobal Kay, and Max Spoor. 2011. *Land Grabbing in Latin America and the Caribbean Viewed from Broader International Perspectives*. New York: United Nations. http://www.tni.org/sites/www.tni.org/files/download/borras _franco_kay__spoor_land_grabs_in_latam__caribbean_nov_2011.pdf.

Boston Common Asset Management. 2003. "Boston Common Asks Newmont Mining to Disclose Risks of Its Environmental and Social Liabilities." News release, December 11. www.bostoncommonasset .com/news/newmont-disclosure.html.

Bourguignon, François, and Christian Morrisson. 2002. "Inequality among World Citizens: 1820–1992." *American Economic Review* 92, no. 4: 727–744.

Brabeck-Lethame, Peter. 2012. "Water Can't Be Free." *Big Think*. www .youtube.com/watch?v=rzaV8tg6hno. Accessed June 18, 2013.

Bradsher, Keith, and Andrew Pollack. 2011. "Nuclear Company to Compensate Evacuees in Japan." *New York Times*. April 15.

Bräutigam, Deborah, and Tang Xiaoyang. 2011. "African Shenzhen: China's Special Economic Zones in Africa." *Journal of Modern African Studies* 49, no. 1: 27–54.

Bronder, Larisa, Igor Kudrik, Alexander Nikitin, Kristin V. Jorgensen, and Vladislav Nikiforov. 2010. "Norilsk Nickel: The Soviet Legacy of Industrial Pollution." Bellona Foundation, St. Petersburg.

Brothers, Caroline. 2011. "U.N. Reports Steady Rise of Refugees." *New York Times*. June 19.

Brown, Desair. 2012. "Expert Answers Your Questions on Fracking." *USA Today*. April 24.

Brunori, Margherita. 2013. "Indonesian Court Gives Land Rights Back to Millions of Indigenous." LandPortal.info. June 21. Accessed June 30, 2013.

Bryson, John R., and Peter W. Daniels, eds. 2007. *The Handbook of Service Industries*. Cheltenham: Edward Elgar Publishing.

Budapest Business Journal. 2013. "Gov't to Extend Eviction Moratorium, Banks Opposed." *Budapest Business Journal*. February 20.

"Bunker Hill Reports Profitable Quarter." 1990. *Spokane Chronicle*. May 2.

Bureau of Labor Statistics. 2012. "Employment, Hours, and Earnings from the Current Employment Statistics Survey (National)." www.bls .gov/data/#employment. Accessed January 5, 2013.

———. 2013. "Labor Force Statistics from the Current Population Survey." *United States Department of Labor.* http://data.bls.gov/pdq /SurveyOutputServlet. Accessed January 1, 2014.

Bureau of Land Management. 1996. "Notice of Intent to Prepare an Environmental Impact Statement (EIS) for the Midnite Uranium Mine (MUM) Reclamation." *Federal Register* 61, no. 18: 2528.

Burgen, Stephen. 2013. "Spain Youth Unemployment Reaches Record 56.1%." *The Guardian.* http://www.theguardian.com/business/2013/aug /30/spain-youth-unemployment-record-high. Accessed January 1, 2014.

Burgers, Paul, and Ari Sustani. 2011. "Oil Palm Expansion in Riau Province, Indonesia: Serving People, Planet, Profit?" Background paper for European Report on Development. http://erdreport.eu/erd /report_2011/documents/researchpapers_susanti-burgers.pdf.

Calhoun, C. 2004. "A World of Emergencies: Fear, Intervention, and the Limits of Cosmopolitan Order." *Canadian Review of Sociology and Anthropology* 41, no. 4: 373–395.

Carrington, Damian. 2012. "The Himalayas and Nearby Peaks Have Lost No Ice in Past 10 Years, Study Shows." *Guardian.* August 2.

Carter, Jimmy. 2011. "Call Off the Global Drug War." *New York Times.* June 17.

Castle, Stephen. 2013. "Irish Legacy of Leniency on Mortgages Nears an End." *New York Times.* March 30.

CBC. 2008. "Bottled Water: Quenching a Planet's Thirst." www.cbc.ca /news/background/consumers/bottled-water.html. Accessed January 22, 2013.

———. 2012a. "Mayor Rob Ford Wants to Banish Gun Convicts from Toronto." *Huffington Post.* July 20.

———. 2012b. "Rob Ford's Ex-con Banishment Plan Won't Fly, Says Minister." CBC/Radio Canada. July 20.

Center for Housing Policy. 2012. "High-Cost Purchase Loans and Census Tract Level Foreclosure Data." www.foreclosure-response.org/maps _and_data/high_cost_maps.html. Accessed July 28, 2012.

Chang, Cindy. 2012. "In World of Prisons, Some Rural Parishes' Econo-mies Hinge on Keeping Their Jails Full." *Times-Picayune.* May 13. http://www.nola.com/crime/index.ssf/2012/05/in_world_of_prisons _some_rural.html.

Chatterjee, Partha. 2011. *Lineages of Political Society: Studies in Postcolonial Democracy*. New York: Columbia University Press.

Cheng, Derek. 2012. "New Private Prison at Wiri Given Green Light." *New Zealand Herald*, March 8.

Chesapeake Energy. 2012. "Hydraulic Fracturing Facts." www.hydraulicfracturing.com/Pages/information.aspx. Accessed July 30, 2012.

Chestney, Nina. 2012. "Club of Rome Sees 2 Degree Celsius Rise in 40 Years." Reuters. May 8.

CIA. 2012. "Country Comparison: Distribution of Family Income—GINI Index." *CIA World Factbook*.

Clark, Colin. 2011. "Improving Speed and Transparency of Market Data." *NYSE EURONEXT* [blog]. http://exchanges.nyx.com/cclark/improving-speed-and-transparency-market-data.

Clarke, Tony. 2007. "Nestlé's Water Wars: The Experience in North America." Polaris Institute, Ottawa.

Clinton, Bill. 1993. "NAFTA Will Create 200,000 American Jobs in Two Years." *Philadelphia Inquirer*. September 19.

CNNMoney Staff. 2013. "S&P 500 Above 1,800. Dow Hits Record Again." *CNNMoney*. http://money.cnn.com/2013/11/22/investing/stocks-markets/. Accessed January 1, 2014.

Colchester, Marcus. 2011. *Palm Oil and Indigenous Peoples in South East Asia*. Rome: International Land Coalition.

Cole, Juan. 2013. "Asia Will Drown, Africa Will Starve in 30 Years: World Bank Report on Global Warming." *Informed Comment* [blog]. www.juancole.com/2013/06/starve-report-warming.html. Accessed November 22, 2013.

CoreLogic. 2013a. "National Foreclosure Report." www.corelogic.com/research/foreclosure-report/national-foreclosure-report-april-2013.pdf. Accessed August 3, 2013.

———. 2013b. "CoreLogic Equity Report: First Quarter 2013." http://www.corelogic.com/research/negative-equity/corelogic-q1-2013-negative-equity-report.pdf. Accessed January 1, 2014.

Corporate Watch. n.d. "Nestle SA: Corporate Crimes." www.corporatewatch.org.uk/?lid=240. Accessed January 22, 2013.

Cotula, Lorenzo. 2011. *The Outlook on Farmland Acquisitions*. Rome: International Land Coalition.

Cotula, Lorenzo, and Kyla Tienhaara. 2013. "Reconfiguring Investment Contracts to Promote Sustainable Development." In K. Sauvant, ed.,

Yearbook on International Investment Law & Policy 2011–2012, 281–310. Oxford: Oxford University Press.

Cotula, Lorenzo, Sonja Vermeulen, Rebeca Leonard, and James Keeley. 2009. "Land Grab or Development Opportunity?: Agricultural Investment and International Land Deals in Africa." Rome: FAO, IIED, and IFAD (Food and Agriculture Organization of the United Nations [FAO], the International Institute for Environment and Development [IIED], and the International Fund for Agricultural Development [IFAD]).

Coumou, D., and S. Rahmstorf. 2012. "A Decade of Weather Extremes." *Nature Climate Change* 2: 491–496.

Crystal Springs Preserve. 2013. "About Us." http://crystalspringspreserve .com/about-us/. Accessed July 13, 2013.

Daley, Suzanne. 2010. "In Spain, Homes Are Taken but Debt Stays." *New York Times.* October 27.

Davies, Nigel. 2012. "Spain's Economy Seen Contracting 1.4 Percent in 2012, 2013." Reuters. November 7.

Davies, Peter J. 2009. "Radioactivity: A Description of Its Nature, Dangers, Presence in the Marcellus Shale and Recommendations by the Town of Dryden to the New York State Department of Environmental Conservation for Handling and Disposal of such Radioactive Materials." Cornell University. www.tcgasmap.org/media/Radioactiv ity%20from%20Gas%20Drilling%20 SGEIS%20Comments%20by %20Peter%20Davies.pdf. Accessed November 23, 2013.

Day, Paul. 2013. "Spain's Economy Shrinks for Seventh Straight Quarter." Reuters. April 30.

Deaton, Angus. 2013. *The Great Escape: Health, Wealth, and the Origins of Inequality.* Princeton, NJ: Princeton University Press.

Deddy, Ketut. 2006. "Community Mapping, Tenurial Rights and Conflict Resolution in Kalimantan." In Fadzilah Majid Cooke, ed., *States, Communities and Forests in Contemporary Borneo.* Canberra: Australian National University Press.

Demelle, Brendan. 2011. "Natural Gas Industry Rhetoric versus Reality." *DeSmogBlog.* www.desmogblog.com/natural-gas-industry-rhetoric -versus-reality. Accessed July 30, 2012.

Dempsey, Daniel. 2013. "Seeing in the Dark: The Rise of Dark Pools, and the Danger Below the Surface." http://tabbforum.com/opinions/ seeing-in-the-dark-the-rise-of-dark-pools-and-the-danger-they -present.

DeNavas-Walt, Carmen, Bernadette D. Proctor, and Jessica C. Smith. 2011. *Income, Poverty, and Health Insurance Coverage in the United States: 2010.* U.S. Census Bureau, Current Population Reports. Washington, DC: U.S. Government Printing Office.

De Schutter, Oliver. 2011. "The Green Rush: The Global Race for Farmland and the Rights of Land Users." *Harvard International Law Journal* 52, no. 2: 504–559.

Dewan, Shaila. 2013. "A City Invokes Seizure Laws to Save Homes." *New York Times.* July 30.

Diaz, R. J., and R. Rosenberg. 2008. "Spreading Dead Zones and Consequences for Marine Ecosystems." *Science* 321, no. 5891: 926–929.

Diggs, Morse. 2013. "Atlanta Police Chief Seeks to Banish Convicted Prostitute." KDFW, Dallas, TX. January 28.

Doe Run Peru. n.d. "History of the Company." www.doerun.com.pe /content/pagina.php?pID=764. Accessed January 3, 2013.

Doe Run Resources Corporation. 2006. "United States Securities and Exchange Commission: Form 10-K." Securities and Exchange Commission. www.sec.gov/Archives/edgar/data/1061112 /000110465906018264/a06–5938_110k.htm#Item2_Properties _131244.

Dossou, Paulin Jésutin, Simon B. Y. Allagbe, Tatiana DeSouza, Grégoire Noudaikpon, and Alexis N. Tovissohe. 2011. *Evolution and Impacts of Coastal Land Use in Benin: The Case of the Sèmè-Podji Commune.* Rome: International Land Coalition.

Drajem, Mark. 2012. "Fracking Tied to Unusual Rise in Earthquakes in U.S." *Bloomberg.* April 12.

Duffy, P. B., and C. Tebaldi. 2012. "Increasing Prevalence of Extreme Summer Temperatures in the U.S." *Climatic Change* 111, no. 2: 487–495.

Duruibe, J. O., M. O. C. Ogwuegbu, and J. N. Egwurugwu. 2007. "Heavy Metal Pollution and Human Biotoxic Effects." *International Journal of Physical Sciences* 2, no. 5: 112–118.

eAfrica. 2005. "Case Study: Private Prisons." South African Institute of International Affairs, August. www.saiia.org.za/archive-eafrica/case -study-private-prisons.html.

Earthworks. 2012. "Fort Belknap Reservation." www.earthworksaction .org/voices/detail/fort_belknap_reservation. AccessedJuly 30, 2012.

Easterly, William. 2014. *The Tyranny of Experts: Economists, Dictators, and the Forgotten Rights of the Poor.* New York: Basic Books.

Economic Policy Institute. 2008. "When Income Grows, Who Gains?" The State of Working America. http://stateofworkingamerica.org/who -gains/#/?start=2000&end=2007.

———. 2011a. "Nearly Half of Family Income Goes to the Top Fifth, the Only Income Group with Increased Income Share since 1973." The State of Working America. http://stateofworkingamerica.org/charts /share-of-family-income-by-income-fifth-1947–201.

———. 2011b. "Family Income Growth in Two Eras." The State of Working America. http://stateofworkingamerica.org/charts/real -annual-family-income-growth-by-quintile-1947-79-and-1979 -2010.

———. 2011c. "Wealth Skewed towards the Richest of the Rich." The State of Working America. http://stateofworkingamerica.org/charts /average-wealth-by-wealth-class-in-2009.

———. 2011d. "Share of Total Household Income Growth Attributable to Various Groups, 1979–2007." The State of Working America. http://stateofworkingamerica.org/chart/swa-income-figure-2y-share -total-household/.

———. 2011e. "The Ratio of Average Top 1% Wealth to Median Wealth, 1962–2010." The State of Working America. http://stateofwork ingamerica.org/chart/swa-wealth-figure-6c-ratio-top-1-wealth/.

———. 2011f. "Median Household Wealth, by Race and Ethnicity, 1983–2010 (2010 Dollars)." The State of Working America. http:// stateofworkingamerica.org/chart/swa-wealth-table-6-8-average -median-assets/.

———. 2011g. "Share of Total Household Wealth Growth Accruing to Various Wealth Groups, 1983–2010." The State of Working America. http://stateofworkingamerica.org/chart/swa-wealth-figure-6b-share -total-household/.

———. 2013. "Average Family Income Growth, by Income Group." The State of Working America. http://stateofworkingamerica.org/data. Accessed February 9, 2013.

Economic Times. 2013. "Plachimada Anti-Coca Cola Unit Plans Stir." http://articles.economictimes.indiatimes.com/2013-07-12/news /40536432_1_plachimada-claims-special-tribunal-bill-cola-unit. Accessed January 4, 2014.

Economist. 2011a. "One Degree Over: Data from Crop Trials Underline the Threat Climate Change Poses to Farmers." Editorial, *Economist*. March 17.

————. 2011b. "Shining a Light on Dark Pools." http://www.economist.com/blogs/schumpeter/2011/08/exchange-share-trading. Accessed January 6, 2014.

Eggler, Bruce. 2007. "Despite Promises to Fix It, the Gulf's Dead Zone Is Growing." *Times-Picayune*. June 9.

El Defensor Chieftan. 2009. "Protestors to Fight 'Water Grab.'" www.dchieftain.com/2009/11/18/protesters-to-fight-water-grab. Accessed November 22, 2013.

Ellsworth, W. L., S. H. Hickman, A. L. Lleons, A. McGarr, A. J. Michael, and J. L. Rubinstein. 2012. "Are Seismicity Rate Changes in the Midcontinent Natural or Manmade?" Abstract of oral presentation at the Seismological Society of America 2012 Annual Meeting.

Environment and Process Division. 2004. "Mining-Related Chromate Water Pollution in the Sukinda Watershed (Orissa, India)." Bureau de Recherches Géologiques et Minières, Orléans, France.

Environment News Service. 2010. "Chernobyl Radiation Killed Nearly One Million People: New Book." April 26.

EPA. 1994. "Technical Report: Treatment of Cyanide Heap Leaches and Tailings." EPA530-R-94-037. U.S. Environmental Protection Agency, Office of Solid Waste, Special Waste Branch.

————. 2000. "Chromium Compounds." U.S. Environmental Protection Agency. Technology Transfer Network: Air Toxics Web Site. www.epa.gov/ttnatw01/hlthef/chromium.html.

————. 2006. "Midnite Mine Superfund Site: Record of Decision." Office of Environment Cleanup, EPA Region 10. www.epa.gov/region10/pdf/sites/midnite_mine/midnite-mine-rod-06.pdf. Accessed June 22, 2013.

————. 2008. "Times Beach Site." U.S. Environmental Protection Agency. www.epa.gov/superfund/sites/nplfs/fs0701237.pdf.

————. 2012a. "Plutonium." U.S. Environmental Protection Agency. March 6. www.epa.gov/rpdweb00/radionuclides/plutonium.html.

————. 2012b. "EPA's Recommendations for Enhanced Monitoring for Hexavalent Chromium (Chromium-6) in Drinking Water." U.S. Environmental Protection Agency. http://water.epa.gov/drink/info/chromium/guidance.cfm.

Eskanazi, Stuart. 1998. "The Biggest Pump Wins." *Dallas Observer*. November 19.

EuroHealthNet. 2011. "Greece—Augmentation of 40% Rate of Suicide." Press release, Brussels, September 25.

Eurojobs. 2012. "Quarter of Europe Risks Poverty or Social Exclusion." *Eurojobs* [blog]. December 6. http://blog.eurojobs.com/2012/12 /quarter-of-europe-risks-poverty-or-social-exclusion. Accessed February 8, 2013.

European Commission. 2011. "National Measures and Practices to Avoid Foreclosure Procedures for Residential Mortgage Loans," Commission staff working paper 357. March 31.

———. 2012. "Spain: Deep Adjustment Continues." *European Economic Forecast, Autumn 2012*. Brussels: Directorate General for Economic and Financial Affairs.

———. 2013. "FAQ on the EU-US Transatlantic Trade and Investment Partnership ('TTIP')." http://trade.ec.europa.eu/doclib/docs/2013/may /tradoc_151351.pdf.

European Mortgage Federation. 2007. *Study on the Efficiency of Mortgage Collateral in the European Union*. European Mortgage Federation, Brussels.

Eurostat. 2012a. "At Risk of Poverty or Social Exclusion in the EU27: In 2011, 24% of the Population Were at Risk of Poverty or Social Exclusion." News release 171/2012, December 3.

———. 2012b. "Income and Living Conditions." Dec. 17. http://epp .eurostat.ec.europa.eu/portal/page/portal/income_social_inclusion_liv ing_conditions/introduction.

———. 2012c. "Emigration by Sex, Age Group, and Citizenship." European Commission. http://appsso.eurostat.ec.europe.eu/nui/show .do?dataset-migr_emi1ctz&lang-en. Accessed December 31, 2012.

———. 2013a. *Second Estimate for the First Quarter of 2013. Euro Area GDP Down by 0.2% and EU27 Down by 0.1%, −1.1% and −0.7% Respectively compared with First Quarter of 2012*. Publication no. 86/2013. European Commission.

———. 2013b. Unemployment Statistics. http://epp.eurostat.ec.europa.eu /statistics_explained/index.php/Unemployment_statistics. Accessed August 5, 2013.

———. 2013c. "Data Explorer: Unemployment Rate by Sex and Age Groups—Annual Average, %." http://appsso.eurostat.ec.europa.eu /nui/show.do?dataset=une_rt_a&lang=en. Accessed January 1, 2014.

FAO. 2009. "CROPWAT 8.0 Decision Support System." www.fao.org/nr /water/infores_databases_cropwat.html. Accessed December 6, 2013.

Farrell, Diana, Susan Lund, Christian Fölster, Raphael Bick, Moira Pierce, and Charles Atkins. 2008. *Mapping Global Capital Markets: Fourth Annual Report.* New York: McKinsey and Co.

Fatima, Rabab, and Adnan Ahmed Sirajee. 2009. "Climate Change and Displacement in Bangladesh." International Organization for Migration. November 16.

Favell, A. 2008. *Eurostars and Eurocities: Free Movement and Mobility in an Integrating Europe.* Oxford: Blackwell.

FEANTSA. 2011. *European Observatory on Homelessness.* www .feantsa.org/spip.php?article62&lang=en. Accessed November 29, 2013.

Federal Bureau of Prisons. n.d. "BOP: Inmate Work Programs." U.S. Department of Justice. www.bop.gov/inmate_programs/work_prgms .jsp.

Federal Reserve Bank of St. Louis. 2013a. "Corporate Profits after Tax (without IVA and CCAdj) (CP)." http://research.stlouisfed.org/fred2 /graph/?s[1][id]=CP.

———. 2013b. "Nonfinancial Corporate Business; Total Financial Assets, Level (TFAABSNNCB)." http://research.stlouisfed.org/fred2/series/ TFAABSNNCB.

Ferreira, Francisco H. G., and Michael Walton. 2005. "The Inequality Trap: Why Equity Must Be Central to Development Policy." *Finance and Development* 42, no. 4.

Field, C. B., V. Barros, T. F. Stocker, D. Qin, D. J. Dokken, K. L. Ebi, M. D. Mastrandrea, et al. 2012. *IPCC: Managing the Risks of Extreme Events and Disasters to Advance Climate Change Adaptation.* Special Report of Working Groups I and II of the Intergovernment Panel on Climate Change. Cambridge: IPCC.

Fisher, Max. 2011. "Map: U.S. Ranks Near Bottom on Income Inequality." *Atlantic*, September.

Fitzgerald, Joan. 2009. "Cities on the Front Lines." *The American Prospect.* March 22. http://prospect.org/article/cities-front-lines.

Foster, G., and S. Rahmstorf. 2011. "Global Temperature Evolution 1979–2010." *Environmental Research Letters* 6, no. 4.

Fouillet, A., G. Rey, F. Laurent, G. Pavillon, S. Bellec, C. Ghihenneuc-Jouyaux, J. Clavel, et al. 2006. "Excess Mortality Related to the August 2003 Heat Wave in France." *International Archives of Occupational and Environmental Health* 80, no. 1.

Founda, D., and C. Giannaopoulos. 2009. "The Exceptionally Hot Summer of 2007 in Athens, Greece—A Typical Summer in the Future Climate?" *Global and Planetary Change* 67, nos. 3–4.

Frank, Andre Gunder. 1966. *The Development of Underdevelopment.* New York: Monthly Review Press.

FRED. 2013. "Compensation of Employees: Wages & Salary Accruals (WASCUR)/Gross Domestic Product (GDP)." *St. Louis Federal Reserve.* http://research.stlouisfed.org/fred2/graph/?g=2Xa. Accessed January 1, 2014.

Freeland, Chrystia. 2013. *Plutocrats: The Rise of the New Global Super-Rich and the Fall of Everyone Else.* New York: Penguin Books.

Freeland, Howard J., and Denis Gilbert. 2009. "Estimate of the Steric Contribution to Global Sea Level Rise from a Comparison of the WOCE One-Time Survey with 2006–2008 Argo Observations." *Atmosphere-Ocean* 47, no. 4: 292–298.

Friends of Lead Free Children. 2009. "Friends of Lead Free Children: Helping to Create an Environment for Children to Achieve Their Full Learning Potential." http://friendsofleadfreechildren.org/dominican _programs.html. Accessed July 13, 2013.

Friis, Cecilie, and Anette Reenberg. 2010. *Land Grab in Africa: Emerging Land System Drivers in a Teleconnected World.* GLP Report No. 1. Copenhagen: GLP International Project Office.

Furman Center. 2007. "New Housing Data Continue to Show Signs of Danger for New York City's Homeowners, Furman Center Analysis Concludes." Press release. Furman Center for Real Estate and Urban Policy, New York University. October 15.

Gagnon, Geoffrey. 2004. "Moving Mountains." *Legal Affairs,* September–October.

Ganchev, K., M. Kearns, Y. Nevmyvaka, and J. W. Vaughn. 2009. "Censored Exploration and the Dark Pool Problem." Computer and Information Science, University of Pennsylvania. www.cis.upenn.edu /~mkearns./papers/darkpools-final.pdf.

Gans, Herbert J. 2013. "An Enduring Recession?" *Challenge* 56, no. 1: 72–87.

GAO. 2013. "Corporate Income Tax: Effective Rates Can Differ Significantly from Statutory Rate." Washington, DC.

Ghosh, Palash. 2013. "A Cheap New Drug Decimating Greece's Homeless as Economic Crisis Tightens Grip." *International Business Times.* May 17.

Gillis, Justin. 2013. "Heat-Trapping Gas Passes Milestone, Raising Fears." *New York Times*. May 11.

Gilmore, Ruth Wilson. 2007. *Golden Gulag: Prisons, Surplus, Crisis, and Opposition in Globalizing California*. Berkeley: University of California Press.

Glick, Reuven, and Kevin J. Lansing. "FRBSF Economic Letter: Global Household Leverage, House Prices, and Consumption." 2010. Federal Reserve Bank of San Francisco. January 11.

Global Commission on Drug Policy. 2011. "The War on Drugs and HIV/AIDS: How the Criminalization of Drug Use Fuels the Global Pandemic." www.globalcommissionondrugs.org/reports.

Global Insight. 2007. "The Mortgage Crisis: Economic and Fiscal Implications for Metro Areas." United States Conference of Mayors and the Council for the New American City.

Global Research. 2010. "Coca-Cola Causes Serious Depletion of Water Resources in India." March 24. www.globalresearch.ca/coca-cola -causes-serious-depletion-of-waterresources-in-india/18305. Accessed July 30, 2012.

Godoy, Julio. 2011. "New Sarcophagus for Chernobyl Will Have to Wait Until 2015." Inter Press Service. April 25.

Go Green America. 2011. "Great Pacific Garbage Patch." GoGreenA-mericaTV.com. http://gogreenamericatv.com/wp-content/uploads /2011/11/Great-Pacific-Garbage-Patch-picture.jpg. Accessed July 30, 2012.

Goldstein, Matthew. 2013. "Cheap Money Bankrolls Wall Street's Bet on Housing." Reuters. May 6.

Golovnina, Maria. 2005. "Interview—Norilsk Will Become Cleaner, but Not Overnight." Reuters. October 12.

Gonzalez-Valero, Juan. 2009. "Climate, Land Degradation, Agriculture and Food Security: Means to Adopt." Syngenta report. September 2009. www.wmo.int/wcc3/sessionsdb/documents/WS10_Gonzalez .pdf. Accessed July 30, 2012.

Graeber, David. 2012. *Debt: The First 5,000 Years*. Reprint edition. Brooklyn, NY: Melville House.

GRAIN. 2012. "GRAIN Releases Data Set with over 400 Global Land Grabs." Press release, GRAIN, February 23.

Gray, Ellen. 2012. "Land Stat Top Ten: A Shrinking Sea, the Aral Sea." NASA Earth Science News Team. July 23. www.nasa.gov/mission _pages/landsat/news/40th-top10-aralsea.html.

"Greece Approves Sweeping Public Sector Cuts." 2013. *Telegraph.* July 18.

Guerino, Paul, Paige M. Harrison, and William J. Sabol. 2012. "Prisoners in 2010." Bureau of Justice Statistics, Office of Justice Programs, U.S. Department of Justice. February 9. www.bjs.gov/content/pub/pdf /p10.pdf.

Hakkeling, R. T. A., L. R. Olderman, and W. G. Sombroek. 1991. *World Map of the Status of Human-Induced Soil Degradation: An Explanatory Note.* Wageningen: International Soil Reference and Information Center.

Hall, Deborah. 2010. "Bottled Water Pits Nestlé vs. Greens." *Wall Street Journal.* http://online.wsj.com/article/SB10001424052748704414504 575243921712969144.html. Accessed November 29, 2013.

Hall, Ruth. 2011. "Land Grabbing in Africa and the New Politics of Food." Policy Brief 041. Future Agricultures.

Hankewitz, Gert. 2013. "Foreclosures Peak Last Year." *Postimees: In English.* February 7. http://news.postimees.ee/1129916/foreclosures -peak-last-year. Accessed August 3, 2013.

Hansen, J., M. Sato, and R. Ruedy. 2012. "Perception of Climate Change." *Proceedings of the National Academy of Sciences of the United States* 109: 14726–14727.

Harden, Blaine, and Dan Morgan. 2004. "Debate Intensifies on Nuclear Waste: Lawmakers in Affected States Press Bush Administration on Cleanup." *Washington Post.* June 2.

Harden, Mark. 2012. "Fracking in Colorado Uses a City's Worth of Water, Enviro Report Says." *Denver Business Journal.* June 20.

Harding, R. 2001. "Private Prisons." *Crime and Justice* 28: 265–346.

Hart, B., and D. V. Boger. 2008. "Making an Unsustainable Industry More Sustainable." *Proceedings of the Eleventh International Seminar on Paste 08* 1, no. 1: 3–14.

Hartman, Chester, and Gregory D. Squires, eds. 2013. *From Foreclosure to Fair Lending.* New York: New Village Press.

Harvey, David. 1982. *The Limits of Capital.* Chicago: University of Chicago Press.

Harvey, David W. 2000. "History of the Hanford Site 1943–1990." Pacific Northwest National Laboratory. http://ecology.pnnl.gov/library /History/Hanford-History-All.pdf. Accessed January 4, 2013.

Held, David, and Ayse Kaya. 2007. *Global Inequality: Patterns and Explanations.* Cambridge: Polity.

Hendryx, M. 2009. "Mortality from Heart, Respiratory and Kidney Disease in Coal Mining Areas of Appalachia." *International Archives of Occupational and Environmental Health* 82: 243–249.

Herivel, Tara, and Paul Wright, eds. 2003. *Prison Nation: The Warehousing of America's Poor.* New York: Routledge.

Her Majesty's Prison Service. n.d. "Contracted-out Prisons." www.justice.gov .uk/about/hmps/contracted-out.

HighQuest Partners. 2010. "Private Financial Sector Investment in Farmland and Agricultural Infrastructure." OECD Food, Agriculture and Fisheries Papers, No. 33. August 10.

Home Office. 2012. "Have You Got What It Takes? Working with Prisons." www.homeoffice.gov.uk/publications/police/pcc/working -with-others/working-with-prisons?view=Binary.

Hope, Kerin. 2013. "Greek Deflation Accelerates after Wages Drop." *Financial Times.* http://www.ft.com/cms/s/0/c8564ce8-48ab-11e3 -8237-00144feabdc0.html#axzz2pGr9q4q0. Accessed January 1, 2014.

Hoshaw, Lindsey. 2009. "Afloat in the Ocean, Expanding Islands of Trash." *New York Times.* November 10.

Hovil, Lucy. 2010. *Hoping for Peace, Afraid of War: The Dilemmas of Repatriation and Belonging on the Borders of Uganda and South Sudan.* Research paper No. 196. Geneva: Policy Development and Evaluation Service. United Nations High Commissioner for Refugees.

Humber, Yuriy. 2008. "Kremlin Sidelines Oligarchs in Taking Norilsk Control (Update1)." www.bloomberg.com/apps/news?pid=newsarchive &sid=aLyndimCNJvY. Accessed November 23, 2013.

Hurdle, Jon. 2009. "Pennsylvania Lawsuit Says Drilling Polluted Water." Reuters. November 9.

Huseynova, Shahnaz. 2007. "Azerbaijan: Sumgayit Becomes One of World's Most-Polluted Cities." Radio Free Europe/Radio Liberty. September 18.

Ideas First Research. 2010. "Sector—Metal & Mining: Industry— Ferroalloys." Ideas First Research, Mumbai, India.

IFPRI (International Food Policy Research Institute). 2009. "Outsourc-ing's Third Wave." *Economist.* May 21.

Ifran, Zareena Begum, and Uvaneswari. 2012. "Determination of the Cost-Effective Adsorbents to Remove Toxic Metal Pollutants from Industrial Waste Water." *International Journal of Social Sciences and Interdisciplinary Research* 1, no. 4.

Illinois Department of Public Health. n.d. "Lead in Industry." Illinois Department of Public Health. www.idph.state.il.us/about/epi/getpbout.htm.

ILO. 2012. "Global Unemployment: Trends for Youth 2012." *International Labor Organization*. Geneva, CH.

ILO and OECD. 2013. "Short-term Labour Market Outlook and Key Challenges in G20 Countries: Statistical Update for the Meeting of G20 Labour and Employment Ministers." July 18–19. Moscow. www.ilo.org/wcmsp5/groups/public/---dgreports/---dcomm/---publ/documents/publication/wcms_217546.pdf.

IMF. 2006. *Global Financial Stability Report: Market Developments and Issues*. Washington, DC: International Monetary Fund.

———. 2008. *Global Financial Stability Report: Containing Risks and Restoring Financial Soundness*. Washington, DC: International Monetary Fund.

———. 2012a. *Global Financial Stability Report: Restoring Confidence and Progressing on Reforms*. Washington, DC: International Monetary Fund. www.imf.org/External/Pubs/FT/GFSR/2012/02/pdf/text.pdf.

———. 2012b. "World Economic and Financial Surveys." *World Economic Outlook Database*. www.imf.org/external/pubs/ft/weo/2012/01/weodata/index.aspx. Accessed December 31, 2012.

Inman, Phillip, and Helena Smith. 2012. "Greek Economy to Shrink 25% by 2014." *Guardian*. September 18.

Instituto Nacional de Estadística. 2011. "Economically Active Population Survey." www.ine.es/en/inebmenu/mnu_mercalab_en.htm. Accessed November 29, 2013.

———. 2013a. "Labour Market." Instituto Nacional de Estadística (Spain).

———. 2013b. "Notas De Prensa: 30 de Abril de 2013." Instituto Nacional de Estadística (Spain). April 30. www.ine.es/prensa/cntr0113a.pdf.

Integrated Pollution Prevention and Control. 2012. "A Teaching Case: The Basel Ban and Batteries." www.commercialdiplomacy.org/case_study/case_batteries.htm.

International Atomic Energy Agency. n.d. "Frequently Asked Chernobyl Questions." www.iaea.org/newscenter/features/chernobyl-15/cherno-faq.shtml. Accessed January 4, 2013.

International Center for Prison Studies. 2011. "World Prison Population List." University of Essex. www.apcca.org/uploads/9th_Edition_2011.pdf.

International Energy Agency. 2012. "Global Carbon-Dioxide Emissions Increase by 1.0 Gt in 2011 to Record High." www.iea.org/news roomandevents/news/2012/may/name,27216,en.html. Accessed June 29, 2013.

International Land Coalition. *Commercial Pressures on Land.* http://www .landcoalition.org/cpl.

International Monetary Fund. 2013. World Economic Outlook Database: April 2013 edition. http://www.imf.org/external/ pubs/ft/weo /2013/01/weodata/index.aspx.

IPPC. 2003. "Integrated Pollution Prevention and Control (IPPC): Reference Document on Best Available Techniques for the Tanning of Hides and Skins." European IPPC Bureau (EIPPCB). http://eippcb.jrc .es/reference/BREF/tan_bref_0203.pdf.

ISDA (International Swaps Derivatives Association). 2008. Data on Credit-Default Swaps. http://www2.isda.org/.

Isidore, Chris. 2012. "Corporate Profits Hit Record as Wages Get Squeezed." *CNNMoney.* http://money.cnn.com/2012/12/03/news /economy/record-corporate-profits/. Accessed January 1, 2014.

Islamzade, Arif. 1994. "Sumgayit: Soviet's Pride, Azerbaijan's Hell." *Azerbaijan International* 2, no. 3: 26–27, 30.

Jackson, Robert, Avner Vengosh, Thomas H. Darrah, Nathaniel R. Warner, Adrian Down, Robert Poreda, Stephen G. Osborn, Kaigung Zhao, and Jonathan D. Karr. 2013. "Increased Stray Gas Abundance in a Subset of Drinking Water Wells Near Marcellus Shale Gas Extraction." *Proceedings of the National Academy of Sciences of the United States* 110, no. 28: 11213–11214.

Jamasmie, Cecilia. 2012. "Doe Run Peru to Be Liquidated After Rejected Restructuring of La Oroya Smelter." Mining.com. www.mining.com/doe -run-peru-to-be-liquidated-after-rejectedrestructuring-of-la-oroya-smelter.

Johnson, Kirk. 2011. "E.P.A. Links Tainted Water in Wyoming to Hydraulic Fracturing for Natural Gas." *New York Times.* December 8.

Johnston, David Cay. 2005. *Perfectly Legal: The Covert Campaign to Rig Our Tax System to Benefit the Super Rich—and Cheat Everybody Else.* New York: Penguin Group.

———. 2011. "Where's the Fraud, Mr. President?" Reuters. December 13.

———. 2013. "Corporate Tax Rates Plummet as Profits Soar." The National Memo. July 16

Jones, Graydon. 1989. "Work Will Resume at Crescent Mine." *Spokane Chronicle.* April 28.

Jones, P. D., D. H. Lister, and Q. Li. 2008. "Urbanization Effects in Large-Scale Temperature Records, with an Emphasis on China." *Journal of Geophysical Research* 113, no. D16: 1–12.

Jorgensen, Dan. 2006. "Hinterland History: The Ok Tedi Mine and Its Cultural Consequences in Telefolmin." *Contemporary Pacific.* September 22.

Jowit, Juliette. 2008. "Is Water the New Oil?" *Observer.* November 1.

Joyce, Christopher. 2012. "Quakes Caused by Waste from Gas Wells, Study Finds." National Public Radio, April 11, 2012.

Jubilee Debt Campaign. 2009. "2. How Big Is the Debt of Poor Countries?" http://jubileedebt.org.uk/faqs-2.

———. 2012. *The State of Debt: Putting an End to 30 Years of Crisis.* Jubilee Debt Campaign, London.

———. 2013. "How Big Is the Debt of Poor Countries?" Jubilee Debt Campaign, London. http://jubileedebt.org.uk/faqs-2/how-big-is-the -debt-of-poor-countries.

Kahn, Hilary E. 2014. *Framing the Global: Entry Points for Research.* Bloomington: Indiana University Press.

Kaiser, Tania. 2010. "Dispersal, Division and Diversification: Durable Solutions and Sudanese Refugees in Uganda." *Journal of Eastern African Studies* 4, no. 1: 44–60.

Karaian, Jason. 2013. "Spanish Real Estate Has Lost More Than a Third of Its Value, But It's Still Overvalued." *Quartz.* http://qz.com/124088 /spanish-real-estate-has-lost-more-than-a-third-of-its-value-but-its -still-overvalued/. Accessed January 1, 2014.

Karoly, D. J. 2009. "The Recent Bushfires and Extreme Heat Wave in Southeast Australia." *Bulletin of the Australian Meteorological and Oceanographic Society* 22: 10–13.

Katz, M. Jonathan. 2007. "Dominican Town Looks to Clean Up Pollution." *Washington Post.* June 20.

Kaul, B., R. S. Sandhu, C. Depratt, and F. Reyes. 1999. "Follow-up Screening of Lead-Poisoned Children near an Auto Battery Recycling Plant, Haina, Dominican Republic." *Environmental Health Perspectives* 107, no. 11 (November): 917–920.

Keep Tap Water Safe. 2013. "List of Bans Worldwide." http://keep tapwatersafe.org/global-bans-on-fracking/. Accessed January 2, 2014.

Kelleher, James. 2007. "Signs of Life Returning to Times Beach." Reuters. May 25.

Kennedy, Loraine. 2005. "Variations on the Classical Model: Forms of Cooperation in Leather Clusters of Palar Valley, Tamil Nadu." In Keshab Das, ed., *Indian Industrial Clusters,* 103–227. Burlington: Ashgate.

Kenny, J. F., N. L. Barber, S. S. Hutson, K. S. Linsey, J. K. Lovelace, and M. A. Maupin. 2009. "Estimated Use of Water in the United States in 2005." *U.S. Geological Survey Circular* 1344: 52. http://pubs.usgs .gov/circ/1344/.

Keohane, David. 2012. "The Decline of US Shadowing Banking, Charted." *Financial Times.* May 29.

Keranen, Katie M., Heather M. Savage, Geoffy A. Abers, and Elizabeth S. Cochran. 2013. "Potentially Induced Earthquakes in Oklahoma, USA: Links between Wastewater Injection and the 2011 Mw 5.7 Earthquake Sequence." *Geology* 41, no. 6: 699–702.

Kinnard, Christophe, Christian M. Zdanowicz, David A. Fisher, Elisabeth Isaksson, Anne de Vernal, and Lonnie G. Thompson. 2011. "Reconstructed Changes in Arctic Sea Ice over the Past 1,450 Years." *Nature* 479, no. 7374: 509–512.

Kirkham, Chris. 2012. "Private Prisons Profit from Immigration Crackdown, Federal and Local Law Enforcement Partnerships." *Huffington Post.* June 7.

Klauk, Erin. 2013a. "Environmental Impacts at Fort Belknap from Gold Mining." Science Education Center, Carleton College.

———. 2013b. "Political Issues on the Fort Belknap Reservation from Gold Mining." Science Education Center, Carleton College.

———. 2013c. "Exploration and Development History of Gold Mining at the Zortman-Landusky Mine." Science Education Resource Center, Carleton College.

Knobel, Beth. 1997. "Secret Soviet City Opens Its Dirty Doors." *Living on Earth.* August 1.

Knorr Cetina, K., and A. Preda, eds. 2013. *The Oxford Handbook of the Sociology of Finance.* Oxford: Oxford University Press.

Kocjan, John, Don Ogilvie, Adam Schneider, and Val Srinivas. 2012. "The Deloitte Shadow Banking Index." www.deloitte.com/assets/ Dcom-UnitedStates/Local%20Assets/Documents/CFO_Center_FT /US_FSI_The_Deloitte_Shadow_Banking_052912.pdf. Accessed July 28, 2012.

Kopsini, Christina. 2012. "Drugs from Car Batteries." [Greek] *Kathimerini.* August 4. http://news.kathimerini.gr/4dcgi/_w_articles_ell_2_08 /04/2012_478530.

Krainer, John. 2009. "Housing Prices and Bank Loan Performance." FRBSF Economic Letter 2009-06. Federal Reserve Bank of San Francisco. February 6.

Kramer, Anna. 2012. "Q&A: La Oroya's Future." Oxfam America. www .oxfamamerica.org/articles/q-a-la-oroyas-future. Accessed January 8, 2013.

Krippner, G. R. 2011. *Capitalizing on Crisis: The Political Origins of the Rise of Finance*. Cambridge, MA: Harvard University Press.

Krotz, Dan. 2011. "Thawing Permafrost Could Release Vast Amounts of Carbon and Accelerate Climate Change by the End of This Century." Berkeley Lab News Center RSS. August 22.

Krugman, Paul. 2010. "Trade Does Not Equal Jobs." *The Conscience of a Liberal* [blog], *New York Times*. December 6.

Kubiszewski, Ida, Robert Constanza, Carol Franco, Philip Lawn, John Talberth, Tim Jackson, and Camille Alymer. 2013. "Beyond GDP: Measuring and Achieving Global Genuine Progress." *Ecological Economics* 93: 57–68.

Kumhof, Michael, and Romain Rancière. 2010. "Inequality, Leverage and Crises." Working paper WP/10/268. International Monetary Fund, Washington, DC.

LaFlure, Rebecca. 2013. "The Mess Gets Worse at Hanford's Nuclear Site." The Center for Public Integrity. Accessed January 5, 2014. http://www.publicintegrity.org/2013/11/18/13770/mess-gets-worse -hanford-s-nuclear-site.

Lambin, Eric F., and Patrick Meyfroidt. 2011. "Global Land Use Change, Economic Globalization, and the Looming Land Scarcity." *PNAS* 108, no. 9: 3465–3472.

Land Matrix. 2013. "Why Do the Numbers Constantly Change?" Land Matrix. www.landmatrix.org/en. Accessed June 29, 2013.

———. 2014. The Online Public Database on Land Deals. http://land portal.info/landmatrix.

Landes, David S. 1999. *The Wealth and Poverty of Nations: Why Some Are So Rich and Some So Poor*. New York: W. W. Norton & Company.

Leckie, S., Z. Simperingham, and J. Baker. 2011. "Bangladesh's Climate Displacement Nightmare." *Ecologist* [blog]. www.theecologist.org /blogs_and_comments/commentators/other_comments/854868 /bangladeshs_climate_displacement_nightmare.html. Accessed November 29, 2013.

Leistner, Marilyn. 1995. "The Times Beach Story." *Synthesis/Regeneration* 7–8.

Lenntech. 2011. "Chromium and Water: Reaction Mechanisms, Environmental Impact and Health Effects." Delft, Netherlands. www.lenntech.com/periodic/water/chromium/chromium-and-water.htm.

Lerner, Stephen, and Saqib Bhatti. 2013. "Forcing Banks to the Bargaining Table: Renegotiating Wall Street's Relationship with Our Communities." In Chester Hartman and Gregory D. Squires, eds., *From Foreclosure to Fair Lending*, 177–205. New York: New Village Press.

Levring, Peter. 2013. "Denmark Feeds World's Biggest Home Debt Load as Caps Spurned." *Bloomberg*. http://www.bloomberg.com/news/2013-11-14/denmark-feeds-world-s-biggest-private-debt-as-caps-rejected.html. Accessed January 1, 2014.

Levy, Dan, and Prashant Gopal. 2011. "Foreclosure Filings in U.S. May Jump 20% from Record 2010 as Crisis Peaks." Bloomberg. January 13.

Lidsky, Theodore I., and Jay S. Schneider. 2002. "Lead Neurotoxicity in Children: Basic Mechanisms and Clinical Correlates." *Brain: A Journal of Neurology* 126, no. 1: 5–19.

Lima, Joao. 2013. "Bank of Portugal Forecasts Deeper Economic Contraction This Year." March 26. *Bloomberg*. March 26. http://www.bloomberg.com/news/2013-03-26/bank-of-portugal-forecasts-deeper-economic-contraction-this-year.html.

Liu, Yao, and Christoph B. Rosenberg. 2013. "Dealing with Private Debt Distress in the Wake of European Financial Crisis." Working paper 13/44. International Monetary Fund, Washington, DC.

Long, Katy. 2010. *Home Alone? A Review of the Relationship between Repatriation, Mobility and Durable Solutions for Refugees*. Geneva: United Nations High Commissioner for Refugees.

"Louisiana Incarcerated: How We Built the World's Prison Capital." 2012. *Times-Picayune*. May. www.nola.com/prisons.

Lucas, Linda E. 2005. *Unpacking Globalization: Markets, Gender and Work*. Kampala, Uganda: Makerere University Press.

Marcellus Drilling News. 2010. "List of 78 Chemicals Used in Hydraulic Fracturing Fluid in Pennsylvania." June 10. http://marcellusdrilling.com/2010/06/list-of-78-chemicals-used-in-hydraulic-fracturing-fluid-in-pennsylvania.

Marcuse, Peter. 2014. "Blog #43—Who Lost the War on Poverty, and Who Won It?" Peter Marcuse's Blog.WordPress.com.January 28. http://pmarcuse.wordpress.com/2014/01/25/blog-43-who-lost -the-war-on-poverty-and-who-won-it/.

Margulis, Matias E., Nora McKeon, and Saturnino M. Borras. 2013. "Land Grabbing and Global Governance: Critical Perspectives." *Globalizations* 10, no. 1: 1–23.

Mason, Cody. 2012. "Too Good to Be True: Private Prisons in America." Sentencing Project, January. http://sentencingproject.org/doc/publi cations/inc_Too_Good_to_be_True.pdf.

Massey, Steve. 1991a. "Bunker Hill Founder Says Insiders Clean." *Spokane Chronicle.* September 27.

———. 1991b. "Bunker Hill Sale Yields Much Less than Predictions." *Spokane Chronicle.* August 30.

Mattera, Philip. 2006. "Still, Not So Sterling: A Look at Revett Minerals." Clark Fork Coalition and Rock Creek Alliance. www.earthworksac tion.org/files/pubs-others/FS_StillNotSoSterling.pdf.

Mayer, Judith. 2009. "The Trouble with Palm Oil." *Indonesia Today.* www.insideindonesia.org/feature-editions/the-trouble-with-oil-palm. Accessed July 1, 2013.

McClesky, Claire O'Neill. 2012. "Mexico to Build 2 Private Prisons by Year-End." Insight Crime. August 2. www.insightcrime.org/news -briefs/mexico-to-build-2-private-prisons-by-year-end.

McClure, Robert. 2001. "Pegasus Gold—from Boom to Bankruptcy." *Seattle Post-Intelligencer.* June 13.

McCormack, Simon. 2012. "Prison Labor Booms as Unemployment Remains High; Companies Reap Benefits." *Huffington Post.* December 10.

McDonald, Douglas C. 1992. "Private Penal Institutions." *Crime and Justice* 16: 361–419.

McKibben, Bill. 2012. "Global Warming's Terrifying New Math: Three Simple Numbers That Add Up to Global Catastrophe—and That Make Clear Who the Real Enemy Is." *Rolling Stone.* July 19.

McMichael, Philip. 2009. "A Food Regime Genealogy." *The Journal of Peasant Studies* 36, no. 1: 171–196.

McQuaid, John. 2012. "Finally, a Victory against Mountaintop Removal." *Slate.* November 30.

McTighe, Laura. 2012. "The War on Drugs Is a War on Relationships: Crossing the Borders of Fear, Silence and HIV Vulnerability in the

Prison-Created Diaspora." In *Beyond Walls and Cages: Bridging Prison Abolition and Immigrant Justice Movements,* ed. Jenna Loyd, Matthew Mitchelson, and Andrew Burridge. Athens: University of Georgia Press.

———. 2013. "Privatizing Punishment: A Global Analysis of Private Prison Expansion in 2005." (Unpublished paper).

Michigan Citizens for Water Conservation. 2012. "History Highlights." www.savemiwater.org/about/history. Accessed January 22, 2013.

Milanovic, Branko. 2005. *Worlds Apart: Measuring International and Global Inequality.* Princeton: Princeton University Press.

———. 2009. *Global Inequality Recalculated.* Working paper no. 5061. World Bank.

———. 2011. "Global Inequality: From Class to Location, from Proletarians to Migrants." Working Paper no. 5820. World Bank.

———. 2012. "Global Inequality: From Class to Location, from Proletarians to Migrants." *Global Policy* 3, no. 2: 125–134.

Miles, David K., and Vladimir C. Pillonca. 2008. "Financial Innovation and European Housing and Mortgage Markets." *Oxford Review of Economic Policy* 24, 1: 145–175.

Mineral Policy Center. 2000. "Cyanide Leach Mining Packet." August. www4.nau.edu/itep/waste/HazSubMap/docs/Mining/Cyanide_Leach_Packet.pdf. Accessed July 13, 2013.

Mines and Communities. 2003. "Hell on Earth." www.minesandcommunities.org/article.php?a=1409. Accessed June 15, 2013.

Mining Truth. 2012. "How Corporations Evade Liability for Pollution at Closed Mines." *Mining Truth.* www.miningtruth.org/wp-content/uploads/2013/01/How-Corporations-Evade-Liability-Mining-Truth.pdf. Accessed June 23, 2013.

Mishel, Lawrence. 2007. "Who's Grabbing All the New Pie? Economic Snapshots." Economic Policy Institute, Washington, DC. August 1.

———. 2011. "Huge Disparity in Share of Total Wealth Gain since 1983." Economic Policy Institute, Washington, DC. September 15.

———. 2013. "Economy Built for Profits Not Prosperity." Economic Policy Institute, Washington, DC. March 28.

Mishel, Lawrence, and Jared Berstein. 2007. "Economy's Gains Fail to Reach Most Workers' Paychecks." Economic Policy Institute, Washington, DC. August 30.

Mishel, Lawrence, and Josh Bivens. 2011. "Occupy Wall Streeters Are Right about Skewed Economic Rewards in the United States." Economic Policy Institute, Washington, DC. October 26.

Mishel, Lawrence, Josh Bivens, Elise Gould, and Heidi Shierholz. 2012. *The State of Working America*. 12th ed. Ithaca, NY: Cornell University Press.

Mishel, Lawrence, and Heidi Shierholz. 2011. "The Sad but True Story of Wages in America." Issue Brief #297. Economic Policy Institute, Washington, DC. March 14.

Mitchell, Josh. 2013. "More Americans Living in Others' Homes." *Wall Street Journal*. July 22.

Mitchell, Larry D. 2004. "Zortman and Landusky Mines: Water Quality Impacts." Environmental Quality Council, Helena, MT. Accessed January 9, 2013.

Moir, Matt. 2013. "Idle No More and Canada's Prison Apartheid." *The Tyee*. January 2. 2013.

Molnar, Augusta, Keith Barney, Michael DeVito, Alain Karsenty, Dominic Elson, Margarita Benavides, Pedro Tipula, Carlos Soria, Phil Shearman, and Marina France. 2011. *Large Acquisition of Rights on Forest Lands for Tropical Timber Concessions and Commercial Wood Plantations*. Rome: International Land Coalition.

Morris, Tim. 2009. "Louisiana's Incarceration Rate Is No. 1 in Nation." *Times-Picayune*. March 2.

Moyo, Dambisa. 2010. *Dead Aid: Why Aid Is Not Working and How There Is Another Way for Africa*. London: Penguin.

Murphy, Kevin. 1996. "In a Fouled Jungle, Tribes Win One." *New York Times*. June 12.

Murphy, Sophia. 2013. "Land Grabs and Fragile Food Ecosystems: The Role of Globalization." Institute for Agriculture and Trade Policy, Minneapolis, MN.

NASA. "Measuring Vegetation (NDVI & EVI): Feature Articles." *Earth Observatory*. http://earthobservatory.nasa.gov/Features/Measuring Vegetation/measuring_vegetation_2.php.

———. n.d. http://earthobservatory.nasa.gov/Features/WorldOfChange /aral_sea.php.

National Climatic Data Center. 2013a. "Billion-Dollar Weather/Climate Disasters." www.ncdc.noaa.gov/billions/. Accessed November 22, 2013.

———. 2013b. "Drought-August 2013." www.ncdc.noaa.gov/sotc /drought/2013/8. Accessed November 22, 2013.

National Prisoner Statistics Program. 2013. "Prisoners in 2010 (Revised)." Bureau of Justice Statistics, U.S. Department of Justice. http://bjs.ojp .usdoj.gov/index.cfm?ty=pbdetail&iid=2230. Accessed February 8, 2013.

National Wildlife Federation. 2012. "Hard Rock Mining Pollution." National Wildlife Federation. www.nwf.org/Wildlife/Policy/Mining -Loopholes.aspx.

Nellas, Demetris. 2013. "Greek Bill Opens Way for Civil Service Layoffs." Associated Press. April 28.

Neumann, Jeannette. 2013. "Blackstone, Deutsche Bank in Talks to Sell Bond Backed by Home Rentals." *Wall Street Journal.* July 30.

Newmont Mining Corporation. 1998. "Form 10-K." Securities and Exchange Commission. www.sec.gov/answers/form10k.htm. Accessed June 23, 2013.

———. 2012. "Newmont Announces Record Operating Cash Flow of $3.6 Billion and Record Annual Revenue of $10.4 Billion in 2011." Press release. Newmont Mining Corporation, Denver, CO. February 23.

New York Times. 2001. "Mine in Wilderness Approved After 14 Years." *New York Times.* December 28.

Nigeria Intel. 2012. "Privatising the Prisons." Nigeria Intel. December 17. www.nigeriaintel.com/2012/12/17/privatising-the-prisons.

NOAA. 2011. "State of the Climate: Global Hazards for August 2011." National Climatic Data Center, National Oceanic and Atmospheric Administration, Washington, DC.

———. 2012a. "State of the Climate: Global Hazards for July 2012." National Climatic Data Center, National Oceanic and Atmospheric Administration, Washington, DC. www.ncdc.noaa.gov/sotc /national/2012/7 (published online Aug 2012).

———. 2012b. "Wildfires—August 2012." http://www.ncdc.noaa.gov/sotc /fire/2012/8. Accessed January 4, 2014.

———. 2013a. "Billion-Dollar Weather/Climate Disasters." www.ncdc .noaa.gov/billions/. Accessed November 22.

———. 2013b. "Drought-August 2013." www.ncdc.noaa.gov/sotc /drought/2013/8. Accessed November 22, 2013.

———. n.d. http://marinedebris.noaa.gov/sites/default/files/GPmap_2012 _NOAAMDP.jpg.

Noorani, Shehzad. 2008. "Children of the Black Dust." CNN. September 28.

Norilsk Nickel. 2008. "History: Mastering Norilsk Ore Deposits." www .nornik.ru/en/about/history. Accessed June 13, 2013.

Novinite. 2011. "Bulgaria: Foreclosure Auctions Jump in 2011." Novinite [Sofia News Agency]. www.balkaninsight.com/en/article/bulgaria -foreclosure-auctions-jump-in-2011. Accessed August 3, 2013.

Novo, Andre, Kees Jansen, Maja Slingerland, and Ken Giller. 2010. "Biofuel, Dairy Production and Beef in Brazil: Competing Claims on Land Use in São Paulo State." *The Journal of Peasant Studies* 37, no. 4: 769–792.

OECD. 2008. *Growing Unequal? Income Distribution and Poverty in OECD Countries.* Paris: OECD.

———. 2011. *Divided We Stand: Why Inequality Keeps Rising.* Paris: OECD.

———. 2012. "Annex Table 27: General Government Financial Balances." Economic Outlook Annex Tables. www.oecd.org/eco/outlook/economic outlookannextables.htm.

———. 2013a. "Economic Outlook No. 93—June 2013—Flash File." February 8. http://stats.oecd.org/Index.aspx?DataSetCode=EO93 _FLASHFILE_EO93.

———. 2013b. "Income Distribution and Poverty." OECD. Stat Extracts. http://stats.oecd.org/index.aspx?DataSetCode=IDD.

———. 2013c. "Incidence of Involuntary Part Time Workers." http://stats .oecd.org/Index.aspx?DatasetCode=INVPT_I.

———. 2013d. "OECD: Stat Extracts." http://stats.oecd.org/. Accessed January 1, 2014.

———. 2014. "Central Government Debt." OECD.Stat Extracts. http:// stats.oecd.org/index.aspx?queryid-8089.

Office of the United States Trade Representative. 2013a. "Free Trade Agreements." www.ustr.gov/trade-agreements/free-trade -agreements.

———. 2013b. "Negotiations for the Transatlantic Trade and Investment Partnership Have Begun." Press release, July 8. www.ustr.gov /about-us/press-office/blog/2013/july/ TTIP-negotiations-begin.

———. 2013c. "The United States in the Trans-Pacific Partnership." Online fact sheet. www.ustr.gov/about-us/press-office/fact-sheets /2011/november/united-states-trans-pacific-partnership.

Olson-Sawyer, Kai. 2012. "Really? Shale Gas Fracking Uses a Lot of Water? Really!" Grace Communications Foundation. April 3. www.gracelinks .org/blog/901/really-shale-gas-fracking-uses-a-lot-of-water-really.

Ortiz, Isabel, and Matthew Cummins. 2013. *The Age of Austerity: A Review of Public Expenditures and Adjustment Measures in 181 Countries.* New York: Initiative for Policy Dialogue. Geneva: The South Centre.

Oxfam. 2012. "Our Land, Our Lives: Time Out on the Global Land Rush." Oxfam Briefing Note. October.

Pager, Devah, Bruce Western, and Bart Bonikowski. 2009. "Discrimination in a Low-Wage Labor Market: A Field Experiment." Discussion paper No. 4469. Institute for the Study of Labor, Bonn.

Palmer, Lisa. 2013. "Q and A: The Angry Economist." *Green: A Blog about Energy and the Environment. New York Times.* March 1.

Palmer, M. A., E. S. Bernhardt, W. H. Schlesinger, K. N. Eshleman, E. FouFoula-Georgiu, M. S. Hendryx, A. D. Lemly, G. E. Likens, O.L Loucks, M. E. Power, P. S. White, and P. R. Wilcock. 2010. "Mountaintop Mining Consequences." *Science* 327: 148–149.

Papademetriou, D., and A. Terrazas. 2009. "Immigrants and the Current Economic Crisis: Research Evidence, Policy Challenges, and Implications," Migration Policy Institute, Washington, DC.

Parenti, Christian. 2008. *Lockdown America.* London: Verso.

Paris, Costas, Matina Stevis, and Stelios Bouros. 2012. "Eurozone Meets on New Greek Aid Deal." *Dow Jones Financial News.* February 9.

Patoski, Joe Nick. 2011. "Water Policy in Legislature Rode on One Word." *New York Times,* June 9.

Patterson, Scott. 2013. "Dark Pools Face Scrutiny." *Wall Street Journal.* http://online.wsj.com/news/articles/SB10001424127887324069104578527361102049152. Accessed November 25, 2013.

Pender, James S. 2008a. "Community-Led Adaptation in Bangladesh." *Forced Migration Review* 31: 54–55.

———. 2008b. "What Is Climate Change? And How It Will Affect Bangladesh?" Briefing paper. Church of Bangladesh Social Development Programme, Dhaka.

Penn, Ivan. 2008. "The Profits on Water Are Huge, but the Raw Material Is Free." *Tampa Bay Times.* March 16.

Peralta, Eyder. 2011. "Pa. Judge Sentenced to 28 Years in Massive Juvenile Justice Bribery Scandal." National Public Radio. August 11.

Perlez, Jane, and Kirk Johnson. 2005. "Behind Gold's Glitter: Torn Lands and Pointed Questions." *New York Times.* October 24.

Pettit, Kathryn L. S., and Kim Rueben. 2012. "Investor-Owners in the Boom and Bust." MetroTrends. www.metrotrends.org/Commentary/mortgage-lending.cfm. Accessed July 13, 2012.

Pew Center on the States. 2008. *One in 100: Behind Bars in America 2008*. Washington, DC: Pew Charitable Trusts.

———. 2009. *One in 31: The Long Reach of American Corrections*. Washington, DC: Pew Charitable Trusts.

———. 2010. *Prison Count 2010: State Population Declines for the First Time in 38 Years*. Washington, DC: Pew Charitable Trusts.

Phillips, Jonathan D. 2004. "Impacts of Surface Mine Valley Fills on Headwater Floods in Eastern Kentucky." *Environmental Geology* 45, no. 3: 367–380.

Pilkington, Ed. 2008. "The Village at the Tip of the Iceberg." *Guardian*. September 27.

Pino, Isaac, Charlie Kannel, and Tom Gardner. 2012. "How Dow Chemical Can End the Tragedy in Bhopal." *Motley Fool*. July 27.

Pistor, Katharina. 2002. "The Standardization of Law and Its Effect on Developing Economies." *The American Journal of Comparative Law* 50, no. 1: 97–130.

PMEL. 2012. Hawaii Carbon Dioxide Time Series. PMEL Carbon Program, National Oceanic and Atmospheric Administration, Washington, DC.

Porter, Lynn. 2004. "Introduction to Hanford Issues." Hanford Watch. www.hanfordwatch.org/introduction.htm. Accessed January 9, 2013.

Portes, Alejandro. 2010. *Economic Sociology: A Systematic Inquiry*. Princeton, NJ: Princeton University Press.

Pouiller, Francisca. 2010. "Doe Run Workers Protest to Demand Smelter Reopen." Miningweekly.com. June 14.

Powley, Tanya, and Lucy Warwick-Ching. 2012. "Stateless and Super-rich." *Financial Times*. April 28.

Poynter, Bilbo. 2012. "Private Prison Companies Look to Canada as Industry Faces Lawsuits in US." *Guardian*. June 19.

"Prison Population Around the Globe." 2008. [Graphic.] *New York Times*. April 22.

Prison Reform Trust. 2013. "Background to Private Prisons." www.prisonreformtrust.org.uk/ProjectsResearch/Privatesectorprisons. Accessed Jan. 4, 2013.

Productschap Margerine, Vetten en Oliën. 2011. "Fact Sheet Palm Oil." www.mvo.nl/LinkClick.aspx?fileticket=jsFVMZwZzkc%3D. Accessed June 27, 2013.

Provost, Claire. 2012. "New International Land Deals Database Reveals Rush to Buy up Africa." *Guardian*. April 27.

Public Citizen. 2013. "On Anniversary of U.S.-Korea FTA Implementation, U.S. Exports Down 9 Percent, Imports from Korea Up and
Deficit with Korea Swells 30 Percent, Undermining Obama Export
and Job Growth Goals." Press release. March 14. www.citizen.org
/documents/press-release-korea-fta-one-year-anniversary.pdf.

Public Services International Research Unit. 2005a. *Prison Privatisation
Report International*. Report no. 67, March/April. Public Services
International Research Unit, University of Greenwich.

———. 2005b. *Prison Privatisation Report International*. Report no. 68,
May/June. Public Services International Research Unit, University of
Greenwich.

———. 2005c. *Prison Privatisation Report International*. Report no. 69,
July/August. Public Services International Research Unit, University
of Greenwich.

———. 2005d. *Prison Privatisation Report International*. Report no. 70,
Sept./Oct. Public Services International Research Unit, University of
Greenwich.

Putzel, Louis, Samuel Assembe-Mvondo, Laurentine Bilogo Bi Ndong,
Reine Patrick Banioguila, Paolo Cerutti, Julius Chupezi Tieguhong,
Robinson Djeukam, Noël Kabuyaya, Guillaume Lescuyer, and
William Mala. 2011. "Chinese Trade and Investment and the
Forests of the Congo Basin: Synthesis of Scoping Studies in Camer-
oon, Democratic Republic of Congo and Gabon." Working paper
no. 67. Center for International Forestry Research, Bogor,
Indonesia.

Quijano, Aníbal. 2007. "Coloniality and Modernity/Rationality." *Cultural
Studies* 21, nos. 2–3: 168–178.

Ramesh, Randeed. 2009. "Bhopal Water Still Toxic 25 Years After Deadly
Gas Leak, Study Finds." *Guardian*. December 1.

Ravanera, Roel R., and Vanessa Gorra. 2011. *Commercial Pressures on
Land in Asia: An Overview*. Rome: International Land Coalition.

Rawat, Vidya Bhushan, Mamidi Bharath Bhushan, and Sujatha Surepally.
2011. *The Impact of Special Economic Zones in India: A Case Study
of Polepally SEZ*. Rome: International Land Coalition.

Ray, M. K. 2013. "The Water Grab on the Augustin Plains." Sierra Club.
http://southern.nmsierraclub.org/water-grab-on-the-augustin-plains.
Accessed November 22, 2013.

RealtyTrac. 2007. "More than 1.2 Million Foreclosure Filings Reported
in 2006." February 8. www.realtytrac.com/content/press-releases

/more-than-12-million-foreclosure-filings-reported-in-2006-2234. Accessed July 17, 2012.

———. 2008. "U.S. Foreclosure Activity Increases 75 Percent in 2007." January 30. www.realtytrac.com/content/press-releases/us-foreclo sure-activity-increases-75-percent-in-2007-3604. Accessed July 17, 2012.

———. 2009. "2008 Year-End Foreclosure Market Report." February 5. www.realtytrac.com/content/news-and-opinion/2008-year-end -foreclosure-market-report-4621. Accessed July 17, 2012.

———. 2011. "Record 2.9 Million U.S. Properties Receive Foreclosure Filings in 2010 Despite 30-Month Low in December." January 12. www.realtytrac.com/content/foreclosure-market-report/record-29 -million-us-properties-receive-foreclosure-filings-in-2010-despite-30 -month-low-in-december-6309. Accessed July 17, 2012.

———. 2012a. "February 2012 U.S. Foreclosure Market Report: Foreclo sure Tide Rising in Half of Largest Metro Areas." March 13. www .realtytrac.com/content/foreclosure-market-report/february-2012-us -foreclosure-market-report-7069. Accessed July 13, 2012.

———. 2012b. "Foreclosure Trends." www.realtytrac.com/trendcenter. Accessed July 28, 2012.

———. 2013a. "All-Cash and Institutional Investor Purchases down from Year Ago in June but Short Sales Continue to Increase." www .realtytrac.com/content/foreclosure-market-report/us-residential-sales -report-june-2013-7812. Accessed August 3, 2013.

———. 2013b. "Single Family Home Flipping Increases 19 Percent in First Half of 2013 While Profits Soar." www.realtytrac.com/content /foreclosure-market-report/us-residential-sales-report-june-2013 -7812. Accessed August 3, 2013.

Reich, Robert B. 2011. *Aftershock: The Next Economy and America's Future.* New York: Vintage.

Reuters. 2013. "PNG Government Takes Full Ownership of Ok Tedi Mine." http://www.reuters.com/article/2013/09/19/png-oktedi -idUSL3N0HF0VC20130919. Accessed January 4, 2014.

Right to Water and Sanitation. 2010. "Case against Coca-Cola Kerala State: India." August 20. www.righttowater.info/ways-to-influence /legalapproaches/case-against-coca-cola-kerala-state-india. Accessed January 9, 2013.

Rignot, E., I. Velicogna, M. R. van den Broeke, A. Monaghan, and J. T. M. Lenaerts. 2011. "Acceleration of the Contribution of the Greenland

and Antarctic Ice Sheets to Sea Level Rise." *Geophysical Research Letters* 38, no. 5: L05503.

Robles, Frances. 2007. "Pollution Sickens Children in Dominican Republic." *Miami Herald*. March 13.

Rodriguez, Michelle Natividad, and Maurice Emsellem. 2011. *65 Million "Need Not Apply": The Case for Reforming Criminal Background Checks for Employment.* National Employment Law Project, New York.

Rogers, Simon, and Lisa Evans. 2011. "World Carbon Dioxide Emissions Data by Country: China Speeds Ahead of the Rest." *Guardian*. January 31.

Romm, Joe. 2011. "Shale Shocked: 'Highly Probable' Fracking Caused U.K. Earthquakes, and It's Linked to Oklahoma Temblors." Think Progress. http://thinkprogress.org/climate/2011/11/02/360014/shale -fracking-earthquakes. Accessed June 26, 2013.

Roth, Mitchel P. 2006. *Prisons and Prison Systems: A Global Encyclopedia.* Westport, CT: Greenwood, 2006.

Rothkopf, David J. 2009. *Superclass: The Global Power Elite and the World They Are Making.* New York: Farrar, Straus and Giroux.

Royal Tropical Institue. 2012. "Indonesia: Food Security and Land Governance Tenure." IS Academy on Land Governance for Equitable and Sustainable Development, Netherlands Ministry of Foreign Affairs, Amsterdam.

Rubio, Blanca. 2003. *Explotados y Excluidos: Los Campesinos Latino-americanos en la Fase Agroexportadora Neoliberal.* Mexico City: Plaza y Valdés, S.A. de C.V.

Ruditsky, Jake. 2004. "Toxic Felis: A Visit to Russia's Most Polluted City." *The Exile* (Moscow). June 24.

Rulli, Maria Cristina, Antonio Saviori, and Paolo D'Odorico. 2013. "Global Land and Water Grabbing." *Proceedings of the National Academy of Sciences of the United States* 110, no. 3: 892–897.

Rupp, D. E., P. W. Mote, N. Massey, C. J. Rye, and M. Allen. 2012. "Did Human Influence on Climate Make the 2011 Texas Drought More Probable?" *Bulletin of the American Meteorological Society* 93, no. 7 (July): 1053–1057.

Saez, Emmanuel. 2010. "Striking It Richer: The Evolution of Top Incomes in the United States (Updated with 2008 Estimates)." Department of Economics, University of California, Berkeley.

Salem-News. 2013. "US Energy Department Announces It Still Plans to Use Hanford as a National Radioactive Waste Dump." http://www

.salem-news.com/articles/december132013/hanford-waste.php.
Accessed January 5, 2014.

Samek, Kelly. 2004. "Unknown Quantity: The Bottled Water Industry and Florida's Springs." *Journal of Land Use* 19, no. 2: 569–595.

Sampaniotis, Theodosios. 2013. "Greek Real Estate Market: Prices and Activity Decline Escalates, Uncertainty Increases." *Eurobank*. http://www.eurobank.gr/Uploads/Reports/GREECE%20Macrofebruary%202013.pdf. Accessed January 1, 2014.

Sample, Ian. 2007. "Global Food Crisis Looms as Climate Change and Population Growth Strip Fertile Land." *Guardian*. August 31.

Sangham, A. S., and the Plachimada Struggle Solidarity Committee. 2010. "A Call to Struggle . . . for Water . . . for Life." *Kerala Letter* [blog]. http://keralaletter.blogspot.com/2010/01/call-to-strugglefor-waterfor-life.html. Accessed July 30, 2012.

Santer, B. D., K. E. Taylor, T. M. L. Wigley, J. E. Penner, P. D. Jones, and U. Cubasch. 1995. "Towards the Detection and Attribution of an Anthropogenic Effect on Climate." *Climate Dynamics* 12, no. 2: 77–100.

Santoso, Puji, and Jon Afrizal. 2004. "Two Killed, Five Injured in Riau Land Disputes." *Jakarta Post*. November 24.

Sassen, Saskia. 1988. *The Mobility of Labor and Capital: A Study in International Investment and Labor Flow*. Cambridge: Cambridge University Press.

———. 2001. *The Global City: New York, London, Tokyo*. Revised 2nd ed. Princeton, NJ: Princeton University Press.

———. 2008a. "A Bad Idea: Using a Financial Solution to the Financial Crisis." *Huffington Post*. November 20.

———. 2008b. "Mortgage Capital and Its Particularities: A New Frontier for Global Finance." *Journal of International Affairs* 62, no. 1: 187–212.

———. 2008c. *Territory, Authority, Rights: From Medieval to Global Assemblages*. 2nd ed. Princeton, NJ: Princeton University Press.

———. 2008d. "Two Stops in Today's New Global Geographies: Shaping Novel Labor Supplies and Employment Regimes." *American Behavioral Scientist* 52, no. 3: 457–496.

———. 2010. "A Savage Sorting of Winners and Losers: Contemporary Versions of Primitive Accumulation." *Globalizations* 7, no. 1: 23–50.

———. 2011a. *Cities in a World Economy*. Revised 4th edition. Thousand Oaks, CA: Sage/Pine Forge.

———. 2011b. "The Global Street: Making the Political." *Globalizations* 8, no. 5 (October): 565–571.

———. 2012. "Interactions of the Technical and the Social: Digital Formations of the Powerful and the Powerless." *Information, Communication & Society*. DOI:10.1080/1369118X.2012.667912.

———. 2013. "Global Finance and Its Institutional Spaces." In Karin Knorr Cetina and Alex Preda, eds., *The Oxford Handbook of the Sociology of Finance*. Oxford: Oxford University Press.

———. Forthcoming. *Ungoverned Territories*. Cambridge, MA: Harvard University Press.

Sassen, Saskia, and Natan Dotan. 2011. "Delegating, Not Returning, to the Biosphere: How to Use the Multi-scalar and Ecological Properties of Cities." *Global Environmental Change* 21, no. 3: 823–834.

Schuur, Edward A. G., and Benjamin Abbott. 2011. "Climate Change: High Risk of Permafrost Thaw." *Nature* 480: 32–33.

Schwartz, Mike. 2004. "Bottled Water Conflicts." Department of Geography, University of Wisconsin, Eau Claire.

Schwartzkopff, Frances. 2013. "Denmark Races to Prevent Foreclosures as Home Prices Sink." Bloomberg.com. March 18.

Scott, James C. 1999. *Seeing Like a State: How Certain Schemes to Improve the Human Condition Have Failed*. New Haven: Yale University Press.

Scott, Robert E. 2010. "Trade Policy and Job Loss." Working paper no. 289. Economic Policy Institute, Washington, DC.

———. 2012. "The China Toll: Growing U.S. Trade Deficit with China Cost More than 2.7 Million Jobs between 2001 and 2011, with Job Losses in Every State." Briefing paper #345, Economic Policy Institute, Washington, DC.

———. 2013. "No Jobs from Trade Pacts." Economic Policy Institute, Washington, D.C.

Seager, R., M. F. Ting, I. M. Held, Y. Kushnir, J. Lu, G. Vecchi, H.-P. Huang, N. Harnik, A. Leetmaa, N. C. Lau, C. Li, J. Velez, and N. Naik. 2007. "Model Projections of an Imminent Transition to a More Arid Climate in Southwestern North America." *Science* 316, no. 5828: 1181–1184.

"Sea Level." *The Guardian*. Guardian News and Media. http://www.theguardian.com/environment/sea-level.

SEC. 2013. "Release No. 34-68842." www.sec.gov/rules/sro/finra/2013/34-68842.pdf. Accessed November 25.

Selcraig, Bruce. 1998. "This Reclamation Plan Uses Waste to Bury Waste." *High County News* 122. January 19.

Sen, Amartya. 2000. *Development as Freedom*. New York: Anchor.

Sen, Arjun. 2003. "Heat on Cold Drinks." *Statesman*. August 12.

Sender, Henny Arash Massoudi, and Anjli Raval. 2013. "US Housing Groups to Launch IPOs." *Financial Times*. May 13.

Serrano, Fernando. 2008. "Environmental Contamination in the Homes of La Oroya and Concepcion and Its Effects in the Health of Community Residents." United Nations, Office of the High Commissioner for Human Rights, Geneva.

Shah, Shahid. 2009. "Corporate Farming Raises Concern among Local Growers." *The News (Pakistan)*. January 28.

Shepard, D. with M. Anuradha. 2010. *(Mis)Investment in Agriculture: The Role of the International Finance Corporation in the Global Land Grab*. Oakland Institute. http://www.oaklandinstitute.org/.

Sherman, Arloc, and Chad Stone. 2010. "Income Gaps Between Very Rich and Everyone Else More than Tripled in Last Three Decades, New Data Show." Center on Budget and Policy Priorities. June 25. Center on Budget and Policy Priorities, Washington, DC.

Shinn, Mary Beth. 2010. "Homelessness, Poverty, and Social Exclusion in the United States and Europe." *European Journal of Homelessness* 4 (2010).

Sierra Club: Southern New Mexico Group. 2013. "The Water Grab on the Augustin Plains." http://southern.nmsierraclub.org/water-grab-on -the-augustin-plains. Accessed November 22, 2013.

Sills, Ben, and Andre Tartar. 2013. "Spain Recession Seen Ending by 2014 as Austerity Eases." Bloomberg.com. June 13.

Smeeding, Timothy M. 2002. "Globalization, Inequality, and the Rich Countries of the G-20: Evidence from the Luxembourg Income (LIS)." Working paper no. 48. Center for Policy Research, http://dx .doi.org/10.2139/ssrn.1809030.

Smith, Jim. 2011. "A Long Shadow over Fukushima." *Nature* 472, no. 7 (April 5).

Smith, Merrill. 2004. "Warehousing Refugees: A Denial of Rights, a Waste of Humanity." In *World Refugee Survey 2004*. Arlington, VA: U.S. Committee for Refugees.

Smith, Yves. 2013. "New Whistleblower Describes How Bank of America Flagrantly Violates Dual Tracking, Single Point of Contact Requirements in State/Federal Mortgage Settlement." *Naked Capitalism* [blog], February 21.

Smyth, Sharon. 2013. "Spain Home Expropriation Plans Seen Violating EU Bailout." *Bloomberg Businessweek*. May 12.

Snyder, Howard N. 2011. "Arrest in the United States, 1980–2009." Bureau of Justice Statistics, U.S. Department of Justice. September 22.

Solomon, S., D. Qin, M. Manning, Z. Chen, M. Marquis, K. B. Averyt, M. Tignor, and H. L. Miller, eds. 2007. *Climate Change 2007: The Physical Science Basis*. Contribution of Working Group I to the Fourth Assessment Report of the Intergovernmental Panel on Climate Change. Cambridge: Cambridge University Press.

Stamatis, Georgios. 2012. "Homeless in Greece in the Current Financial Crisis: What Perspectives?" University of Athens. http://crisis.med .uoa.gr/elibrary/13.pdf.

Stiffarm, Dean L. 2005. "Community Involvement Conference and Training: The Zortman & Landusky Goldmines." Fort Belknap Indian Community–Environmental Department, Harlem, Montana. www.epancic.org/2005/download/presentations/ballroom_a/thu /stiffarm.pdf. Accessed January 9, 2013.

Stiglitz, Joseph E. 1999. *Freefall: Freemarkets and the Sinking of the Global Economy*. New York: W. W. Norton & Company.

———. 2012. *The Price of Inequality*. New York: W. W. Norton & Company.

———. 2013. "Globalisation Isn't Just about Profits. It's About Taxes Too." *The Guardian*, May 27. http://www.guardian.co.uk/comment isfree/2013/may/27/globalisation-is-about-taxes-too.

Stiglitz, Joseph E., and Mary Kaldor, eds. 2013. *The Quest for Security: Protection without Protectionism and the Challenge of Global Governance*. New York: Columbia University Press.

Stott, P. A. 2000. "External Control of 20th Century Temperature by Natural and Anthropogenic Forcings." *Science* 290, no. 5499: 2133–2137.

Stott, P. A., G. S. Jones, N. Christidis, F. Zwiers, G. Hegerl, and H. Shiogama. 2011. "Single-Step Attribution of Increasing Frequencies of Very Warm Regional Temperatures to Human Influence." *Atmospheric Science Letters* 12, no. 2: 220–227.

Stott, P. A., D. A. Stone, and M. R. Allen. 2004. "Human Contribution to the European Heatwave of 2003." *Nature* 432, no. 7017: 610–614.

Sudbury, Julia, ed. 2005. *Global Lockdown: Race, Gender, and the Prison-Industrial Complex*. New York: Routledge.

Summerill, Joseph. 2011. "Housing Federal Prisoners in Local Jails." Statement of Joseph Summerill Before the Committee on Appropriations: Commerce, Justice, Science, and Related Agencies. March 11.

Sutcliffe, Bob. 2004. "World Inequality and Globalization." *Oxford Review of Economic Policy* 20, no. 1: 15–37.

———. 2007. "Postscript to the Article 'World Inequality and Globalization.'" World Bank, Washington, DC.

Sydor, Guy. 2004. "The World's Highest Railroad." http://www.peruhotel.com/english/article.php3?idarticle=13. Accessed January 9, 2013.

Tagliabue, John. 2013. "Parts of Low Country Are Now Quake Country." *New York Times*. March 27.

Tarlock, Dan A. 2004. *Bottled Water: Legal Aspects of Groundwater Extraction.* Madison, Wisconsin: State Environmental Resource Center.

Tax Justice Network. 2011. "The Cost of Tax Abuse." November. www.tackletaxhavens.com/Cost_of_Tax_Abuse_TJN_Research_23rd_Nov_2011.pdf.

Teubal, Miguel. 2006. "Expansión del Modelo Sojero en la Argentina. De la Producción de Alimentos a los Commodities." *Realidad Económica.* No. 220.

Texas A&M University. 2013. "Texas Water Law." http://texaswater.tamu.edu/water-law. Accessed July 13, 2013.

Theodorikakou, O., A. Alamanou, et al. 2012. "Homelessness in Greece—2012: An In-Depth Research on Homelessness in the Financial Crisis." Klimaka NGO—Greece. European Research Conference: Access to Housing for Homeless People in Europe, York, September 21. www.slideshare.net/FEANTSA/seminar-3-klimaka.

Thompson, Derek. 2013. "Europe's Record Youth Unemployment: The Scariest Graph in the World Just Got Scarier." *Atlantic.* May.

Thompson, Mark. 2012. "Spanish Economy Shrinks Again." CNNMoney. October 23.

Townsend, P. K., and W. H. Townsend. 2004. "Assessing an Assessment: The Ok Tedi Mine." www.maweb.org/documents/bridging/papers/townsend.patricia.pdf.

Tsukimori, Osamu, and Nathan Layne. 2011. "Areas near Japan Nuclear Plant May Be Off Limits for Decades." Reuters. August 27.

UNCTAD. 2008. *World Investment Directory*, volume 10: *Africa.* New York: United Nations.

UNDP. 2005. *A Time for Bold Ambition: Together We Can Cut Poverty in Half: UNDP Annual Report*. New York: UNDP.

———. 2008. *Human Development Report 2007–2008*. New York: UNDP.

———. 2013. *Human Development Report 2013*. New York: UNDP.

UNEP/GRID. 2006. *Planet in Peril: An Atlas of Current Threats to People and the Environment*. Arendal, Norway: UNEP/GRID.

UNHCR. 2012a. *Global Trends 2011*. Geneva : United Nations High Commissioner for Refugees.

———. 2012b. "Annex Tables." *Global Trends 2011*. www.unhcr.org/pages/4fd9a0676.html. Accessed January 2, 2013.

UNICEF. 2012. "Progress on Drinking Water and Sanitation." www.unicef.org/media/files/JMPreport2012.pdf. Accessed June 18, 2013.

United Nations Framework Convention on Climate Change. 2013. "A Summary of the Kyoto Protocol." http://unfccc.int/kyoto_protocol/background/items/2879.php. Accessed June 18, 2013.

Urban, Rob, and Sharon Smyth. 2012. "Greek Banks Follow Euripides to Help Borrowers: Mortgages." *Bloomberg Businessweek*. July 26.

U.S. Committee for Refugees. 2009. *World Refugee Survey 2009*. Arlington, VA: U.S. Committee for Refugees.

U.S. Energy Information Administration. 2012a. "Assumptions to the Energy Outlook 2012: Coal Modual." www.eia.gov/forecasts/aeo/assumptions/pdf/coal.pdf. Accessed January 9, 2013.

———. 2012b. "Total Energy: Annual Energy Review." www.eia.gov/totalenergy/data/annual/showtext.cfm?t=ptb0701. Accessed January 9, 2013.

U.S. International Trade Commission. 2013. USITC Interactive Tariff and Trade DataWeb. Data for 2000–2013, year-to-date, April, downloaded June 21 via spreadsheet. http://dataweb.usitc.gov/.

Van Lynden, G. W. J. 2004. "European and World Soils: Present Situation and Expected Evolution." *Proceedings of I International Conference: Soil and Compost Eco-biology, León, Spain*.

van Onselen, Leith. 2013. "Three Headwinds for the US Housing Recovery." *MacroBusiness*. www.macrobusiness.com.au/2013/07/factors-that-may-thwart-the-us-housing-recovery. Accessed August 3, 2013.

Varchaver, Nicholas, and Katie Benner. 2008. "The $55 Trillion Question." CNN Money. September 30.

Vergano, Dan. 2007. "Climate Change Threatens New Dust Bowl in Southwest." *USA Today*. April 6.

Vermeulen, Sonja, and Nathalie Goad. 2006. *Towards Better Practice in Smallholder Palm Oil Production*. Natural Resources Issues Series 5. London: IIED.

Vidal, John. 2012. "Chinese Food Security May Be Motivating Investments in Africa." *Guardian*. May 10.

Viñas, Maria-José. 2012. "Satellites See Unprecedented Greenland Ice Sheet Surface Melt." NASA. www.nasa.gov/topics/earth/features /greenland-melt.html. Accessed July 30, 2012.

Visser, Oane, and Max Spoor. 2011. "Land Grabbing in Post-Soviet Eurasia: The World's Largest Agricultural Land Reserves at Stake." *Journal of Peasant Studies* 38, no. 2: 299–323.

von Braun, Joachim. 2008. "Food and Financial Crises: Implications for Agriculture and the Poor." *Washington DC: International Food Policy Research Institute (IFPRI) Food Policy Report* 20. http://www .ifpri.org/PUBS/agm08/jvbagm2008.asp.

von Braun, Joachim, Akhter Ahmed, Kwadwo Asenso-Okyere, Shenggen Fan, Ashok Gulati, John Hoddinott, Rajul Pandya-Lorch, Mark W. Rosegrant, Marie Ruel, Maximo Torero, Teunis van Rheenen, and Klaus von Grebmer. 2008. "High Food Prices: The What, Who, and How of Proposed Policy Actions." *Washington DC, International Food Policy Research Institute (IFPRI) Policy Brief*. http://www.ifpri .org/pubs/ib/foodprices.asp.

von Braun, Joachim, and Ruth Meinzen-Dick. 2009. "'Land Grabbing' by Foreign Investors in Developing Countries: Risks and Opportunities." *Washington DC: International Food Policy Research Institute (IFPRI) Policy Brief* 13. http://www.ifpri.org/publication/land -grabbing-foreign-investors-developing-countries.

Voyant Solutions Pvt. Ltd. 2009. "Final Report for City Corporation cum Business Plan for Ranipet Town." 2009. http://municipality.tn.gov.in /ranipet/Ranipet.pdf. Accessed January 9, 2013.

Wagenhofer, Erwin. 2005. *We Feed the World*. Allegro Film Produktions-firma GmbH. www.youtube.com/watch?v=qyAzxmN2s0w. Accessed June 18, 2013.

Wald, Matthew L. 2010. "Analysis Triples U.S. Plutonium Waste Figures." *New York Times*. July 11.

Walmsley, R. 2011. *World Population List*, 9th ed. Essex: International Centre for Prison Studies

Walsh, Bryan. 2007. "Dzerzhinsk, Russia." The World's Most Polluted Places. *Time*. www.time.com/time/specials/2007/article/0,28804
,1661031_1661028_1661021,00.html. Accessed January 9, 2013.

Warner, Koko, Olivia Dun, and Marc Stal. 2008. "Field Observations and
Empirical Research." *Forced Migration Review* 31: 13–15.

Warnock, Veronica Cacdac, and Francis E. Warnock. 2008. "Markets and
Housing Finance." Social Science Research Network. http://papers
.ssrn.com/sol3/papers.cfm?abstract_id=981641. Accessed July 28,
2012.

———. 2012. "Developing Housing Finance Systems." Reserve Bank of
Australia Annual Conference Volume pp. 49–67. http://www.rba.gov
.au/publications/confs/2012/pdf/warnock-warnock.pdf. Accessed
January 8, 2014.

Warren, L. H. 1940. "Leather Buffers' Nodes." *Journal of the American
Medical Association* 114, no. 7 (February 17): 571.

Washington State Department of Ecology. 2008. "Hanford Quick Facts."
http://web.archive.org/web/20080624232748/http://www.ecy.wa.gov
/features/hanford/hanfordfacts.html.

———. 2013. "Ecology Statement on Notification of More at Risk
Consent Decree Milestones." http://www.ecy.wa.gov/programs/nwp
/sections/tankwaste/twtreatment/pages/20131008_statement.html.
Accessed January 5, 2014.

Wassener, Bettina. 2011. "Raising Awareness of Plastic Waste." *New York
Times*. August 14.

Watkins, Thayer. 2013. "The Chaebol of South Korea." San Jose State
University faculty webpage, www.sjsu.edu/ faculty/watkins/chaebol
.-htm.

Wellington Water Watchers. 2011. "Nestlé Waters Canada, Permit to Take
Water." www.wellingtonwaterwatchers.ca/nestle-waters-canada
-permit-to-take-water/. Accessed November 23, 2013.

Western, Bruce, and Becky Pettit. 2010. "Incarceration & Social Inequality." *Daedalus,* Summer 2010.

White, Alan. 2013. "Foreclosure Crisis in Europe vs US." Credit Slips: A
Discussion on Credit, Finance, and Bankruptcy. www.creditslips.org
/creditslips/2011/08/foreclosure-crisis-in-europe-vs-us.html. Accessed
February 8, 2013.

White, Ben, Saturnino M. Borras Jr., Ruth Hall, Ian Scoones, and Wendy
Wolford. "The New Enclosures: Critical Perspectives on Corporate
Land Deals." *Journal of Peasant Studies* 39, nos. 3–4: 619–647.

White House. 2010. "The U.S.-South Korea Free Trade Agreement: More American Jobs, Faster Economic Recovery Through Exports" (fact sheet). www.whitehouse.gov/ sites/default/files/fact_sheet_overview _us_korea_free_trade_ agreement.pdf.

WHO. 2005. "Chernobyl: The True Scale of the Accident." World Health Organization, Geneva.

———. 2010. "Dioxins and Their Effect on Human Health." World Health Organization, Geneva.

Wiener Bravo, E. 2011. "The Concentration of Land Ownership in Latin America: An Approach to Current Problems." CISEPA contribution to ILC Collaborative Research Project on Commercial Pressures on Land. Rome: ILC.

Wigley, T., and B. Santer. 2012. "A Probabilistic Quantification of the Anthropogenic Component of Twentieth Century Global Warming." *Climate Dynamics*.

Williams, Laura. 2012. *Housing Landscape 2012*. National Housing Conference, Washington, DC.

Wolman, David. 2006. "Train to the Roof of the World." *Wired* 14, no. 7 (July).

World Bank. 2005. "Increasing Aid and Its Effectiveness." In *Global Monitoring Report: Millennium Development Goals: From Consensus to Momentum*, 151–188. Washington, DC: World Bank.

———. 2006. *Global Economic Prospects 2006: Economic Implications of Remittances and Migration*. Washington, DC: World Bank.

———. 2008. *Global Monitoring Report 2008*. Washington, DC: World Bank.

———2012. *Turn Down the Heat: Why a 4° Warmer World Must Be Avoided*. Washington, DC: World Bank.

———. 2013a. "Europe and Central Asia Housing Finance Crisis Prevention and Resolution: A Review of Policy Options." Working paper no. 78346. World Bank, Washington, DC.

———. 2013b. *Turn Down the Heat: Climate Extremes, Regional Impacts, and the Case for Resilience*. Washington, DC: World Bank.

———. 2013c. "GDP Per Capita (Current US$)." http://data.worldbank. org/indicator/NY.GDP.PCAP.CD?page=1. Accessed January 1, 2014.

World Food Programme. 2013. "10 Things You Need to Know about Hunger in 2013." World Food Programme, Rome.

World Nuclear Association. 2012. "Chernobyl Accident 1986." www.world -nuclear.org/info/chernobyl/inf07.html. Accessed January 9, 2013.

Wyly, Elvin, Markus Moos, Daniel Hammel, and Emanuel Kabahizi.
2009. "Cartographies of Race and Class: Mapping the Class-
Monopoly Rents of American Subprime Mortgage Capital." *International Journal of Urban and Regional Research* 33, no. 2 (June):
332–354.

Xing, Yuqing. 2010. "Facts About and Impacts of FDI on China and
the World Economy." *China: An International Journal* 8, no. 2:
309–327.

Yusuf, Hamid. 2012. "Land Administration System in Indonesia." Paper
presented at the 17th ASEAN Valures Association Congress. www
.aseanvaluers.org/PDF/Land%20Administration%20System%20in
%20Indonesia.pdf. Accessed July 1, 2013.

Zarchin, Tomer. 2009. "International Legal Precedent: No Private Prisons
in Israel." *Haaretz.* November 9.

Zeiss, Geoff. 2011. "Large Water Diversion Projects, Environmental
Impact and Convergence." *Between the Poles: All about Infrastructure*
[blog]. http://geospatial.blogs.com/geospatial/2011/03/large-water
-diversion-projects-and-the-environment.html. Accessed June 30,
2013.

Zoomers, A. 2010. "Globalisation and the Foreignisation of Space: Seven
Processes Driving the Current Global Land Grab." *Journal of Peasant
Studies* 37, no. 2 (April): 429–447.

Zuber, Helen. 2012. "Mortgage Nightmares: Evictions Become Focus of
Spanish Crisis." *Der Spiegel.* December 22.

Notes

1. Shrinking Economies, Growing Expulsions

1. Sassen 2008a; 2008b; 2008c, chapters 4 and 7; 2013.
2. Oxfam 2012, 1–2; see also Atkinson et al. 2011.
3. IMF 2012a, 82; Johnston 2013 on U.S. corporations.
4. Sassen 2008c, chapter 5.
5. Sassen 2001, chapter 8; Sassen 2011.
6. Sassen 1988.
7. Johnston 2005, 2013; GAO 2013; CNNMoney Staff 2013.
8. Johnston 2013 writes that a July 1, 2013, report to Congress suggests the rate on large profitable firms may be even lower than what is shown in publicly available IRS data. The 2010 net tax rate was really just 12.6 percent, according to the Government Accountability Office—the investigative arm of Congress—which had access to secret documents.
9. Large corporate firms do extensive lobbying for laws and regulatory rules that get little or no attention in the mainstream news. GE spent $39.3 million just on Washington lobbying in 2010, more than $73,000 per senator and representative. ExxonMobil has spent on average almost $23 million annually lobbying Washington between 2008 and 2010. Walmart has spent between $6.2 million and $7.8 million lobbying Washington each year since 2008. See also Mishel 2013.
10. Tax Justice Network 2011.
11. For a short description of the report, see Johnston 2011; Isidore 2012.
12. Sassen 2008c, chapter 5; 2013.
13. Kubiszewski et al. 2013.
14. Ortiz and Cummins 2013; see also Samir Amin 2010; Portes 2010.

15. This is a whole subject in itself, with a rapidly growing research litera-ture (for one of the most comprehensive treatments, see Bryson and Daniels 2007). It is impossible to develop the subject here beyond a few summary statements (for a detailed discussion and extensive list of sources see Sassen 2001, chapters 5 and 6, and Sassen 2013; see also Sassen 2012 on digital technology). In my reading, the growth in the demand for service inputs, and especially bought service inputs, in all industries is perhaps the most fundamental condition making for change in advanced economies. One measure can be found in the value of bought service inputs in all industries. For this purpose I analyzed the national accounts data over different periods—beginning with 1960—for several industries in manufacturing and services. For in-stance, the results showed clearly that this value increased markedly over time. It has had pronounced impacts on the earnings distribution, on industrial organization, and on the patterns along which economic growth has spatialized. It has contributed to a massive growth in the demand for services by firms in all industries, from mining and manu-facturing to finance and consumer services, and by households, both rich and poor.

16. For instance, data analyzed by Smeeding (2002) for twenty-five devel-oped and developing countries showed that since 1973 the incomes of those in the top 5 percent have risen by nearly 50 percent, while in-comes of those in the bottom 5 percent have declined by approximately 4 percent. According to the U.S. Bureau of the Census, from 1970 to 2003 the aggregate national income share of the top 5 percent in the United States went from 16 to 21 percent, and for the top 20 percent from 41 percent to 48 percent. All these figures will tend to underesti-mate inequality insofar as the top earners also have non-salary-based gains in wealth, and the bottom of the scale tends to exclude many of the poor who lack any source of income and are dependent on friends and family, or become homeless and dependent on charities.

17. Mishel 2007; Stiglitz 2012; Fisher 2011.

18. Sassen 2001; Sassen 2011.

19. The key sources for the data discussed in this section are Atinc et al. 2006; World Bank 2013c; Stiglitz 2012; Held and Kaya 2007; Mila-novic 2005, 2011; Arestis, Sobreira, and Oreiro 2011; Sutcliffe 2004, 2007; OECD 2008, 2011; Saez 2010; FRED 2013; Bourguignon and Morrison 2002.

20. Milanovic 2011; Atinc et al. 2006.

21. Atinc et al. 2006, 64.
22. Economic Policy Institute 2011a, 2011b, 2011c, 2011d, 2011e, 2011f, 2011g; EPI 2013.
23. Mishel and Bivens 2011.
24. Economic Policy Institute 2008.
25. Mishel and Bivens 2011; Allegretto 2011.
26. Mishel and Bivens 2011; Allegretto 2011.
27. Sources for the following discussion can be found at BBC News 2012; Paris, Stevos, and Bouros 2012; Inman and Smith 2012; Bensasson 2013; Blackstone et al. 2012; Lima 2013; Greece 2013; Hope 2013.
28. ILO 2012; ILO and OECD 2013, 5 and Figure 3; Eurojobs 2012.
29. ILO and OECD 2013, figure 2, Panel C; see also OECD 2013b, 2013c.
30. Inman and Smith 2012; Nellas 2013; Bakalidou 2013.
31. Portugal, Spain, and Ireland have far more private sector debt than Greece. As a result, while government debt in Portugal is less than that of Greece, relative to GDP, total debt (including private sector debt) is actually larger. See generally OECD 2011, 2008.
32. Data for this section can be found at Davies 2012; Day 2013; Sills and Tartar 2013; Thompson 2012; and "Wrong Way" [graphic], *Wall Street Journal,* available at http://si.wsj.net/public/resources/images/ WO-AI754B_EUECO_G_20120214184204.jpg.
33. According to a June 2013 Eurostat press release, GDP fell by 0.2 percent in the euro area (EA17) and by 0.1 percent in the European Union (EU27) during the first quarter of 2013, compared with the previous quarter (Eurostat 2013a).
34. Further information for this section can be found in Thompson 2013; Instituto Nacional de Estadística 2011, 2013a, 2013b; and OECD. Stat Extracts, http://stats.oecd.org/Index.aspx?DatasetCode=INVPT _I; Bolanos 2012.
35. Instituto Nacional de Estadística 2011, see also European commission 2012; Burgen 2013.
36. Papademetriou and Terrazas 2009.
37. Immigrants' mobility contrasts with the immobility of natives, and provides evidence to support prevailing theories on the relatively limited migration across EU member states (see Favell 2008; OECD 2013c, 2013d).
38. Daley 2010; Zuber 2012; European Commission 2011.
39. In this report "default rates refer to the percentage of mortgage loans over 90 days in arrears in relation to outstanding mortgage loans in a

Member State, unless otherwise indicated. Data relates to the total number of contracts in default to the total number of outstanding contracts, unless otherwise indicated" (Instituto Nacional de Estadística 2011, 12). See also Smyth 2013; Karaian 2013; Sampaniotis 2013.

40. Eurostat 2012a; see also Eurostat 2012b, 2013b, 2013c. Looking at each of the three elements contributing to being at risk of poverty or social exclusion, 17 percent of the population in the EU-27 in 2011 were at risk of poverty even after social transfers. The highest rates of being at risk of poverty were observed in Bulgaria, Romania, and Spain (all 22 percent) and Greece (21 percent), and the lowest in the Czech Republic (10 percent), the Netherlands (11 percent), Austria, Denmark, and Slovakia (each 13 percent). It is important to note that risk of poverty is a relative measure and that the poverty threshold varies greatly among EU member states. The threshold varies also over time, and it has fallen in recent years in a number of member states due to the economic crisis.

41. As regards the indicator on low work intensity, 10 percent of the population under age fifty-nine in the EU-27 lived in households where the adults worked less than 20 percent of their total work potential during the past year. Belgium (14 percent) had the largest proportion of those living in very low work intensity households, and Cyprus (5 percent) the lowest.

42. See Shinn 2010 and, generally, FEANTSA 2011.

43. EuroHealthNet 2011. Most suicides, attempted and real, have occurred in the greater Attica region (surrounding Athens) and on the island of Crete (where a number of businessmen with no prior history of mental illness took their own lives over a period of eighteen months). Another increase concerns rates of substance use among Greece's homeless population, which has worsened public health crises such as HIV/AIDS. See Ghosh 2013; Klimaka 2012; Stamatis 2012.

44. See UNHCR 2012b for a glossary of the UNHCR categories of displaced peoples.

45. Smith 2004; see also Hovil 2010; Long 2010; Kaiser 2010.

46. Brothers 2011; UNHCR 2012a, 2012b.

47. Besides UNHCR reports, the sources for this section on the environmental aspect are Calhoun 2004; Pender 2008a; Leckie et al. 2011; Warner, Dun, and Stal 2008.

48. Warner, Dun, and Stal 2008, 13 (emphasis added).

49. While this section largely examines how imprisonment functions as a force of expulsion, it is worth noting that the language of "banish-

ment" has been deployed in recent times by mayors and police chiefs alike when trying to advance exclusionary carceral policy. In the summer of 2012, the mayor of Toronto was trying to figure out a way to banish people with gun charges from the city, including using immigration deportation laws. Justifying the proposal, he explained, "I don't care if you're white, pink or purple. I don't care what country you're from. I don't care if you're a Canadian citizen or not. All I'm saying is if you're caught with a gun and convicted of a gun crime, I want you out of this city" (CBC 2012a, 2012b). In January 2013, the police chief of Atlanta, Georgia, proposed a similar banishment policy, this time for anyone with two or more prostitution convictions (Diggs 2013).

50. Sources for this section on privatization of prisons: United States, Guerino, Harrison, and Sabol 2012; Mexico, McCleskey 2012; New Zealand, Cheng 2012; Peru, Associated Press 2010; South Africa, eAfrica 2005; United Kingdom, Her Majesty's Prison Service n.d. See also Nigeria Intel 2012; Home Office 2012; Moir 2013; Zarchin 2009; Sudbury 2005; Prison Population around the Globe 2008; Prison Reform Trust 2013.

51. Sources for this section are Pew Center on the States 2008, 2009; Rodriguez and Emsellem 2011; National Prisoner Statistics Program 2013; Parenti 2008; Pager et al. 2009; Herivel and Wright 2003; Gilmore 2007; Western and Pettit 2010.

52. Walmsley 2011; Roth 2006; Snyder 2011; Alexander 2010; Amin 2012.

53. A team of reporters at the Times Picayune established these numbers. The full eight-part series is available online at www.nola.com/prisons/. See also Chang 2012, "In World of Prisons, Some Rural Parishes' Economies Hinge on Keeping Their Jails Full," www.nola.com/crime/index.ssf/2012/05/in_world_of_prisons_some_rural.html; www.opensocietyfoundations.org/sites/default/files/socioeconomic-impact-pretrial-detention-02012011.pdf.

54. This section on privatized prisons in the United States uses findings and data examined in McDonald 1992; Harding 2001; Austin and Coventry 2001; Mason 2012; Kirkham 2012.

55. This section is based on McTighe 2012, 2013; Public Services International Research Unit 2005a, 2005b, 2005c, 2005d; Peralta 2011.

56. Sassen 2008c, chapter 4.

57. Peralta 2011.

58. On use of prisoners as exceptionally low-wage work camps, see Federal
Bureau of Prisons n.d.; McCormack 2012; Summerill 2011. See also the
Times-Picayune's 2012 eight-part series on incarceration in Louisiana,
"How We Built the World's Prison Capital," at www.nola.com/prisons.

2. The New Global Market for Land

1. This is a subject I examine in *Ungoverned Territories* (forthcoming). On
contracts see Cotula and Tienhaara 2013; Margulis et al. 2013; Pistor
2012; Shephard and Anuradha 2010; IFPRI 2009; Zoomers 2010.
2. I provide a detailed critical account of these various policies and the
literatures they have engendered in Sassen 1988, 2001, 2010.
3. Sassen 1988. For broader historical accounts see Bertola and Ocampo
2013; Chatterjee 2011; Quijano 2007; Scott 1999; Landes 1999; Rubio
2003; McMichael 2009; White et al. 2012.
4. See Sassen 2008c, chapters 1, 8, and 9 for a development of the theo-
retical, methodological, and historical aspects.
5. This section is based on a larger research project (Sassen 2008d) that
seeks to show how the struggles by individuals, households, entrepre-
neurs, and even governments are micro-level enactments of larger processes of economic restructuring in developing countries launched by
the IMF and World Bank Programs, as well as in WTO law implementation during the 1990s and onward.
6. By 2003, debt service as a share of exports only (not overall government revenue) ranged from extremely high levels for Zambia (29.6 percent) and Mauritania (27.7 percent) to significantly lowered levels
compared with the 1990s for Uganda (down from 19.8 percent in
1995 to 7.1 percent in 2003) and Mozambique (down from 34.5 percent in 1995 to 6.9 percent in 2003).
7. Jubilee Debt Campaign 2012, 2013.
8. UNDP 2005, 2008, 2013; see also Ferreira and Walton 2005.
9. For overviews of the data, see UNDP 2005, 2008; World Bank 2005;
Atinc et al. 2006, 2013; Attinc et al. 2006; Behrman et al. 2011; Lucas
2005; Sassen 2008d, 2010.
10. Land Matrix, landmatrix.org (accessed July 29, 2012); Anseeuw, Wily,
et al. 2012; Anseeuw, Boche, et al. 2012. See also DeSchutter 2011; FAO
2009; Cotula et al. 2009; Borras and Franco 2012; IFPR 2011; Margulis et al. 2013; on particular legal aspects see Pistor 2012.
11. See also Provost 2012; Xing 2010.

12. GRAIN 2012.
13. HighQuest Partners 2010.
14. Aabø and Kring 2012, 2.
15. Oxfam 2012, 1.
16. Murphy 2013, 5.
17. Ravanera and Gorra 2011.
18. Hall 2011 and Cotula et al. 2009. Beyond Africa, see Visser and Spoor 2011; Novo et al. 2010; Shah 2009; Teubal 2006.
19. Cotula 2011; Ravanera and Gorra 2011.
20. Wiener Bravo 2011.
21. Molnar et al. 2011.
22. Ibid.
23. Putzel et al. 2011.
24. Colchester 2011.
25. For Benin, see Dossou et al. 2011; for India, see Rawat, Bhushan, and Surepally 2011.
26. Bräutigam and Tang 2011.
27. According to Rulli, Saviori, and D'Odorico 2013, "about 0.31×10^{12} m^3/yr of green water (i.e., rainwater) and up to 0.14×10^{12} m^3/yr of blue water (i.e., irrigation water) are appropriated globally for crop and livestock production in 47×10^6 ha of grabbed land worldwide (i.e., in 90% of the reported global grabbed land)."
28. The share of the primary sector (which includes prominently mining and agriculture) in inward FDI stock increased to 41 percent in 2006, up from 5 percent in 1996; in contrast, the share of the manufacturing sector almost halved, to 27 percent from 40 percent, over that period. (UNCTAD 2008).
29. For comprehensive data, see UNCTAD 2008.
30. On the other side, the World Food Programme spent $116 million to provide 230,000 tons of food aid between 2007 and 2011 to the 4.6 million Ethiopians it estimated were threatened by hunger and malnutrition. This coexistence in a single country of profiting from food production for export and hunger, with the taxpayers of the world providing food aid, is a triangle that has repeated itself starting in the post–World War II war decades (Sassen 1988).
31. Friis and Reenberg 2010.
32. Ibid. Note that the graphs presented in Figures 2.7 and 2.8 are not contained in Friis and Reenberg 2010 but have been constructed by the author using their data.

33. Sun Biofuels actually failed in Tanzania and shut down in 2011, which led to severe and sudden shocks to the local economy.
34. Colchester 2011, 1; Productschap Margerine, Vetten en Oliën 2011, 1.
35. Productschap Margerine, Vetten en Oliën 2011, 1.
36. Colchester 2011, 2–3.
37. Ibid., 1.
38. Ibid., 2.
39. Burgers and Sustani 2011, 1, 11. See Vermeulen and Good for alternatives.
40. Mayer 2009.
41. Royal Tropical Institute 2012, 3.
42. Yusuf 2012, 7.
43. Ibid., 13.
44. Ibid.
45. Deddy 2006, 91; Asian Human Rights Commission 2012.
46. Mayer 2009.
47. Colchester 2011, 18.
48. Asian Human Rights Commission 2012.
49. Ibid.
50. Ibid.
51. Santoso and Afrizal 2004.
52. Brunori 2013.

3. Finance and Its Capabilities

1. I develop this proposition in Sassen 2008b, 2013. These sources also contain extensive bibliographies on all key aspects of the subject of this chapter. See also generally Stiglitz 1999; Knorr and Preda 2013; Graebner 2012; Hartman and Squires 2013; Krippner 2011; Lerner and Bhatti 2013; IMF 2006, 2008, 2012a, 2012b.
2. Sassen 2001, chapter 4; 2008c, chapters 5 and 7. A key feature of finance is that it can extract robust profits from international transactions even in the face of massive job losses. Thus, in the United States the sector has profited from so-called Free Trade Agreements (FTAs) that, though presented as job creators (e.g., White House 2010), are not (e.g., Scott 2010, 2013; European Commission 2013; Office of the United States Trade Representative 2013a, b, c; Public Citizen 2011, 2013). Nor will the new Transpacific FTA create the promised jobs.
3. For a fuller development and extensive bibliography, see Sassen 2013.

4. Sassen 2008c, 348–65. On particular issues in the relation of finance and banking to housing see, e.g., van Onselen 2013; Goldstein 2013; Smith 2013; Krainer 2009; Kumhof and Rancière 2010; Neumann 2013.

5. See generally Center for Housing Policy 2012; Core Logic 2013; Furman Center 2007; Hankiewitz 2013; Levy and Gopal 2011; Mitchell 2013. On racial discrimination, see Wyly et al. 2009 and several chapters in Aalbers 2012. On details about foreclosure notices, see Realty Trac 2007, 2008, 2009, 2011, 2012a, 2012b, 2013a, 2013b.

6. Global Insight 2007; Pettit and Reuben 2012; but see also Dewan 2013. This is only one component of the financial system. There are many components of finance that consist of interactions between rich and powerful investors where these mechanisms of primitive accumulation are not an issue. But there are some other major components that also are subject to such mechanisms, notably pension funds and mutual funds, which often have to pay multiple little fees and commissions that add up to significant and unwarranted losses for the pensioners and the consumers who buy shares in mutual funds. Finally, much of the loss due to subprime mortgage foreclosures fell on bondholders, not on banks.

7. More detail can be found in Sassen 2008a; White 2013; Schwartzkopff 2013; Liu and Rosenberg 2013; Novinite 2011; Miles and Pillonca 2008; Glick and Lansing 2010; Warnock and Warnock 2008, 2012.

8. Arrighi 1994.

9. Farrell et al. 2008.

10. On the global potential of housing mortgage finance see generally European Mortgage Federation 2007; World Bank 2008, 2013a; Miles and Pillonca 2008; Glick and Lansing 2010; Neumann 2013. Elsewhere (Sassen 2008b, 2013) I examine diverse and extensive data that show the potential for global finance to use this particular type of subprime mortgage worldwide, given its invention of instruments that delink the capacity to pay the mortgage from investors' profit.

11. Sassen 2008c, chapter 7; Varchaver and Benner 2008, based on data from ISDA.

12. Sassen 2001, chapter 4.

13. Ganchev et al. 2009; SEC. 2013; Kocjan et al. 2012; Keohane 2012.

14. Alvarenga 2013.

15. Patterson 2013.

16. Clark 2011.

17. Patterson 2013.

4. Dead Land, Dead Water

1. Bai et al. 2008, 223. In this paragraph all other quotes are from World Bank 2013b. Additional sources are World Bank 2012, 2013b; Hakkeling, Olderman, and Sombroek 1991.

2. Sources for this section are Bai et al. 2008; Hakkeling, Olderman, and Sombroek 1991; Van Lynden 2004.

3. Bai et al. 2008. Although the Normalized Difference Vegetation Index provides no information about the *type* of environmental degradation taking place, it is possible to get some measure of this because the index is mapped as a continuous surface; thus, "the drivers may be revealed by correlation with other geo-located biophysical and socioeconomic data" (ibid., 224); NASA web.

4. Sources for this section are World Bank 2013b; Coumou and Rahmstorf 2012; Stott, Stone, and Allen 2004; Founda and Giannaopoulos 2009; Karoly 2009; Barriopedro et al. 2011; NOAA 2011, 2013a, 2013b; Rupp et al. 2012; Hansen, Sato, and Ruedy 2012.

5. The five hottest summers in Europe since 1500 all occurred after 2002, with 2003 and 2010 being exceptionally hot (Barriopedro et al. 2011). The death toll of the 2003 heat wave is estimated at 70,000 (Field et al. 2012), with daily excess mortality reaching up to 2,200 in France (Fouillet et al. 2006). The heat wave in Russia in 2010 resulted in an estimated death toll of 55,000, of which 11,000 deaths were in Moscow alone, and more than 1 million hectares of burned land (Barriopedro et al. 2011). In 2012 the United States, experienced a devastating heat wave and drought period (NOAA 2012a, 2012b); by the end of July about 63 percent of the contiguous United States was affected by drought conditions, and the January-to-July period was the warmest ever recorded. That same period also saw numerous wildfires, setting a new record for total burned area (NOAA 2012b).

6. All quotes in this paragraph are from World Bank 2013b.

7. Solomon et al. 2007; Wigley and Santer 2012; Hansen, Sato, and Ruedy 2012.

8. Foster and Rahmstorf 2011, among others, show that if one removes known factors that affect short-term temperature variations (solar variability, volcanic aerosols, El Niño, and others), natural factors cannot explain warming. Hence it can be largely attributed to anthropogenic factors—man-made factors. See also Santer et al. 1995; Stott 2000; Duffy and Tebaldi 2012; Jones, Lister, and Li 2008; Stott et al. 2011; Sample 2007.

9. UNEP/GRID 2006, 27.
10. Borodkin and Ertz 2004; Bronder et al. 2010, 9; Blacksmith Institute 2013a, 2013b; Norilsk Nickel 2008; Mines and Communities 2003; BBC News 2007; Golovnina 2005; Bronder et al. 2012.
11. Bronder et al. 2010.
12. Norilsk Nickel 2008; Borodkin and Ertz 2004.
13. Cole 2013, 5, 22.
14. Abel 1997; Klauk 2013c; EPA 1994, 1; Mineral Policy Center 2000.
15. Perlez and Johnson 2005; Mitchell 2004, 10; Klauk 2013a, 2013b; McClure 2001; Stiffarm 2005.
16. Jones 1989; Massey 1991a, 1991b; *Spokane Chronicle* 1990; Associated Press 1991; Mining Truth 2012.
17. Bureau of Land Management 1996, 2528; Newmont Mining Corporation 1998, 2013; Selcraig 1998; "Mine in Wilderness" 2001.
18. Leistner 1995; EPA 2008; Kelleher 2007.
19. Blacksmith Institute 2013b; Huseynova 2007.
20. Blacksmith Institute 2011a.
21. Lidsky and Schneider 2002; Illinois Department of Public Health n.d.; Blacksmith Institute 2011c, 2011d.
22. This is confirmed by the Blacksmith Institute 2011c, 2011d.
23. Robles 2007; Friends of Lead Free Children 2009; Blacksmith Institute 2013f; Kaul et al. 1999, 917.
24. Doe Run Peru n.d.
25. Serrano 2008; Jamasmie 2012; Pouiller 2010; Kramer 2012.
26. Kramer 2012; Wolman 2006; Sydor 2004; Doe Run Peru n.d.; Doe Run Resources Corporation 2006, 2012.
27. Lenntech 2011; Blacksmith Institute 2011a, 2011c, 2011f; IPPC 2003; Kennedy 2005; Blackman and Kildegaard 2003; Warren 1940.
28. Voyant Solutions 2009; Blacksmith Institute 2013c.
29. Key sources are Hart and Boger 2008; Townsend and Townsend 2004; UNEP/GRID 2006; National Wildlife Federation 2012; Duruibe, Ogwuegbu, and Egwurugwu 2007; Blacksmith Institute 2011a, 2011e.
30. Brown 2012; Hurdle 2009; see also note 28. Since 2012 over fifteen more regions banned fracking. For updates visit *Keep Tap Water Safe* 2013.
31. Kenny et al. 2009; Harden 2012; Marcellus Drilling News 2010; Olson-Sawyer 2012; Johnson 2011; Chesapeake Energy 2012; Demelle 2011; Jackson et al. 2013.
32. Belcher and Renikoff 2013; Davies 2009.

33. Keranen et al. 2013; Ellsworth et al. 2012; Drajem 2012; Joyce 2012; Romm 2011; Tagliabue 2013.
34. McQuaid 2012; Aurora Lights 2013; Palmer et al. 2010; Hendryx 2009; U.S. Energy Information Administration 2012a, 2012b; Bureau of Labor Statistics 2012; Gagnon 2004; Aurora Lights 2013.
35. Townsend and Townsend 2004; Jorgenson 2006; Murphy 1996; Bice 2013.
36. Belton 2006; Blacksmith Institute 2007; ARMZ Uranium Holding Co. 2012.
37. BBC News 2011; Blacksmith Institute 2007; World Nuclear Association 2012; International Atomic Energy Agency n.d.; WHO 2005; Environment News Service 2010; Godoy 2011.
38. Harvey 2000; Harden and Morgan 2004; EPA 2012a; Wald 2010; Porter 2004; Washington State Department of Ecology 2008.
39. Tsukimori and Layne 2011; Smith 2011; Bradsher and Pollack 2011.
40. Pino, Kannel, and Gardner 2012; Bhopal Census Highlights 2011.
41. Sources for this section on dead water zones are World Bank 2013b; Diaz and Rosenberg 2008; Eggler 2007.
42. World Bank 2013b.
43. NOAA 2013b.
44. Wassener 2011; Hoshaw 2009.
45. Jowit 2008; World Food Programme 2013; UNICEF 2012.
46. Sources for this introductory section on Nestlé are CBC 2008; Hall 2010; Wagenhofer 2005; Brabeck-Lethame 2012; Tarlock 2004.
47. Wagenhofer 2005.
48. Brabeck-Lethame 2012.
49. Tarlock 2004.
50. Clarke 2007.
51. Crystal Springs Preserve 2013; Samek 2004; Schwartz 2004; Penn 2008.
52. Eskanazi 1998; Patoski 2011; Texas A&M University 2013.
53. Clarke 2007; Michigan Citizens for Water Conservation 2012.
54. Corporate Watch n.d.
55. Wellington Water Watchers 2011.
56. El Defensor Chieftan 2009; Ray 2013.
57. Sources for the section on Coca-Cola are Right to Water and Sanitation 2010; Sen 2003; Global Research 2010.
58. Blomfield 2007; Knobel 1997; Blacksmith Institute 2013d; Ruditsky 2004; Walsh 2007.

59. Ideas First Research 2010; Blacksmith Institute 2013e; EPA 2012b; Environment and Process Division 2004.
60. Ballantyne et al. 2012; Rogers and Evans 2011; International Atomic Energy Agency n.d.; Gillis 2013; Ifran and Uvaneswari 2012; McKibben 2012.
61. McKibben 2012.
62. Chestney 2012; Economist 2011a.
63. Seager et al. 2007; Mingfang Ting interviewed in Vergano 2007.
64. Zeiss 2011; Gray 2012.
65. Carrington 2012. For an explanation see Freeland and Gilbert 2009; "Sea Level," Guardian, www.guardian.co.uk/environment/sea-level.
66. Viñas 2012; Rignot et al. 2011.
67. Kinnard et al. 2011; Pilkington 2008; Schuur and Abbott 2011.

v2 přímitive accy

Acknowledgments

Many people and many events have contributed to this book, too many to name. In a project that took years, there are a vast number of organizations and individuals I would like to thank; they are mostly recognized in the text, even if not always by their names. When it comes to the work of *making* a manuscript, I am particularly grateful to Walker Kahn for his great work on the case studies and throughout the preparation of the manuscript, to Laura Mc-Tighe for her research on prisons, to Anna Zamora for her indefatigable work with the tables and graphs, and to Eunkyong Shin, Mary Joseph, Sarah Partridge, and Jared Conrad-Bradshaw for all their help. A big debt goes to my editor, Ian Malcolm, and his assistant, Joy Deng; the copyeditor, Sue Warga; and the production editor, Melody Negron. All errors are mine.

Home: 116
"immaterial" 117 (c.f. virtual)
credit-default swaps ₹₿ 122
82 new hunger
citizenship 83
remittances 90
extractive logic 10

Index

Children: in poverty, 51; social exclusion of, 51; austerity measures and, 91; cancer in, 157; illness in, 157; lead poisoning in, 165, 167, 168; battery recycling by, 166; in leather tanning work, 172; uranium poisoning, 182; abandoned, 214

China: middle class growth, 17–18; middle sector growth, system of, 17; government debt, 21; unemployment, 39, 40; prisons and imprisonment in, 67; land acquisition investors, 80, 101, 102, 107, 108; special economic zones (SEZs), 102; housing finance, 122; superprime market for the very rich, 134; financial capital, positives in, 147; rising sea levels, Ho Chi Minh City, 188; industrial emissions, 201

Chromium pollution, 169–172, 199–200

Ciavarella, Mark (kids-for-cash" judge), 69

Circuito das Aguas springs, 196

Climate change: displaced persons from, 55, 63, 207; causes of, 200–201; altering, possibility of, 207–208

Climate change, effect on: displaced persons population, 55; desertification, 62, 152, 189, 203–204; land degradation, 152–154; poverty, 153–154; food insecurity/malnourishment, 154; groundwater recharge, 154; agricultural production, 188, 202–203; land temperature, rise in, 201–202; fresh water bodies, 203–204; ocean acidity, 204–205; ocean levels, 204–207; methane gas

production, 207; permafrost thaw, 207

Coal mining. See Mountaintop removal mining

Columbia River, 184, 185

Conceptually subterranean trends, subterranean trends: 5, 6, 8, 63, 119, 150, 217

Copper mining, 156–157, 168

Corporate tax reductions, 19–21

Corporations: profits and assets, growth in, 19–21; prison labor, benefit from, 74; financial crisis, impact on, 141

Corrections Corporation of America (CCA), 68, 72

Costa Rica, 71

Côte d'Ivoire, 56

Credit default swaps, 127, 138, 141–143

Credit Suisse, 144

Crystal Springs Recreation Preserve, 194

Cuadrilla Resources, 178

Cummins, Matthew, 24

Cyanide gas, 186–187

Cyanide heap leaching, 159–161

Cyprus, 50

Czech Republic: poverty and social exclusion, population at risk, 51; prisons and imprisonment in, 69–70; ratio of household credit to personal disposable income, 132

Dallara, Charles, 41

Dark pools, 143–145

Dawn Mining, 162–163

Dead land, 2, 12, 16, 81, 83, 149, 150, 173, 210, 215, 222

Dead water, 149, 150, 210, 222

Debt: growth in governments, 21–23, 27; need for, 146